The Book of Daily Prayer

Morning and Evening, 2001

Kim Martin Sadler
Editor

United Church Press
Cleveland, Ohio

United Church Press, Cleveland, Ohio 44115
© 2000 by United Church Press

Hymn lyrics are primarily from *The New Century Hymnal* (Cleveland, Ohio: The Pilgrim Press, 1995); alterations copyright © The Pilgrim Press and are used by permission.

Biblical quotations are primarily from the New Revised Standard Version of the Bible, © 1989 by the Division of Christian Education of the National Council of the Churches of Christ in the U.S.A., and are used by permission. Adapted for inclusivity.

Printed in the United States of America on acid-free paper

05   04   03   02   01   00   5   4   3   2   1

Library of Congress Cataloging-in-Publication Data

The book of daily prayer : morning and evening, 2001 / Kim Martin Sadler, editor.
p.   cm.
ISBN 0-8298-1383-7 (alk. paper)
1. Prayers. 2. Devotional calendars. I. Sadler, Kim Martin.
BV 245.B586 1997
248'.8—dc80   95-51065
CIP

Contents

Introduction

The year 2000 was a year of transition and change. Celebrations of the new millennium circled the globe. Doomsayers predicted the end of the world. Some of us prepared for Y2K, only to be left with cases and cases of bottled water and canned goods. And if that was not enough, the presidential election, stock market volatility, new career choices, medical and technological advances, births and deaths—all had an impact on our lives.

In the midst of this ever-changing world, I am grateful that I can rely on the constant presence, love, and comfort of our Savior, Jesus Christ. Isaiah tells us to "trust in God forever, for in God we have an everlasting rock." You can trust in this rock, and depend on this rock, for God never changes. I will continue to stand upon this rock. I offer you this rock. Pass it on to others through your prayers and supplications.

Blessings,

Kim Martin Sadler

How to Use *The Book of Daily Prayer*

The Book of Daily Prayer is to be used for daily devotion in the morning and evening. To use the book as a personal devotional guide, begin by reading the scripture passage for the day, followed by the opening morning prayer.

Read the meditative prayer next. This prayer is written in a style known as "praying the scripture," which allows your meditative prayer to be more than an interpretation of the day's reading.

The intercessory morning prayer, which follows the meditative prayer, is to be offered for those in need of God's blessings and for other personal concerns. It may be followed by the Prayer of Our Savior or another suggestion by the author. Both morning and evening devotional times end with a closing prayer.

Those who use *The Book of Daily Prayer* in a group setting can follow the same pattern described for personal use. One person can read the scripture verses aloud, and another can lead the prayers. The meditative prayer may be said in unison or read silently. You may decide that each group member will share her or his prayer concerns during intercessory prayer. The Prayer of Our Savior and the closing prayer may be recited by the entire group in unison.

You are encouraged to develop your own methods of using this devotional guide. For example, you may wish to form prayer partnerships with others who use this book. You may choose to sing familiar hymns at the beginning and end of prayer. Or it might be helpful to maintain a prayer list that you can use during intercessory prayer.

MONDAY, JANUARY 1
(Read Luke 3:15–17)

(Morning)
Mighty Redeemer, cleanse my eyes so they may see your presence in this new time.

(Evening)
Mighty Redeemer, what will I resolve to see in others? The faults that we all bear?
Or the opportunity to love despite human frailty?

O Living Waters, the future seems veiled, but let me be a bearer of good news—
that the God of hosts lives and is a cleanser of souls! Let me resolve to cleanse
my life of the sins that prevent me from loving fully. Let me resolve to cleanse
my heart of despair, knowing that you alone, God, are a bearer of light where
there is darkness. Let me show others in this new time through words and
deeds that I am a follower of Jesus Christ.

(Morning)
Provider of life, put a new song in my heart.
Give me direction where I need guidance.
Let me be a beacon of light to someone who has become lost along the way.
(Prayers of Intercession)

(Evening)
Provider of life, how glorious is your name above all others. Thank you for life.
(Prayers of Intercession)

Prepare me, God, for the beginning of a new season.
(Pray the Prayer of Our Savior.)

(Morning)
O faithful and gracious God, provide tender mercies this day, and renew my spirit that I may be instrumental in renewing the spirit of others. In accordance to your will, Jesus. In the name of Jesus. Amen.

(Evening)
God, I thank you and praise your holy name, for your everlasting love flows freely. In the name of Jesus. Amen.

TUESDAY, JANUARY 2
(Read Luke 3:21–22)

(Morning)
Sweet Lily of the Valley, let me pause throughout this day
and pray for someone in need.

(Evening)
Sweet Lily of the Valley, did I remember to give thanks
to you today for answered prayers?

O God, too often my prayers begin with a plea for help. Let me always remember before praying to give thanks to you for the many prayers you have already answered in my life. Let me remember to pray for the needs of others less fortunate than myself. Let me remember the importance and power of intercession. And even when I feel too anxious or weary to pray, guide me to pray anyway.

(Morning)
O Sovereign God, allow me to take time today to pray earnestly
for someone who is unwilling or unable to ask.
(Prayers of Intercession)

(Evening)
Thank you, Jesus, for your prayer life. Help me to grow stronger in my prayer life.
Help me to pray as you do.
(Prayers of Intercession)

Prayer changes things.
(Pray the Prayer of Our Savior.)

(Morning)
I praise the wonderful and marvelous name of our Savior. How good it is to know your goodness is everlasting. Thank you for listening to my silent prayers when I cannot speak. In the name of Jesus. Amen.

(Evening)
Thank you, God, for my blessings. Thank you, God, for answering the prayers of others in need. In the name of Jesus. Amen.

WEDNESDAY, JANUARY 3
(Read Isaiah 43:1–7)

(Morning)
Blessed Savior, as I go forward this day,
may I take comfort in knowing you are walking right beside me.

(Evening)
Blessed Savior, thank you for never leaving me and never forsaking me.
Protect me from fearful thoughts as I sleep.

As I go through this life, I have so often been trapped by fear—the fear of failure, the fear of disapproval, the fear of reproach, even the fear of blessings. Let me remember that in your name, blessed Jesus, I find courage. You, Creator, will place a shield of protection around me. You, Holy One, will uphold and console me.

(Morning)
God, you continue to strengthen me, to comfort me, to love me.
For this, I will forever bless your name. In you, I find the spirit of love, not fear.
(Prayers of Intercession)

(Evening)
Through another day, you have shown me that despite my resistance to surrender all
to you, I can still find a safe haven in your love.
(Prayers of Intercession)

If God is with me, who shall be against me?
(Sing "Blessed Assurance" or another familiar song.)

(Morning)
Help me, God, to brush aside fear, and to boldly proclaim the way of salvation to someone today. In accordance with your will, Jesus. In the name of Jesus. Amen.

(Evening)
Thank you, Jesus, for surrounding me with a hedge of safety. You are my Rock. You are my High Tower. I lift up your name above all others. I glorify your name. In the name of Jesus. Amen.

THURSDAY, JANUARY 4
(Read Psalm 29:1–3)

(Morning)
Sovereign God, thank you for awakening me to live among your creation.
You alone are worthy of all praise.
I will gladly worship your name for the life you breathe into me daily.

(Evening)
Sovereign God, all plans did not go as smoothly as anticipated. However, I thank
you for teaching me patience and for allowing me to wait on you. I am grateful.

O Wonderful Counselor, I ask so much of you. I expect everything when I am
owed nothing and am unworthy to even speak your name. Show me, God, how
I can give of myself freely to you. Help me to give of my time to work in your
vineyard. Grant me the ability to give of my finances to uphold your Word. Let
me praise you when I am tired and full of despair. Open a place in my life so
that I can experience you anew.

(Morning)
Precious Savior, let me find new reasons to stop and give praise.
Help me show others how to worship you continually.
(Prayers of Intercession)

(Evening)
Royal High Priest, for how you bless me; for when you bless me;
for being an ever-present help when I need you; for salvation, I thank you.
(Prayers of Intercession)

You alone, God, are worthy to be praised.
(Sing "Bless God, O My Soul" or another familiar hymn.)

(Morning)
You allow me to see a new morning,
God. All good things I achieve today
are a testament to your grace and
power. In the name of Jesus. Amen.

(Evening)
Thank you for the blessings of this day. I
worship you. I adore you. I give my life
to you. I love you. In the name of Jesus.
Amen.

FRIDAY, JANUARY 5
(Read Psalm 29:4–9)

(Morning)
Savior, help me to listen to you today amid the noise.

(Evening)
Savior, as I sleep, speak to me in your small, sweet voice.

Gracious God, you often speak to me, but I don't always hear. Allow me to remain still and listen to your voice. Let me hear your will and not my own. The path that you set for me is holy and good and righteous. Enable me, with strength, to boldly live the Word of God.

(Morning)
Sweet Jesus, thank you for allowing me another opportunity to serve.
Glory to your name.
(Prayers of Intercession)

(Evening)
Great Majesty, thank you for still caring for me
despite my selfish thoughts and actions.
(Prayers of Intercession)

Please let me be a doer of the Word and not just a hearer.
(Pray the Prayer of Our Savior.)

(Morning)
I begin this morning desiring to hear your Word through others around me. May I remember that you place people in my life to teach me your way. Let me open my ears to hear the lessons of today. In accordance with your will, Jesus. In the name of Jesus. Amen.

(Evening)
Thank you, God, for this time to rest. May my mind and body be renewed as I sleep. May I wake with a bountiful spirit. In accordance with your will, Jesus. In the name of Jesus. Amen.

SATURDAY, JANUARY 6
(Read Psalm 29:10–11)

(Morning)
Giver of peace, when trials emerge, you are my refuge.
Let me look to you for encouragement.

(Evening)
Giver of peace, thank you for your faithfulness today.
You are the God of all comfort.

When tribulations abound and help seems at a distance, may I not look to myself for all of the answers. I am simply not strong or wise enough. Let me remember to whom I belong, and let me call on the name of Jesus in times of trouble. For you, God, are the peace giver, and when I am at my weakest, you provide unyielding strength. You, who called peace into stormy waters, are able to calm my fears. Glory to your wonderful name.

(Morning)
May I be grateful for the obstacles you bring my way.
I know that I have been made stronger by depending on you.
(Prayers of Intercession)

(Evening)
As long as I continue to trust you, God, I can weather any storm.
(Prayers of Intercession)

In Christ, all things are possible.
(Sing "Leaning on the Everlasting Arms" or another favorite hymn.)

(Morning)
Help me, God, to see that I can find peace in any situation. Help me remember that I am never alone today. In accordance with your will, Jesus. In the name of Jesus. Amen.

(Evening)
Thank you, Jesus, for salvation and for being my battle shield. I win with you. In the name of Jesus. Amen.

SUNDAY, JANUARY 7
(Read Acts 8:14–17)

(Morning)
Gracious God, do I allow myself to be guided by the Holy Spirit,
or am I leading the way?

(Evening)
Gracious God, I humble myself before you. Holy Spirit, work within me.
Help me to let go and follow your lead.

God, you have provided me with a voice, a vision, a compass, and a conscience. It is the Holy Spirit—a beacon that gives light and guidance in the night. Help me to become reacquainted with the Holy Spirit. Let it rise up in my soul and renew my life.

(Morning)
God, may I be guided by the Holy Spirit within me.
Let me pray for healing for someone in need today.
(Prayers of Intercession)

(Evening)
You, God, are awesome. You provide for my every need. Thank you for those you
guided to pray for me throughout my life.
(Prayers of Intercession)

Pray continually and believe faithfully.
(Pray the Prayer of Our Savior.)

(Morning)
Help me, God, to pray more consistently; live firmly in your Word; listen to you more carefully; love you more deeply; trust you fearlessly; praise and worship your name faithfully; and forgive and love myself steadfastly. In the name of Jesus. Amen.

(Evening)
Faithful God, I will forever thank you and worship you. You saved my life. Show me your plan for my life, and help me fulfill your design for it. In the name of Jesus. Amen.

MONDAY, JANUARY 8
(Read John 2:1–4)

(Morning)
O God, in what ways today will you say to me, my hour has come?
Am I ready to hear your call?

(Evening)
O God, as I reflect on this day, thank you for the moments I heard your voice.
Teach me to recognize the sound of your voice more often.

God, am I prepared to hear your voice saying to me, "Your hour has come"?
So often, I conclude I am not ready to take the next step in my faith journey. I
focus on my failures and perceived weaknesses. I question my abilities and
gifts. What will it take for me to renew my faith in you and in myself? Perhaps
it is in the process of moving forward that I experience the refreshment of the
Spirit and the courage to embrace your call.

(Morning)
O God of faith and possibilities, may your blessing rest upon these for whom I pray.
(Prayers of Intercession)

(Evening)
Spirit of God, I express my gratitude for the many ways faith overruled doubt today.
(Prayers of Intercession)

God's call comes in unexpected ways from unexpected places!

(Morning)
In the celebrations and the busyness of
this day, may I always give you praise
for your abundant goodness and love. In
Jesus' name. Amen.

(Evening)
May I rest in the confidence of your call
upon my life and your persistent faith in
pursuing me until I respond. In Jesus'
name. Amen.

TUESDAY, JANUARY 9
(Read John 2:5–11)

(Morning)
O God, fill me with your living water this morning
so I might be a sign of your glory to every person I meet this day.

(Evening)
O God, thank you for the many reasons I found today to believe in you.
And in those moments of disbelief, thank you for loving me anyway.

I do not need to look far to see signs of your glory, loving God. The sun and the stars speak to the bright light of your splendor. The beauty of the trees, the flowers, the mountains, the prairie, and all that you have made, O Creator, proclaim your grandeur. Even in days of despair, your love for me speaks of the divine majesty. I cannot help lifting up my heart and soul in praise when contemplating your glory!

(Morning)
O Spirit of Jesus, may your gift of provision reach all these for whom I pray.
(Prayers of Intercession)

(Evening)
Thank you for the sweetness of prayer at the end of the day.
(Prayers of Intercession)

Everywhere there are brilliant signs of God's glorious works!

(Morning)
May I be your good wine in someone's unpleasant day. In Jesus' name. Amen.

(Evening)
I end this day grateful for the revelation of your magnificent will. In Jesus' name. Amen.

WEDNESDAY, JANUARY 10
(Read Isaiah 62:1–3)

(Morning)
O God, give me a new name for every circumstance I encounter
and a new name for each person I meet today.

(Evening)
O God, I give thanks to you for the circumstances and the people I called
by the new names given by you. In the moments when I did not honor
your presence, I confess my need for more of your grace.

God of Zion, I must not keep silent about your goodness. How can I rest when there are so many who have not yet heard of or believed in the name of your Child, Jesus Christ? I pray the sound of your voice will echo through my thoughts and emanate through my mouth. I ask that your salvation through Christ might shine through my life like a burning torch. Let me embrace the name you have given me, O God.

(Morning)
May an abundance of your Spirit rest on each person for whom I pray.
(Prayers of Intercession)

(Evening)
Your name is above all names.
Thank you for allowing me to be called by your name.
(Prayers of Intercession)

Every person is a crown of beauty in the hand of God.

(Morning)	(Evening)
I am honored to claim your name throughout this day, O Christ. In Jesus' name. Amen.	As I fall asleep in your embrace, I once again call out your name and listen as you call out mine. In Jesus' name. Amen.

THURSDAY, JANUARY 11
(Read Isaiah 62:4–5)

(Morning)
Mighty God, I wake up this morning with a
smile on my face because you delight in me.

(Evening)
Mighty God, let me rest in your arms this night confident in your love and delight.

What a mighty God I serve! In all of your greatness and majesty, you, the Almighty, still find time to notice each individual. How amazing and over-whelming is the extravagant love that the Spirit of Christ showers on me. I am humbled by your delight exhibited to all who are created in your image. Not only do you delight in me, O God; you rejoice over me. I will never fully understand this mystery.

(Morning)
O Spirit of joy, I pray for those who need to experience your delight.
(Prayers of Intercession)

(Evening)
For those I met this day who seem unable to embrace the fullness of your joy,
I now pray.
(Prayers of Intercession)

God delights in me!

(Morning)
May your delight in me transform each encounter I have today into one that produces rejoicing. In Jesus' name. Amen.

(Evening)
I close my eyes with a sense of holy contentment because you delight in me. In Jesus' name. Amen.

FRIDAY, JANUARY 12
(Read Psalm 36:5–10)

(Morning)
Steadfast and faithful God, as I prepare for another day of walking
side by side with you, remind me how precious is your steadfast love.

(Evening)
Steadfast and faithful God, at the end of the day
I can still praise you for your steadfast love and faithfulness.

Great is your faithfulness, my Sustainer! When I make choices that contradict your will, you do not leave me. When I ignore your voice, you continue to speak. When I rely on my own strength, you remain ready to offer your power. God, your steadfast love extends to every corner of my life. I pray my faithfulness will grow to approach that of Jesus Christ. Empower my every effort to witness to your steadfast love.

(Morning)
Today, make me your fountain of life to every individual who crosses my path.
(Prayers of Intercession)

(Evening)
For all of the people I observed today who seemed overwhelmed
by the dimness of this world, I pray they might discover your light.
(Prayers of Intercession)

In God's love we discover truth and righteousness.

(Morning)
May your light shine through me in all the arenas I find myself today. In Jesus' name. Amen.

(Evening)
Gratitude overflows from the deepest recesses of my soul as I consider how often I take refuge in the shadow of your wings. In Jesus' name. Amen.

SATURDAY, JANUARY 13
(Read 1 Corinthians 12:1–7)

(Morning)
Loving God, I pray that I might model the inclusive love of Jesus Christ this day.

(Evening)
Loving God, forgive me for any ways I failed to demonstrate
that you are a God who loves all people.

Why do I live in a world where confusion and division often reign? O God, your desire for oneness was evident when you created everyone in your image. When the awareness of your creative design was blurred, you sent Jesus Christ as the reconciler par excellence. The example of Jesus Christ provides me with a way to authentically live out your unity. Your Holy Spirit offers me the power, day by day, to be an agent of reconciliation in the world in which I live.

(Morning)
Give me your Holy Spirit so I will not be led astray by the idolatry
of this world or lead others astray through my own weakness.
(Prayers of Intercession)

(Evening)
I pray, as my world of relationships expands,
I might offer love to each as you would.
(Prayers of Intercession)

Although there are many different gifts, various callings as activists, and multiple opportunities for service, there is only one God.

(Morning)
Guide me to the ways that I might serve
you this day. In Jesus' name. Amen.

(Evening)
As I feel sleep coming, I once again
thank you for including me in your
love. In Jesus' name. Amen.

SUNDAY, JANUARY 14
(Read 1 Corinthians 12:8–11)

(Morning)
Holy Spirit, bring to mind the many gifts you have bestowed upon me.

(Evening)
Holy Spirit, with gratitude I express my delight in the ways you used my gifts today.

God, you give abundantly to all who are faithful to your call. You provide gifts to enrich and empower the calling of each person and each community. Help me identify my gifts. Give me confidence to use my gifts in ways that bring glory to you. Nurture and develop my faith to be more effective in serving you.

(Morning)
Activate my gifts today that I may be a blessing to someone.
(Prayers of Intercession)

(Evening)
Tonight I offer a prayer of thanksgiving for each person
who spoke your word of wisdom to me at just the right moment.
(Prayers of Intercession)

**The Spirit has given everyone gifts for use
in building the community of God.**

(Morning)
May I be used as a source of your healing power today. In Jesus' name. Amen.

(Evening)
I now enter the solitude before sleep overcomes me. I am humbled by how you trust me enough to confer on me gifts for ministry. In Jesus' name. Amen.

MONDAY, JANUARY 15
(Read 1 Corinthians 12:12–26)

(Morning)
O God, I awoke with the postholiday, midwinter, Monday morning blues.
Your Spirit meets my spirit at this early morning hour.
It awaits the dawn and speaks as I prepare to meet this day.

(Evening)
O God, thank you for working your good in the events of these days. I rejoice in
those that I was able to name, and I rest in your promise for the good that my eyes
could not see. Now, I take my rest for the night.

I am not alone. The Word of God affirms my completeness and wholeness as I
go to a world in which I, by the Spirit, am one with all persons baptized into
the body of Christ. We who form the body of Christ are many. In this, my day
is met with gladness. Thank you, Spirit of oneness, who came to my loneliness
before the day began. The same Spirit gives to all of us morning drink and
nurture for the day's needs. God, I marvel at your wisdom. How interesting is
your creating Spirit who seeks to bring all to new harmony.

(Morning)
Spirit Divine, ever creating, in the giving and in the receiving,
may a new earth be shaped. In the name of the Spirit of holiness, I pray.
(Prayers of Intercession)

(Evening)
Forgive me, Spirit of holiness, for not always contributing to the new earth begun by
our Sovereign Christ, whose body I and others celebrated in communion.
Fear robbed me of love's power. Grant to me another day for love's gain.
(Prayers of Intercession)

To each is given the manifestation of the Spirit for the common good.

(Morning)	(Evening)
I go forth into this day seeking the Spirit of God in the common good with joyful anticipation of my contribution to your new earth. Thank you, God, for including me in the body of Christ. In the name of Jesus I pray. Amen.	I accept your forgiveness of my sins for this day, and in that grace may I rest soundly. May I find new courage for the living of the body of Christ in the world that awaits me tomorrow. Spirit of all gifts, hear this prayer. In the name of Jesus I pray. Amen.

TUESDAY, JANUARY 16
(Read 1 Corinthians 12:27–31)

(Morning)
Dear God, I know I was baptized into the body of Christ.
Help me to know who I am in that body and what gift the Spirit has given to me that
I am to offer to my community of faith.

(Evening)
Dear God, one love came to me by your Spirit this day. I know my part in the body
of Christ as ever changing and being renewed, like old cells in my body that die and
are replaced by new ones.

Dear God, in this passage I am asked to seek the greater gifts and a more
excellent way. Accept my prayer for the gift of healing. I want the members of
my congregation to be at peace with one another. Grant that my desire for
peace will be the seed for the giving of the gift of healing. The passage says
that some have deeds of power. God, accept my desire for my congregation to
work together for the good of all its members. Spirit of God, instruct me in the
ways of your leadership as I claim my place within the body of Christ.

(Morning)
Spirit of God, empower me as a member of the body of Christ to live in unity and
harmony with the other members of my congregation.
(Prayers of Intercession)

(Evening)
This day, accept my deeds of love as deeds of power for the coming of your new
earth and the renewing of the congregation of which I am a member.
(Prayers of Intercession)

"Now you are the body of Christ and individually members of it."

(Morning)
God, I come to you. Awaken my desire to claim anew the power of Jesus Christ in my life. Show me today your most excellent way of living as one member among the many members of the body of Christ. In the name of Jesus, I pray. Amen.

(Evening)
Jesus, again this day, I have become aware that you are the Way. Thank you for being my guide into new understandings and new relationships. In the name of Jesus, I pray. Amen.

WEDNESDAY, JANUARY 17
(Read Psalm 19:1–6)

(Morning)
Maker of all that exists, your early morning sky speaks to me of how big you are,
and my heart sighs in amazement at your artistry.

(Evening)
Maker of all that exists, Artist of my morning promise,
thank you for the beauty of this day. I looked up to you and found you faithful.

Maker of the heavens, in reading this psalm, I remember Dr. Preston Bradley's closing words for each radio broadcast: "Keep looking up." I am looking up to your artistic creation this January early morning sky. A gentle, fragile, cool snowflake, innocent of a world of hardships, floats down, and I connect. I listen as many flakes of your artistic hand, in union with one another, find for themselves new power and strength as they come to rest in the towns, cities, and countryside. Today, I seek to gather in the company of others as one of many snowflakes seeking to tell your possibilities.

(Morning)
Creator God, how marvelous are your creative works.
Assist me to know myself as one of your marvelous handiworks.
(Prayers of Intercession)

(Evening)
Creator God, I marvel at your handiwork. Assist me to listen now as the moon and
stars speak to me of your gospel of justice for the whole of creation.
(Prayers of Intercession)

**"The heavens are telling the glory of God;
and the firmament proclaims God's handiwork."**

(Morning)
My God, today I need your shade of power, for I fear that the day's experience may be as a sun's blinding rays upon new snow. May the glory of your heaven be known this day upon your earth. In the name of Jesus, I pray. Amen.

(Evening)
I asked my God, "I did wrong today. Can you forgive me even this?" And the God who painted the sky above me heard my prayer and replied, "The Word that spangled the stars into the vast heaven can revive your soul. It is my pleasure to do so." In the name of Jesus, I pray. Amen.

THURSDAY, JANUARY 18
(Read Psalm 19:7–14)

(Morning)
Perfect God, praise be to your awesome management of life's activities
when I trust in your truth and do not err in my day's journey.
Direct me toward people and places where the purpose is to be a part of your reign.

(Evening)
Perfect God of order and good precepts, my hope is that your dominion is possible.
May I be secure in this hope, and may I be courageous for the living out of this hope.

Dear God, when your promise and will for my life become my daily living, I am refreshed as the morning dew and see possibilities beyond my previous imagining. It is wonderful to know you with such awe. The right way becomes a joy and not a chore. Let me not be caught up with the negative energy of persons who are curt, contemptuous, and condescending. Let my thoughts and actions be congenial, cordial, and courteous, as a courageous person who holds the glory of your goodness in awe and reverence.

(Morning)
Instruct me in the wisdom of living by your decrees. Show me my errors, that I
might rejoice in the knowledge of truth and know and obey your law.
(Prayers of Intercession)

(Evening)
God of all that is right and just, instruct me in my night's rest that my dreams may
see the vision of a world in which courage overcomes fear, and courteous behavior
overcomes contemptuous behavior.
(Prayers of Intercession)

**"Let the words of my mouth and the meditation of my heart
be acceptable to you, O God, my rock and my redeemer."**

(Morning)
God, mentor me in a just way of living. As I look to Jesus as my example, come, Holy Spirit, and rekindle within me the fire of holy living, that my soul may be revived. In the name of Jesus, I pray. Amen.

(Evening)
I accept your forgiveness of my sins for this day, and in that grace may I rest soundly. May I find new courage for the living of the body of Christ in the world that awaits me tomorrow. Spirit of all gifts, hear this prayer. In the name of Jesus, I pray. Amen.

FRIDAY, JANUARY 19
(Read Luke 4:14–21)

(Morning)
Spirit of the living God, come unto me, and anoint me for the living of this day.

(Evening)
Spirit of the living God, unto you I entrusted this day's activities
and my spoken word. I pray that you found favor with me.
May my deeds lead to the release of persons who are bound by oppression.

God of my Sunday praise and worship, with great joy we shared what you had given to us, the "others." A burst of joy, a sharing explosion, beginning from your community of faith in worship. Thanks be to you, great and wondrous God.

(Morning)
Loving God, grant unto me victory from my own sins
and self-respect to face my oppressors.
(Prayers of Intercession)

(Evening)
God, it was good to be in your company this day.
Now watch over me as I sleep, that I may again walk with you tomorrow.
(Prayers of Intercession)

Today, may your Holy Word be fulfilled in my living out my discipleship.

(Morning)
Spirit of the living God, assist me in claiming my own freedom, that I might be witness to your release of others. I pray for those who are in prison, either by their own free will or by the oppressive will of others. Renew your Spirit upon this, your child. In the name of Jesus, I pray. Amen.

(Evening)
May this year be the year of your favor, I pray. For I witnessed this day people blind to your goodwill, poor people, and people oppressed and in captivity. May I be in your favor, my gracious God, so that your reign will come quickly. In the name of Jesus, I pray. Amen.

SATURDAY, JANUARY 20
(Read Nehemiah 8:1–3, 5–6)

(Morning)
O God, that I might come to love your Word with hearing ears and bent knees,
in prayer from dawn till noon. May this worship root me to stir the earth
with actions of love into the beauty of the night.

(Evening)
O God, I come now to rest. Your Word this day was true
and your presence sufficient for life's events.

The story of Ezra reading Moses' law book to the descendants of Abraham returning from exile reminds me of returning home for a family gathering. All of us gathered around the old family album retelling the stories. The elders shared stories of people and places that I knew as my heritage, stories I would hear and retell when I became the elder. We, like Ezra, had moments of joy and sorrow as we shared together our present and our past; we sang. Then when someone called, "It's ready," we blessed you, our God, as the most senior among us offered grace before the meal.

(Morning)
Holy God, may your Word instruct me and guide me
to know my past as a part of my present.
(Prayers of Intercession)

(Evening)
I spent the day listening to your Word, holy God, and I discovered
moments of praise and moments of worship with others.
(Prayers of Intercession)

**My holy God, I will seek to understand your Word for the workplace,
for the play place, and for places even within your church place.**

(Morning)
Although a busy day awaits me, I pray that I may take time to hear your Word, my God, and to name the event as time with you. In the name of Jesus, I pray. Amen.

(Evening)
Parent God, your child came to you in pride, and you showed me my shame. By your Spirit, I received knowledge of myself and wisdom for a new life. In the name of Jesus, I pray. Amen.

SUNDAY, JANUARY 21
(Read Nehemiah 8:8–10)

(Morning)
God, may I find sense in the reading and the hearing
of your Word today in church, and may I understand.

(Evening)
God, I end the day in thanksgiving, for your Word
has filled me and I understood much.

My God, even as the people of Israel returned to you in worship, may my presence with my church family be a holy time of worship. I also weep tears of sadness, for when I hear your Holy Word, I am in want of your holiness. Turn my weeping into joy, and grant unto me and all within your church strength for the renewing of our day. May I, as one among the worshiping people who feast upon your Word, receive strength to spend our afternoon and night sharing our food with the hungry people of my town in joy (Jesus first, others second, and myself last).

(Morning)
God who feeds the hungry, feed me from your cup of holy peace,
that I may this day be to others a messenger of your peace.
(Prayers of Intercession)

(Evening)
Forgive me, God, for falling short of your holiness.
I took little risk in sharing with my neighbor in need.
(Prayers of Intercession)

"This day is holy to God; do not mourn or weep."

(Morning)
Dear God, as I go this day to eat and drink at your place of worship with my brothers and sisters, may our dining together give us strength to follow your will. And may we provide also for those who are without provision. In the name of Jesus, I pray. Amen.

(Evening)
To be honest with you, God, is work. It leaves me tired. May I now sleep by your grace to awaken tomorrow to claim the new day with new grace. In the name of Jesus, I pray. Amen.

MONDAY, JANUARY 22
(Read Luke 4:21–30)

(Morning)
Gracious God, as the night has surrendered to the breaking forth of the day,
help my selfish will to surrender to the breaking forth of your Spirit.

(Evening)
Gracious God, as night once again rolls in,
let me rest in your Spirit that has guided me through the day.

Sovereign God, there are times I assume I know you because I know how you have moved in the past. By that assumption, I often limit the new and fresh ways in which you desire to move in and for me in the present. Forgive me, and help me to be open and welcoming to your Spirit.

(Morning)
You, God, are full of grace and mercy.
Knowing this, I pray for all who are in need this day.
(Prayers of Intercession)

(Evening)
God, if I would not let you do all you wanted to do in me today,
work on me through the night.
(Prayers of Intercession)

With a yielded will, I pray.
(Pray the Prayer of Our Savior.)

(Morning)
God, help me to walk this day in a way that will bring praise to your name. In Jesus' name. Amen.

(Evening)
By your Spirit, grant my flesh's longing for a good night's rest. In Jesus' name. Amen.

TUESDAY, JANUARY 23
(Read Jeremiah 1:4–5)

(Morning)
God, you knew me before I was. You also know this new day that I now begin.
I trust you to lead me through this day.

(Evening)
God, you were there at every turn in this day.
As you walked with me through the day, abide with me through the night.

To be so totally known by you, O God, is sometimes a very overwhelming thought, but at the same time it is a comforting one. Because you know me, I have no need to pretend or to exert my energy to try to be who or what I am not. I know you have a purpose for my life. Help me to know and to be myself, fulfilling your purpose.

(Morning)
God, you know the needs of all for whom I pray this day.
O God, I know you are able to meet those needs.
(Prayers of Intercession)

(Evening)
God, what a glorious day this has been, even with its highs and its lows.
Refresh both my body and my spirit through the night.
This praise and prayer I lift up for all.
(Prayers of Intercession)

With blessed assurance, I pray.
(Pray the Prayer of Our Savior.)

(Morning)
Creator God, you are my Maker and the Maker of this day; therefore, with joy, hope, and peace I start today's journey. In Jesus' name. Amen.

(Evening)
The night is not hidden from your knowing, so now I rest. In Jesus' name. Amen.

WEDNESDAY, JANUARY 24
(Read Jeremiah 1:6–8)

(Morning)
Loving God, you have brought forth a new day. Help me to know you are with me.
Let me walk in the peace of this day and not in fear.

(Evening)
Loving God, thank you for being present with me this day.
Now let me rest in your continued presence in the cover of the night.

Loving God, I often have excuses, which seem legitimate, for not letting your will be done in me. I offer these excuses out of a feeling of inadequacy and often out of fear. Thank you for not letting me get away with my excuses. Thank you for speaking to my heart, assuring me that you are with me, and for desiring to use me for your purpose.

(Morning)
Loving and caring God, I am aware of the fear and anxiety that I and others face as we go forth to do your will. For them and me I pray.
(Prayers of Intercession)

(Evening)
God, as I come to the end of another day, I am reminded again of the loving care you provide for me. I give you thanks now as I prepare to rest.
(Prayers of Intercession)

With joy, I pray.
(Pray the Prayer of Our Savior.)

(Morning)	(Evening)
Thank you, God, for this day. Help me to be a willing servant, yielding myself completely to you. In Jesus' name. Amen.	As tonight's rest renews my body, renew your Spirit in me. In Jesus' name. Amen.

THURSDAY, JANUARY 25
(Read Jeremiah 1:9–10)

(Morning)
Merciful God, once again you have touched me with your loving hand. You have given me another day, a day full of wonderful possibilities and awesome responsibilities. Help me to give glory to your name as I live out this day.

(Evening)
Merciful God, today you have touched me so many times and in so many ways. Thank you.

God, being faithful to you in your service requires that I sometimes pluck out and pull down. Sometimes I must destroy and overthrow, and I must also build and plant. I am aware I cannot do this in my own strength—each day I need your touch. With one touch you give me courage, strength, and determination. With one touch you fill my mouth and heart with your Word. It is with this courage, strength, and determination, and by your Word that I remain faithful to you.

(Morning)
Merciful God, extend your loving touch to those for whom I pray today.
(Prayers of Intercession)

(Evening)
God, your Word has been a comfort to me today,
and at times it made me uncomfortable. Thank you.
(Prayers of Intercession)

With joy, I pray.
(Pray the Prayer of Our Savior.)

(Morning)
God, I know there is much work to be done today to promote your realm in the here and now. Help me to do all I can today to that end. In Jesus' name. Amen.

(Evening)
My body is tired, God, but even as I sleep tonight, my spirit says yes to your will. In Jesus' name. Amen.

FRIDAY, JANUARY 26
(Read Psalm 71:1–6)

(Morning)
Strong God, today and every day, let me lean on you.
My hope and my trust are in you.

(Evening)
Strong God, you were my protection all day long. Now watch over me as I sleep.

My life is often made difficult by outside situations and circumstances over which I have no control. In those difficult times, I find myself wanting to escape and find a hiding place. The places I find are places where I attempt to hide from life; therefore, I do not live life fully. However, when I turn to you, God, my Rock, my Refuge, my Fortress, I find not a place to hide from life, but a place to receive strength to live life.

(Morning)
I call on you this morning, God. Hear my prayer and the prayers of all your people.
(Prayers of Intercession)

(Evening)
Thank you, God, for today's journey and for bringing me safely to its end.
(Prayers of Intercession)

In the comfort of your peace, I pray.
(Pray the Prayer of Our Savior.)

(Morning)
God, today is as new to me as life when I was born. As you have been with me each new day of my life, be with me today also. In Jesus' name. Amen.

(Evening)
God, I have been blessed this day, and I look forward now to a good night's rest. In Jesus' name. Amen.

SATURDAY, JANUARY 27
(Read 1 Corinthians 13:1–7)

(Morning)
Loving God, I woke up this morning with the power of your love in my heart and my surroundings. Help me to show love to everyone I meet today.

(Evening)
Loving God, your love within me made this day shine bright. May that same enduring love give me peace that I might rest now that night has come.

God, help me to remember the love you have for me when I deal with others. When I am impatient, help me to remember your love. When I am unkind to others, help me to remember your love. When I am envious, boastful, arrogant, or rude, help me to remember your love. When I am irritable or resentful, help me to remember your love. Thank you for your love. Without it whatever I may possess or accomplish in life is void.

(Morning)
Out of your love, in my heart for all people, I pray.
(Prayers of Intercession)

(Evening)
I pray for everyone I encountered on my journey today.
(Prayers of Intercession)

In love, I pray.
(Pray the Prayer of Our Savior.)

(Morning)
God, today is as new to me as life was when I was born. As you have been with me each new day of my life, be with me today also. In Jesus' name. Amen.

(Evening)
God, I have been blessed this day, and I look forward now to a good night's rest. In Jesus' name. Amen.

SUNDAY, JANUARY 28
(Read 1 Corinthians 13:8–13)

(Morning)
God of abiding love, thank you for your love, which has endured the test of time.
May I, this day, abide in your love.

(Evening)
God of abiding love, thank you for this day that has ended.
Now I desire to rest in your love and peace that never end.

I praise you, God, for your great love. The magnitude of your love for me is beyond my understanding. Because of this, I am even more grateful for it. My prayer is that in my understanding, I might imitate the love you have for me as a love for all humanity.

(Morning)
Loving God, may the light of your love shine upon all who are in need today.
(Prayers of Intercession)

(Evening)
Thank you, God, for the ability to love even those who were hard to love.
(Prayers of Intercession)

In abiding love, I pray.
(Pray the Prayer of Our Savior.)

(Morning)
God, as I start out this new day, I am sustained by the assurance of your love. In Jesus' name. Amen.

(Evening)
God, this has been a good day. Nevertheless, like many good things, it has ended. Thank you for your love that never ends. It is in the comfort of your love that I sleep tonight. In Jesus' name. Amen.

MONDAY, JANUARY 29
(Read Luke 5:1–5)

(Morning)
Jesus, when I meet you in my work today,
will I be ready to trust what you ask me to do?

(Evening)
Jesus, have I been humble enough to step over my pride
and do what you have asked of me in my work today?

Faith and work are not mutually exclusive. Yet I know sometimes I have not responded when you challenged me in my work, Jesus. I have left undone an act of kindness or avoided making a decision with integrity because I was not willing to do what you asked of me. Jesus, when I hear your voice in my work today, lift me from discouragement and apathy. Help me to respond as you would have me respond.

(Morning)
Jesus, you used the tools at hand to be present to the people around you.
Help me to follow your example as I lift up the work and lives
of the people I meet in my work each day.
(Prayers of Intercession)

(Evening)
Loving Laborer, thank you for your presence in the work done this day.
(Prayers of Intercession)

Jesus continues to work among us, challenging us by his presence.

(Morning)
Remembering Simon Peter's example, I ask for the faith to trust what you ask of me, Jesus. I begin this day willing to cast my net wide. In the Savior's name. Amen.

(Evening)
I watched for and felt your presence in the work done today, Jesus. At the close of the day, I thank you for the gift of rest. In the Savior's name. Amen.

TUESDAY, JANUARY 30
(Read Luke 5:6–11)

(Morning)
Giver of all good gifts, am I worthy to receive the bounty
you will show me this day?

(Evening)
Giver of all good gifts, have I shared your gifts with those around me this day?
Or have I sunk beneath the weight of my selfishness?

I often give in to the temptation of believing I have earned what I have. Material things, success—our society tells us these things come through hard work or perhaps by good luck. It is easy to give in to the sin of feeling, "I am owed; I deserve this." Forgiving God, help me to leave behind the ways of self-centeredness. Help me to lead my life so I may truly follow you.

(Morning)
Patient Teacher, help me to discern the gifts I receive
through the people who are in my prayers today.
(Prayers of Intercession)

(Evening)
Patient Teacher, I thank you for the gifts I have received
through your generous presence this day.
(Prayers of Intercession)

Jesus called his disciples to do difficult and wonderful things.

(Morning)
I begin this day like a fishing expedition, hopeful but unsure of what I will catch. Help me to overcome my fears to do unselfishly what I am asked to do. In the Savior's name. Amen.

(Evening)
I have received the gift of this day now coming to a close. I am grateful for being caught in the net of your calling. Allay my fears, patient Teacher, and lead me to rest. In the Savior's name. Amen.

WEDNESDAY, JANUARY 31
(Read Isaiah 6:1–8)

(Morning)
God of hosts, will I respond willingly this day when I hear your voice calling,
"Whom shall I send, and who will go for us?"

(Evening)
God of hosts, today did I overcome my fear and awe to do the tasks you gave me?

I do not find it an easy thing to come into your presence, God. Doing so means having to wear my imperfections in the presence of your greatness; my sins in the presence of your goodness. Purify me, all-knowing God. Blot out my guilt. Strengthen me in my resolve to serve you with my best, pure self.

(Morning)
All-knowing God, I have been too ready to focus on the sins
of others while ignoring the sins I have committed against them.
Help me to seek the forgiveness of those I have sinned against.
(Prayers of Intercession)

(Evening)
God of new beginnings, I thank you for the opportunities to hear your voice today.
(Prayers of Intercession)

God is an awesome God.
(Sing "Here I Am, Lord" or another familiar hymn.)

(Morning)
I begin this day with your voice reverberating in my very being. May my initial impulse to respond grow into a deliberate and purposeful desire to heed your voice. In the Savior's name. Amen.

(Evening)
I embrace sleep this night, all-knowing God, aware that the source of my strength is the source of all that is glorious in this world. I am grateful for your presence as I lay this day to rest. In the Savior's name. Amen.

THURSDAY, FEBRUARY 1
(Read Isaiah 6:9–13)

(Morning)
O God, your ways are not the ways of humankind. What will happen today to
unstop my ears, to open my eyes, and to make my dull mind comprehend your
Word? What will make me turn and be healed?

(Evening)
O God, did I spend today unrelenting in my contrariness,
intractable in my refusal to take your Word into my heart?
What signs of your power made their way into my consciousness?

God, what is there in human nature that clings to contrariness? Why don't
I choose to hear your voice, to see your wonders, to seek awareness of your
presence? What is it in me that must be brought to desolation before I can
turn my face to your glory? I long to turn my face toward you, O God. Give
me strength.

(Morning)
Powerful, immutable God, I pray for those who do your work in this world,
your voices, your eyes, your healers on this earth.
(Prayers of Intercession)

(Evening)
Powerful, immutable God, I give thanks for those in my life
who have been as your messengers to me.
(Prayers of Intercession)

Even in desolation, God's promise endures.
(Sing "Immortal, Invisible, God Only Wise" or another familiar hymn.)

(Morning)
I begin this day with good intentions. I
pray for the gift of watchfulness, the
gift of listening, the gift of clarity of
thought, the gift of renewal. God, don't
turn away. In the Savior's name. Amen.

(Evening)
I receive the healing restfulness that is a
gift from my God. God watches over me,
listening to my very breath, soothing my
troubled mind, healing my spirit. God,
you did not turn away. In the Savior's
name. Amen.

FRIDAY, FEBRUARY 2
(Read Psalm 138:1–3)

(Morning)
Loving Creator, how can I truly express my gratitude for your steadfast love
and your faithfulness? How can I appreciate the breadth of all
for which I have to be grateful?

(Evening)
Loving Creator, have I been attuned to your gifts of steadfast love and faithfulness
this day? Have I received these gifts with gratitude?

I don't take enough time for thankfulness, Generous One. I let daily demands
distract me from the responsibility and joy of thankfulness and praise. Each
time I call out to you, your answer to my call resounds simple and clear, strengthening my very soul. Your gift of steadfast love and faithfulness is something to
celebrate! I will rejoice in you this day.

(Morning)
Loving Creator, you have given me much for which to be grateful.
I celebrate your gifts to me with praise and thanksgiving.
(Prayers of Intercession)

(Evening)
Loving Creator, I celebrate with gratitude the signs of your
steadfast love and faithfulness in my life today.
(Prayers of Intercession)

Praise God in all you do.
(Sing or speak the words of the Doxology.)

(Morning)
I know my soul's strength lies in you,
loving Creator. Guide me in your
steadfast ways. In the Savior's name.
Amen.

(Evening)
I rest in the comfort of your steadfast
love and faithfulness, O my God. I
praise your holy name and rejoice in
the end of this day. In the Savior's
name. Amen.

SATURDAY, FEBRUARY 3
(Read Psalm 138:4–8)

(Morning)
Steadfast and faithful God, I don't like to ask for help,
but where would I be without you? Stretch out your hand to me.
Deliver me from the midst of trouble, and help me to fulfill your purpose for me.

(Evening)
Steadfast and faithful God, I felt your right hand on mine today.
Did I fulfill your purpose for me?

Even with every proof conceivable, I judge you by human standards. I doubt you. Like a child, I still need reassurance that you will not forsake me. Reassure me, steadfast and faithful God. Strengthen my soul in your purpose for me. Regard me, one of your lowly, and preserve me against the wrath of my enemies. Do not forsake me.

(Morning)
Steadfast Companion, you never have failed to answer my call.
I pray today for the strength to be steadfast and faithful.
(Prayers of Intercession)

(Evening)
Steadfast Companion, people who live by your example are at work in your world.
I lift them up in gratitude.
(Prayers of Intercession)

Wash away my fears, steadfast and faithful God.

(Morning)	(Evening)
I approach this day with my hand in yours, steadfast and faithful God. Though I walk in the midst of trouble, I will call upon you. Fulfill your purpose for me. In the Savior's name. Amen.	I will rest in the refuge of your right hand, steadfast and faithful God. I am comforted, knowing you have not forsaken me. In the Savior's name. Amen.

SUNDAY, FEBRUARY 4
(Read 1 Corinthians 15:1–11)

(Morning)
Redeemer, your name gives hope to me, a sinner.
How will your grace shape me, full of faults and failings as I am?

(Evening)
Redeemer, did I look beyond familiar facts to find the good news today?

I need to hear your story over and over again, Jesus. The facts are harsh, but full of hope. You lived in human pain and suffering, but you transformed it into the good news I long for and want to believe. I know I have not earned the title "Follower of Jesus," but by your grace I wish to embrace it. Extend your grace to me, Redeemer, and help me to be worthy.

(Morning)
Jesus, your friends spoke of you often, even after you were no longer with them.
Today, I remember my family and friends who have died.
(Prayers of Intercession)

(Evening)
Not everything I remember about today feels like good news. Loving Redeemer,
help me to learn from the day's sins, and give me the grace to work harder.
(Prayers of Intercession)

What is your favorite story about Jesus? Reread it.

(Morning)	(Evening)
Jesus, today I will look and listen for your good news in my life. I will try to discern your grace in the world around me, in what I read and hear, and in the people I meet. In the Savior's name. Amen.	I rest this evening remembering even in death, Jesus, you did not leave your friends without hope. I will sleep in the assurance of your grace in my life. In the Savior's name. Amen.

MONDAY, FEBRUARY 5
(Read Luke 6:17–19)

(Morning)
Divine Healer, how healthy am I? Am I open to receive your healing power today?

(Evening)
Divine Healer, what kind of patient have I been today?
Have I ignored the care of your healing presence, the power of your workings?
Or have I reached out to receive your healing virtue?

Holy Healer, now I remember how through the feeding of my mind with impure thoughts, I became troubled with anxiety or vexed by unattained goals. I have ignored the prescriptions you have written for my vexed spirit. So often I forget that wholeness of life comes from you. Humble my thinking that I may meditate on your Word, seek your presence, and be healed from my thoughts and ways. I want to be free and open to your Spirit.

(Morning)
Spirit of health and life, I pray through your limitless power and grace,
you will bring wholeness in the lives of those for whom I pray.
(Prayers of Intercession)

(Evening)
Miraculous Healer of all unclean spirits, I thank you
for the signs of your healing touch that I witnessed this day.
(Prayers of Intercession)

**"And all in the crowd were trying to touch him,
for power came out from him and healed all of them."**
(Sing "He Touched Me" or another familiar hymn.)

(Morning)	(Evening)
I begin this day with an awareness that the One who makes life whole and complete is near me. May I receive the One's cleansing power and be healed. Thanks be to Christ. Amen.	I come to evening time, giving thanks for the working of your healing grace. I lie down now in contentment, asking to be revived through the power of your presence. Thanks be to Christ. Amen.

TUESDAY, FEBRUARY 6
(Read Luke 6:20–26)

(Morning)
Teacher, what kind of disciple am I? Am I willing to receive your teachings today?

(Evening)
Teacher, what kind of disciple have I been today?
Have the discomforts of discipleship pushed me away from you?
Or have I been a faithful follower in the midst of difficulties?

I am mindful of how I become timid for you when faced with various forms of opposition, the fear of failure, or ridicule from people. Sometimes I forget that happiness comes from you; too often I hold back in fear. Give confidence where I have doubt, and equip me to trust in your grace. I want to be a participating disciple in your purpose on earth.

(Morning)
Giver of happiness, I pray your unexplainable peace will bring purpose
and quietness to the lives of those for whom I pray.
(Prayers of Intercession)

(Evening)
Giver of happiness, I thank you for the relationships I shared this day
that bear testimony to your way of peace and happiness.
(Prayers of Intercession)

God works in mysterious ways.
(Sing "He Leadeth Me" or another familiar hymn.)

(Morning)
I begin this day open to the way you lead me. May the experiences through which you lead me anchor my faith. May your will be done in me. Thanks be to Christ. Amen.

(Evening)
I lie down in the gift of your peace, commending to you the cares of this day to be renewed by a season of rest. Thanks be to Christ. Amen.

WEDNESDAY, FEBRUARY 7
(Read Jeremiah 17:5–10)

(Morning)
Searcher of the heart, in whom do I place my trust?
Am I ready to depend on you above all else?

(Evening)
Searcher of the heart, where did I place my trust today?
Did the parched soil cause my spirit to become desolate?
Or have I been like a tree planted by the waters, producing much fruit?

I remember now how in good as well as troubled times, I directed my trust away from you. I chose to forsake you and trust in people. False trusts caused me to experience spiritual drought and spiritual loss. Deliver me from dry places that I may trust in you, caring God. I want to be a bearer of spiritual fruit and stand the tests of life.

(Morning)
Spirit of life and fruitfulness, I pray that in your marvelous way,
you may bring forth new hearts in the lives of those for whom I pray.
(Prayers of Intercession)

(Evening)
Redeemer of hearts, I thank you for evidence
of your redeeming grace at work today.
(Prayers of Intercession)

God works in mysterious ways.
(Sing "'Tis So Sweet to Trust in Jesus" or another familiar hymn.)

(Morning)
I begin this day open to your spiritual power. May your spiritual strength prepare my heart, that I may trust in you and be a bearer of spiritual fruit this day. Thanks be to Christ. Amen.

(Evening)
As I seek to be refreshed in your rest, I place all the cares of this day at your feet; I kneel to pray and let go. Thanks be to Christ. Amen.

THURSDAY, FEBRUARY 8
(Read Psalm 1:1–3)

(Morning)
Knower of ways, which path am I traveling? Am I ready to walk where you lead?

(Evening)
Knower of ways, which way have I traveled today?
Have I followed where evil counsel directed and dictated?
Or have I delighted in your direction according to your Word?

I remember now how I was enticed by evil counsel and lived in association with those who have no regard for you or your teachings. Sometimes I forget that true happiness is a free gift from you, loving God. Direct my spirit that I may open up and reflect on your Word for my guide in life. I want to bring forth fruit of an unfading life.

(Morning)
Divine Counselor, I pray that in your miracle-working power, through your Word, you may bring forth delight in the lives of those for whom I pray.
(Prayers of Intercession)

(Evening)
Director of paths, I am grateful for the tokens
of your presence that I witnessed today.
(Prayers of Intercession)

God works in mysterious ways.
(Sing "Take My Life, God, Let It Be" or another familiar hymn.)

(Morning)
I begin this day reflecting on your Word as a guide for my life. May your directions be a delight to my heart, that I may bear spiritual fruit in every situation in life. Thanks be to Christ. Amen.

(Evening)
As I close the book on this day, may my stewardship of life usher me into a peaceful rest. May the activity of sleep renew my strength. Thanks be to Christ. Amen.

FRIDAY, FEBRUARY 9
(Read Psalm 1:4–6)

(Morning)
Guide of life, how deep is my love for your Word?
Am I ready to be directed in your way today?

(Evening)
Guide of life, have I followed your directions today?
Have I been blown as the chaff when caught up in the wind?
Or have I been anchored in the security of the congregation of the blessed?

Sometimes I am prone to wander from the instructions of the Word of life, and I follow the way of evil counsel, which sometimes appears to be rewarding on the surface. Yet when I follow the directions of your Word, I find prosperity, stability, and security are experienced by a lifestyle that reflects divine instructions. I want to be a spiritual fruit bearer and be known by you, Creator God.

(Morning)
Sustainer of life, I pray that in your mysterious working, you may bring forth spiritual fruit and security in the lives of those for whom I pray.
(Prayers of Intercession)

Preserver of the way, I thank you for the signs of nurturing
and protective power that I observed today.
(Prayers of Intercession)

God works in mysterious ways.
(Sing "He Hideth My Soul" or another familiar hymn.)

(Morning)
I begin this day open to the word you are giving. Direct my way. May this guidance lead me in the path that your will may be done in my life. Thanks be to Christ. Amen.

(Evening)
I lie down in your security, placing in your hand the cares of this day, seeking to be renewed through the Christ. Thanks be to Christ. Amen.

SATURDAY, FEBRUARY 10
(Read 1 Corinthians 15:12–19)

(Morning)
Resurrection Power, how strong is my faith in you?
Can I withstand the onslaught of all the doubting forces I face?

(Evening)
Resurrection Power, what kind of faith have I possessed today?
Have the winds of doubt prevented me from living a victorious life?
Or have I been a strong testimony of faith in you?

My memory is fresh with the times I have become so obsessed with materialism that my faith wavered and my outlook on life became worldly. In such moments, I tend to ignore your great creative power and the faithfulness of your promises. Steady my faith that I will refuse to doubt any of your Word.

(Morning)
Deliverer of life, I pray through your great grace,
you will quicken the faith in the lives of those for whom I pray.
(Prayers of Intercession)

(Evening)
Renewer of life, I thank you for the signs of your
resurrected presence that I witnessed today.
(Prayers of Intercession)

"For if the dead are not raised, then Christ has not been raised."
(Sing "If God Is Dead" or another familiar hymn.)

(Morning)
I begin this day willing to give testimony to the reality of your presence. May these statements be used to move someone from doubt to faith. Thanks be to Christ. Amen.

(Evening)
I pull the curtain on this day and place all of my small efforts in your hands to be blessed by you. Thanks be to Christ. Amen.

SUNDAY, FEBRUARY 11
(Read 1 Corinthians 15:20)

(Morning)
Resurrection Power, what is the measure of my joy in your great power?
Am I poised to proclaim your greatness today?

(Evening)
Resurrection Power, what kind of witness have I given to you today?
Have I been so concerned about how I could enjoy life that I forgot to declare
the greatness of the Giver and the Sustainer of life?

I remember how through the cares of this world, the obsession of material things, or the hollow ring of the applause of people, I have lost my focus on you. In such moments, I forget that true life comes from you; too often I live only in the now. Rekindle my hope in you, and free me for greater service through the resurrection power of Jesus Christ.

(Morning)
Spirit of eternal life, I pray that in your life-giving way,
you may bring forth living waters in the lives of those for whom I pray.
(Prayers of Intercession)

(Evening)
Giver of everlasting life, I rejoice in the expressions of
your presence I observed today.
(Prayers of Intercession)

God works in mysterious ways.
(Sing "He Lives" or another familiar hymn.)

(Morning)
I begin this day open to the words of hope that you speak to me. May these words be my guide as I reflect on a living hope in you. Thanks be to Christ. Amen.

(Evening)
I lie down in the comfort of your presence, ready to be revived through your gift of sleep. Thanks be to Christ. Amen.

MONDAY, FEBRUARY 12
(Read Genesis 45:3–7)

(Morning)
Holy Guide, you have given us families and loved ones. Help us to bring them joy.

(Evening)
Holy Guide, you lead us on strange paths, and we know not where we go.
Our lives snake through grim journeys, but you respond in love.
You take our dreary moments and speak through them.

Thinking of the life of Joseph reminds me of circuitous journeys I have taken against my will—journeys where I was convinced that nothing good could ever result but later learned that it did. On the other hand, I think of a journey I was convinced would bring good, yet it did not. Holy Guide, like Joseph, I must remind myself that good may yet come; this journey may yet have a message for me. I am thankful to have moved to new journeys, for you, O God, will not forsake me.

(Morning)
God of the troubled and confused, you bring peace beyond comprehension.
Thank you for being.
(Prayers of Intercession)

(Evening)
God, help me to reach out and forgive my brothers and sisters,
for I may have need of their forgiveness as well.
(Prayers of Intercession)

"God sent me before you to preserve life."

(Morning)
As this day unfolds, I am reminded of how much I need your guidance. Lead me, God. In the name of the Christ. Amen.

(Evening)
The pain of this day is lessened when compared to the pain of others. Thank you for reminding me that I have you. In the name of the Christ. Amen.

TUESDAY, FEBRUARY 13
(Read Genesis 45:8–11, 15)

(Morning)
Holy Binder of hearts and lives, as your grace brought Joseph
from victim to victor, you raise us from sadness to joy.

(Evening)
Holy Binder of hearts and lives, you give us more
than we need and often more than we ask. Reunite us in your love.

If Joseph could forgive and reunite with those who betrayed him, then I must at least reach out to those I may have overlooked or forgotten. I can look for the human family united through Christ. Life, after all, is about relationships. God, with your help, my soul can be free of those long-standing grudges families often harbor. Through the power of your love, I will search for Christ in my siblings and strengthen relationships.

(Morning)
God, you bring us together as family. Help us not to become lost in self.
(Prayers of Intercession)

(Evening)
God, you bring us together as family. Help us not to become lost in self.
(Prayers of Intercession)

"So it was not you who sent me here, but God."

(Morning)
What do you require of me but to live justly, love mercy, and walk humbly with you? In the name of the Christ. Amen.

(Evening)
Your mercy cascades upon me like a peaceful storm. Enrich my soul through the joys and the frustrations this day held. In the name of the Christ. Amen.

WEDNESDAY, FEBRUARY 14
(Read Psalm 37:1–8)

(Morning)
O God, evil sometimes seems to win, but you rise above it and then it loses. Your love outshines the shadows within a human heart, and evil is destroyed.

(Evening)
O God, I am committed to you. You have opened my soul and my mind.

Commitment frightens us, but you require it of us. Through giving us Christ, you have shown us the ultimate commitment. I will commit my life to you and trust you because I know you will act in my best interest.

(Morning)
Free my heart from envy and anger as I face this day. It is a good day to live for you.
(Prayers of Intercession)

(Evening)
Life was good today. You were there to hear my prayers. Thank you for listening.
(Prayers of Intercession)

"Refrain from anger, and forsake wrath."

(Morning)
This day begins with peace. This day begins with joy. Love filters quickly down from you, O God. Plant these virtues in my soul. In the name of the Christ. Amen.

(Evening)
Rest at day's end brings a chance to reflect; bring feelings of your expansive peace, your joy, and your love. Make tomorrow even better than today. In the name of the Christ. Amen.

THURSDAY, FEBRUARY 15
(Read Psalm 37:9–11, 39–40)

(Morning)
God of refuge, raise my hope and my humility as I face this day.
Let me not be vain. Deliver me from evil.

(Evening)
God of refuge, hear our prayers of confusion. Bring us the calm
that follows the storm. Show us your goodness in a new and joyful way.

I anger as I see the cruelty some show toward others. I ask why anyone would want to hurt another. You bring comfort to the suffering, and you remove their pain. I know you are a loving God who does want anyone to suffer. I shudder to hear someone's sideline advice, "It's God's will," when an individual is in pain. I pray that the person will come to know you better.

(Morning)
Morning breaks anew on the just and the unjust. You are our hope;
your righteousness prevails against the wicked. I pray they will turn to you.
(Prayers of Intercession)

(Evening)
You have given us this day to mend relationships and reach out. Thank you for
binding our souls to those we love and loving those we have just met.
(Prayers of Intercession)

Trust in God and wait quietly for the divine Spirit.

(Morning)	(Evening)
Evil fades in your goodness. Its season is short, and good returns triumphant. In the name of the Christ. Amen.	In the blessed quietness, I find that your goodness belies your presence. You are my God, triumphant. In the name of the Christ. Amen.

FRIDAY, FEBRUARY 16
(Read 1 Corinthians 15:35–38)

(Morning)
Caring One, for both of our lives, we give thanks.
For our brief residence on earth and for our eternal life, we are blessed by Christ's love.

(Evening)
Caring One, like the seed in the ground, like the moth in the cocoon, the soul has
two lifetimes: one fragile, one eternal. For those with faith, you, O God, are in both.

Our annual spiritual journey toward Easter recalls Christ's role in both of our lives.

(Morning)
Just as you have sown our lives on earth, let us follow your example
by sowing our message to others. Help us to enrich both lives
of those around us by sharing your message.
(Prayers of Intercession)

(Evening)
God of love, Parent of ultimate sacrifice, help us to remember your pain and
suffering as you watched the world reject your Child. Help us to put our own
suffering into perspective as we reflect on your sorrow and the sorrow of your
children suffering around the world.
(Prayers of Intercession)

Some may ask how the dead can be raised. Thanks be to Christ, we know.

(Morning)	(Evening)
Bring us out of our cocoons. Nurture our hearts as we seek to grow. In the name of the Christ. Amen.	Thanks be to Christ who elevates us to kinship with Christ and gives life beyond death. In the name of the Christ. Amen.

SATURDAY, FEBRUARY 17
(Read 1 Corinthians 15:42–50)

(Morning)
Heavenly Creator, thank you for your eternal being
and for inviting us to be a part of it.

(Evening)
Heavenly Creator, I am grateful that the body spiritual
will not have the flaws of the body earthly. Thank you for transcending us
beyond physical imperfections and suffering.

Creator God, this passage brings to mind two kinds of bodily weakness. While the scripture surrounding these verses focuses on the weaknesses of human nature, I am reminded of those who have genuine physical weaknesses—from ailments such as depression to debilitating diseases that weaken the body and try the soul. Verses 51–52 give comfort to those with either kind of weakness: "We will all be changed in a moment, in the twinkling of an eye, at the last trumpet."

(Morning)
Through making us human, you imbued us all with a kinship.
As you did with the first human beings, you have given us the precious gift of life.
As you did through Christ, you have given us the promise of the life to come.
(Prayers of Intercession)

(Evening)
Another day has passed with some people hating others—and all for no cause.
Help us to willingly eradicate prejudice and to inspire others who have bound
themselves in hatred. Help me to show them your joyous plan of diversity.
(Prayers of Intercession)

"What is sown is perishable, what is raised is imperishable."

(Morning)
God, you made our physical bodies in your earthly image. You have blessed us with boundless diversity. In the name of the Christ. Amen.

(Evening)
Wise Creator, you have made our spiritual bodies in your heavenly image. Thank you for loving us all equally. In the name of the Christ. Amen.

SUNDAY, FEBRUARY 18
(Read Luke 6:27–38)

(Morning)
Christ, you ask me to do what may seem impossible:
to love and treat kindly someone who has deliberately hurt me.
Help me respond to that person in the way you would respond.

(Evening)
Christ, you challenge us to do the impossible,
yet you promise to reward us for meeting the challenge.

Today's scripture reminds us how we must respond to evil: we are to exhibit selfless, compassionate behavior. To love our enemies is an excellent concept. Our responsibility is to take it beyond concept. God, we are to actualize your love to those we prefer to avoid—whether they differ from us by ethnicity, social level, gender variation, or any other category. In some cases this command means for us to love ourselves, for sometimes we are our own worst enemies and in most need of our prayers.

(Morning)
Wise God, you challenge us and promise to help us meet your expectations.
Give us strength to meet them.
(Prayers of Intercession)

(Evening)
Thank you for focusing our lives and thoughts on love, not hate.
Help us to lessen the hate in this world.
(Prayers of Intercession)

"Be compassionate, as your God is compassionate."

(Morning)
God, help us to focus on the needs of others and forget the potential enemy within. In the name of the Christ. Amen.

(Evening)
Christ, you have reminded us that what goes around comes around. Help us to deal fairly with others, and guide them to be fair with us. In the name of the Christ. Amen.

MONDAY, FEBRUARY 19
(Read Psalm 99:6–9)

(Morning)
Welcoming God, I awaken to continue my journey into your presence.

(Evening)
Welcoming God, I rejoice in the wonderful ways you greet me and accept me.

God, you are a friend and a guide to your people throughout the ages, and so we praise you with thanks and joy. To countless people who have cried out to you, you have shown your mercy, you have revealed your love, and you have spoken your word. You offer to all who faithfully seek you the assurance of your steadfast love and presence. Greet us in this time as we bring our lives and hopes to you. Reach out to us and draw us near so we can gain strength and courage from your power.

(Morning)
I greet this new day knowing that you hear my prayers, O God.
(Prayers of Intercession)

(Evening)
Even as I rest, O God, you hear those who call your name,
and you greet them in love and mercy.
(Prayers of Intercession)

**As we draw near to you, wonderful God, you draw near to us.
Thank you for your steadfast companionship.**

(Morning)
I sense your nearness, holy God; my spirit stretches for your Spirit, and I listen for your guiding voice. Praise be to Christ. Amen.

(Evening)
In the peace of your protecting embrace, God, I rest and gain new energy for tomorrow. Praise be to Christ. Amen.

TUESDAY, FEBRUARY 20
(Read Luke 9:28–36)

(Morning)
Loving God, from the valleys I travel.
I come now to your holy mountain in search of your transforming word.

(Evening)
Loving God, when I have stumbled on the journey to you,
you have given me strength and courage.

God, Jesus knew the value of taking special time to be with you. He frequently separated himself from the tasks and business of daily living to be renewed in your presence. And you greeted Jesus each time he sought your holy touch and wisdom. He knew you as a loving, intimate Parent, ready to receive and embrace him. Let us hear again Jesus' invitation to draw close to you with him; claim us together with Jesus as your chosen cherished ones.

(Morning)
God, you seek to make yourself known to every person in unique ways.
(Prayers of Intercession)

(Evening)
How have you greeted people today, God?
What blessings have you poured into someone's life?
(Prayers of Intercession)

**I will spend some special time today to be with you,
God, knowing you accept me as your own precious creation.**

(Morning)
God, today I seek to be in your presence.
Let me not miss your voice when you
speak. Praise be to Christ. Amen.

(Evening)
Tonight I will rest comfortably, God,
because I know you will greet me again
in the new day. Praise be to Christ.
Amen.

WEDNESDAY, FEBRUARY 21
(Read Exodus 34:29–35)

(Morning)
Brilliant God, this new day embraces me just as your radiant love encircles me.

(Evening)
Brilliant God, my heart is aglow with your power,
and my soul is aflame with your Spirit.

O God, we confess we often fail to share our faith and show your love because we are uncomfortable talking about spirituality at home, in the workplace, and in the neighborhood. We come to you, but we do not go for you. We cover our faith as Moses covered his face, and we place our relationship with you in a separate compartment of our lives. Forgive us for failing to be courageous when you need us most. Embolden us today. Send us out to live and work for you and for your realm.

(Morning)
Use me to change lives today, God; call me into your service.
(Prayers of Intercession)

(Evening)
Thank you for sending me on a mission for you today, O God.
(Prayers of Intercession)

God, I am a vessel through which you pour love on the world.

(Morning)
Light of the world, today help me introduce even one person to you. Praise be to Christ. Amen.

(Evening)
Light of the world, your radiance pierces the night and brings a new dawn each morning. Praise be to Christ. Amen.

THURSDAY, FEBRUARY 22
(Read Luke 9:37–43)

(Morning)
Empowering God, you are the source of healing and restoring.

(Evening)
Empowering God, you make new the lives of your people whom you cherish.

God, Jesus' life demonstrates that you greet us and make yourself known to each of us for a special purpose. Jesus returned from his mountaintop experience in your presence and immediately healed a child and transformed a family's life. Our relationship with you kindles within us a commitment to loving action in your name. We gain power from your presence and commit to use that power to make a positive difference for others. Guide us to people for whom we can be a special blessing in Christ's name.

(Morning)
Strengthen and encourage me in my work for you, O God.
(Prayers of Intercession)

(Evening)
Thank you for the resources and inspiration you have given me
for devoted service, O God.
(Prayers of Intercession)

I am God's agent of healing and restoration in this world.
(Sing "Spirit of the Living God" or another familiar hymn.)

(Morning)	(Evening)
God, today let me be the instrument of your compassion. Praise be to Christ. Amen.	Thank you, God, for the honor of representing you. Praise be to Christ. Amen.

FRIDAY, FEBRUARY 23
(Read 2 Corinthians 3:12–18)

(Morning)
Open my heart today, God, that I may radiate praise and joy.

(Evening)
Open my heart, tonight, God. You have cleared my vision to see you.

God, you know we create barriers that prevent us from fully experiencing and enjoying our relationship with you. These barriers are veils that leave us unable to gaze at your glorious workings in our lives. We fear trusting you fully. We fear treading into the changed future that you prepare for us. We hesitate to accept your vision of who we can be tomorrow because we have grown comfortable today. Forgive us, we pray. Unlock our vision and creativity. Free us to tap into your creating and renewing force to enjoy all kinds of sight, including foresight, hindsight, and insight—each pointing beyond outer realities to a deeper reality within us.

(Morning)
God, increase our sensitivity to the needs of your people.
(Prayers of Intercession)

(Evening)
Tonight, God, I pray for those who, like me,
are struggling to shed veils and tear down barriers.
(Prayers of Intercession)

**God's glory is revealed to me every day in Jesus Christ,
and my soul is open to receive you, God.**

(Morning)
Inspiring God, help me to stay open to new ideas and to feast on what is fascinating, memorable, and beautiful. Praise be to Christ. Amen.

(Evening)
Inspiring God, reveal to us your hopes for tomorrow. Praise be to Christ. Amen.

SATURDAY, FEBRUARY 24
(Read 2 Corinthians 4:1–2)

(Morning)
Dearest God, I freely offer you all of my hopes and dreams for this new day.

(Evening)
Dearest God, I place all of my successes and failures of this day in your hands.

O God, your loving compassion and forgiveness make it easy to be open and vulnerable in my relationship with you. I fully trust my heart in your tender care, knowing you will never ridicule me, condemn me, or turn away from me. But it is hard to be as honest and truthful in relationships with other people. We often hide our emotional and spiritual core by protecting ourselves from exposure and imagined harm. Reassure us, God; loosen this tight grip that clenches our hearts. Let your love inspire us to develop relationships based on unconditional trust and openness. Empower us with courage to draw from your energy and build love, generosity, and mutual concern into our relationships, just as Jesus did with people in his life.

(Morning)
Help me to risk loving so that I may truly live for you, O God.
(Prayers of Intercession)

(Evening)
Thank you for encouraging me and uplifting me today
as I sought to nurture meaningful connections with people.
(Prayers of Intercession)

I am an expression of God's life and love in the lives of people I meet.

(Morning)
I am excited to go with you into this day, loving God, and meet the people you'll draw to me. Praise be to Christ. Amen.

(Evening)
I thank you for your companionship today, loving God, and I ask that tomorrow I may be a companion to another. Praise be to Christ. Amen.

SUNDAY, FEBRUARY 25
(Read Psalm 99:1–5)

(Morning)
Almighty God, hear my joyful praise today.
With a glad and grateful spirit, I worship you.

(Evening)
Almighty God, the universe is full of divine presence.

God, today I recall and celebrate your mighty acts across the centuries, caring for people and drawing them close to you through faithful love, reaching out to embrace and uplift. You sent Jesus to establish your realm of justice and truth in people's hearts so we may establish it for you in this world. You are always present to offer new beginnings and new opportunities. You bring joy and hope where there were lifelessness and despair. Today, use us to further your purposes; make your intentions for us known, and fulfill your promises in us.

(Morning)
I offer you my life, O God, to use for your goals.
(Prayers of Intercession)

(Evening)
Thank you for this day and all the blessings you have revealed, God.
(Prayers of Intercession)

I love God with all my mind, heart, and spirit. Praise God!
(Sing "Joyful, Joyful, We Adore You" or another familiar hymn.)

(Morning)	(Evening)
This is your holy day, God; I will rejoice and be glad in it. Praise be to Christ. Amen.	Thank you, God, for receiving my praise. I now look forward to another week of partnership with you. Praise be to Christ. Amen.

MONDAY, FEBRUARY 26
(Read Luke 4:1–13)

(Morning)
Jesus, I love you. I know you faced temptation in your life. Help me today to stand tall and not yield to the temptations of life. Guide me today.

(Evening)
Jesus, thank you for coming through for me today. Thank you for giving me the strength to be strong in the face of temptations.

Help me to be full of the Holy Spirit as you were upon your return from the Jordan. Help me to be faithful to you. Show me how to be loyal to you, O God. Teach me how to worship you and serve only you. Help me to stay focused on you, worshiping you in spirit and in truth. Help me in my actions not to put you to the test. Hear my prayers, O God, my Strength and my Redeemer.

(Morning)
I praise you for being a loving God who is a tremendous God of hope.
(Prayers of Intercession)

(Evening)
I need your help to be effective in my daily walk with you.
(Prayers of Intercession)

Thank you, God, for being a prayer-answering God.
(Pray the Prayer of Our Savior.)

(Morning)
Help me to be faithful to you. God, so often I desire loyal friends. Help me to always be loyal and faithful to you. Praise be to Christ, our Savior. Amen.

(Evening)
Help me to stay focused on what you deem to be important. Praise be to Christ, our Savior. Amen.

TUESDAY, FEBRUARY 27
(Read Deuteronomy 26:6–11)

(Morning)
God, in my haste, help me to remember to put you first.
You are the One who opens doors that no one can close. I thank you.
Help me to show my gratitude to you as I share the first fruits and tithes of my life.

(Evening)
God, in your mercy, I thank you that throughout history, you have not been too busy
to hear the cries of your African American children for freedom, justice, and
deliverance from oppression and affliction.

Thank you for being Jehovah Jireh, the provider—a provider of a land of milk
and honey for your children initially found in desperate straits. It is truly amazing how you provide.

(Morning)
I am so grateful for the many hills and valleys through which
you have brought me. Time and time again, I am appreciative of the way
you have made the impossible possible in my life.
(Prayers of Intercession)

(Evening)
Thank you for miracles and divine intervention in my life
and throughout the history of all your people.
(Prayers of Intercession)

"God heard our voice and saw our affliction, our toil, and our oppression."

(Morning)
Show me the way to continue to express
my gratitude to you for all of your
goodness to me and the community of
faith. Praise be to Christ, our Savior.
Amen.

(Evening)
I will praise you all of my life for your
amazing grace. Praise be to Christ, our
Savior. Amen.

WEDNESDAY, FEBRUARY 28
(Read Deuteronomy 26:1–6)

(Morning)
God, we come into the land you have provided for us, and we are grateful.
Help us to always remember that you are the provider.
Help us to always remember to respect the reality that you make the impossible possible.

(Evening)
God, help me to trust your provision. Help me to be faithful
in giving my tithes and not view it as a chore.

God, you provide in mighty ways "lands that we can possess and settle into." I am so thankful. Your provision is beyond my wildest dreams. Help me to comfortably settle into your provision for me.

(Morning)
God, help me to remember there is nothing I can give that compares in any way
with the magnitude of your giving to me.
(Prayers of Intercession)

(Evening)
You have brought me from a mighty long way, loving God. Thank you.
(Prayers of Intercession)

**God, you are a Mother to the motherless and a Father to the fatherless.
I thank you for the way you have brought my ancestors
and my family through history.**
(Pray the Prayer of Our Savior.)

(Morning)
O God, I know you have heard the prayers of my ancestors, and it is awesome to realize that today you hear me too. Praise be to Christ, our Savior. Amen.

(Evening)
God, show me how to settle into the land you have given me to possess. I want to do right and be right. Praise be to Christ, our Savior. Amen.

THURSDAY, MARCH 1
(Read Psalm 91:1–2, 11–16)

(Morning)
Almighty God, it is such a privilege to be alive and know that you are a shelter
for me from the storms of life. What would I do without you?
Where would I be without you?

(Evening)
Almighty God, Jesus, and Holy Spirit, you protect me from seen and unseen
dangers. I praise and thank you.

I can depend on you, God, when I am confronted with unexpected challenges
in my life. As I struggle to make sense of my health trials, I am comforted and
assured by your promises to provide protection, refuge, and deliverance.

(Morning)
God, I am your vessel available to be used by you today.
Thank you for your angels that guard me.
(Prayers of Intercession)

(Evening)
I love you, God. I have called on you and thanked you
for rescuing me in the midst of my dilemmas.
(Prayers of Intercession)

I need you to come through for me in so many ways.
No one else can. I am counting on you, El Shaddai.
(Pray the Prayer of Our Savior.)

(Morning)
God, today I want you to be my
Fortress. Praise be to Christ, our Savior.
Amen.

(Evening)
God, I need you now more than ever.
Thank you for helping me. Praise be to
Christ, our Savior. Amen.

FRIDAY, MARCH 2
(Read Romans 10:8–13)

(Morning)
God, too often I glibly confess that I am a Christian
and you are my Redeemer and Savior.

(Evening)
God, I pray for those around the world who confess you as Redeemer and Savior.

I thank you for the privilege of having met some of your children in China who sacrificed dearly. Help me to remember people who sacrificed as the Christians in China did during the cultural revolution. Bibles and hymnbooks were burned, churches were closed, and times were hard for people of faith.

(Morning)
God, help me to remember to pray for those who do not know you.
(Prayers of Intercession)

(Evening)
God, forgive me when I make artificial barriers or distinctions among us as human beings. Help me to remember I have sisters and brothers around the world in the faith whom I do not know by name; but you do.
(Prayers of Intercession)

**God, I thank you for the witness of the Christian martyrs
throughout the ages.**
(Pray the Prayer of Our Savior.)

(Morning)
God, you know the needs of the people in countries around the world who confess your name. Jesus, be with them in a special way today. Praise be to Christ, our Savior. Amen.

(Evening)
God, how can I make my confession of you as my Redeemer and Savior count in your scheme of things? Praise be to Christ, our Savior. Amen.

SATURDAY, MARCH 3
(Read Deuteronomy 26:10–11)

(Morning)
O God, I am so thankful for your goodness in my life. I thank you for my gifts and talents. I bring to you my tithes and firstfruits of my labor and toil.

(Evening)
O God, show me how to always express my gratitude
for the bounty you provide in my life.

El Shaddai, you are the God who is more than enough. You have heard my cries. You answer in due season. You always come through in your own way. You bring me forth to a land of surprises, a land of milk and honey. Help me to hold on and wait on you. When the answers are not always forthcoming, God, help me to know you will come through.

(Morning)
God, I celebrate the amazing ways you provide for me and your countless children. I celebrate that you have blessed me to live, work, and study in America and abroad. Thank you.
(Prayers of Intercession)

(Evening)
O God, I treasure your friendship and appreciate your loving-kindness in my behalf.
(Prayers of Intercession)

Who am I that I should experience such amazing grace from you, loving God?
(Pray the Prayer of Our Savior.)

(Morning)
God, it is phenomenal the way you have moved in my life. Thank you. Praise be to Christ, our Savior. Amen.

(Evening)
God, I trust you even when you are taking me on a journey that is not always easy for me to understand. Praise be to Christ, our Savior. Amen.

SUNDAY, MARCH 4
(Read Psalm 91:9–10)

(Morning)
God, thank you for your protection of me and your children on the earth.
You are a place of refuge.

(Evening)
God, thank you for being a safe place where I can come and share my concerns.
I feel privileged to be able to come to you in the midst of my trials and storms of
life and experience your protection.

Daily, I am assured by your promises that your angels will look after me as I go
about my life. You are there in the midst of my struggles, victories, and even
dangers. I can depend on you, protecting God, for protection. This knowledge
is comforting and astounding.

(Morning)
Open my eyes that I may see the many ways you protect me today.
(Prayers of Intercession)

(Evening)
God, you protect your children in rural, urban, and suburban areas
as well as in combat zones. Protect your children in schools.
(Prayers of Intercession)

**God, I thank you for the way you protect me as well as
all of your children in the community of faith today.**
(Pray the Prayer of Our Savior.)

(Morning)
God, in a mighty way, protect me from
harm and danger today. Praise be to
Christ, our Savior. Amen.

(Evening)
Thank you for protecting me from evil.
Praise be to Christ, our Savior. Amen.

MONDAY, MARCH 5
(Read Luke 13:31–35)

(Morning)
God, as I wake to another day of life, I will face whatever will come my way with
your help. I give you thanks because I know you will be with me.

(Evening)
God, thank you for helping me through another day of life and all that I faced.
I give you thanks because you were there.

Loving God, we see Jesus facing great danger for simply living out the ministry to which you called him. With the Pharisees' threats against him and with Herod's desire to kill him, my Savior, your Child, faced death because of his teaching, preaching, and healing. Unlike Jesus, we do not face death as the obstacle to living out our ministries.

(Morning)
Help me, God, to recognize the obstacles I face as I live out my Christian beliefs.
(Prayers of Intercession)

(Evening)
I have made it through another day seeking to see more clearly my obstacles.
Recognizing my obstacles, I thank you for the energy
to live my beliefs and to perform my ministries.
(Prayers of Intercession)

As Christ taught me, I pray.
(Pray the Prayer of Our Savior.)

(Morning)
Heavenly Creator, I put myself in your hands today. Teach me the obedience and perseverance I need to follow the example of Jesus. In the light of Christ. Amen.

(Evening)
Loving God, thank you for your presence today in my life. As I retire for the evening, give me the rest I need to wake tomorrow with the energy and strength to live out your will in my life. In the light of Christ. Amen.

TUESDAY, MARCH 6
(Read Genesis 15:1–12, 17–18)

(Morning)
Loving God, I am grateful for another day of life.
Help me to show my gratitude to you.

(Evening)
Loving God, thank you for receiving the gratitude I have shown you today.

God, Abram was your faithful servant. There were times when he did not understand what you asked or talked about. Even though you declared that Abram's heir would inherit the lands, he had no children and therefore did not understand this prophecy. Nevertheless, he gave you thanks and praise without hesitation. For what do we not understand that you are asking us to give thanks?

(Morning)
Even if I do not think I should be grateful,
today I will seek to find something in which I can express my thanks to you, O God.
(Prayers of Intercession)

(Evening)
In every situation, I am looking for blessings in which to be thankful.
God, help me find the blessings that I had not considered before.
(Prayers of Intercession)

Humbly I pray.
(Pray the Prayer of Our Savior.)

(Morning)	(Evening)
Loving God, help me to find the ways you want me to express my thankfulness to you, even when I do not understand the situation. In the light of Christ. Amen.	Gracious God, as the day passes, I am warmed with the list of items I have discovered. Thank you for your love and giving. In the light of Christ. Amen.

WEDNESDAY, MARCH 7
(Read Genesis 15:1–12, 17–18)

(Morning)
Gracious and loving God, as I rise today,
help me give thanks for the blessings you have given me.

(Evening)
Gracious and loving God, thank you once again for all the blessings you have given
me today. Help me to rejoice in the opportunity to rest in the security of your love.

God, I have always been amazed by the biblical stories in which your grace
was revealed somehow through a dream. Abram had a revelation during a dream.
Once again it was during sleep that you blessed one of your children. Sometimes in our waking hours we worry and pray without ceasing over problems
and situations that we cannot control. But when we lay our heads down to rest
in your hands, we will be refreshed and made ready to face a new day.

(Morning)
God, knowing that I will face many questions for which I will not have answers,
I pray that you will be with me in these situations.
(Prayers of Intercession)

(Evening)
Thank you, God, for giving me the wisdom to figure out when I need to
let go of the situations I can no longer control, and for making me know
that your loving arms will carry me forward into a restful night's sleep.
(Prayers of Intercession)

Confidently I pray.
(Pray the Prayer of Our Savior.)

(Morning)
Send me off, O loving God, with the
assurance that you will stand by my
side this day. In the light of Christ.
Amen.

(Evening)
Almighty God, thank you for the insight
with which you blessed me today. Now I
ask you to help me reach a deep restful
sleep, so that perhaps within that time of
rest you will bless me again. In the light
of Christ. Amen.

THURSDAY, MARCH 8
(Read Psalm 27)

(Morning)
God, you are "my light and my salvation; whom shall I fear?"
Even in my times of trials and tribulation, whom shall I fear if I have you?

(Evening)
God, finally, as this day comes to an end, the light of your salvation still shines.
Of whom should I be afraid?

There are times when we face life's trials and tribulations. We forget the words of the psalmist reminding us that you are always with us and that, therefore, we have no reason to fear. God, one of your greatest gifts to us is other human beings, though sometimes it is in these relationships that we find trials and tribulations. But like the psalmist, I can proclaim, "Whom shall I fear if I trust in you?"

(Morning)
"I believe that I shall see the goodness of God in the land of the living.
Wait for God, be strong, and let your heart take courage; wait for God."
(Prayers of Intercession)

(Evening)
"I believe that I shall see the goodness of God in the land of the living.
Wait for God, be strong, and let your heart take courage; wait for God."
(Prayers of Intercession)

As Christ prayed, I pray.
(Pray the Prayer of Our Savior).

(Morning)	(Evening)
Be with me, O God, as I encounter all the relationships that represent any trial in my life. Help me to trust in you; then I will fear no longer. In the light of Christ. Amen.	Thank you, God, for giving me the strength to love others through trying times. It is through sharing your love with everyone in my life that I receive your blessings. In the light of Christ. Amen.

FRIDAY, MARCH 9
(Read Psalm 27)

(Morning)
Creator God, as the new day rises, so shines the light of your salvation.
Of whom should I be afraid?

(Evening)
Creator God, as this day comes to an end, your light of salvation still shines.
Of whom should I be afraid?

It is painfully true that the trials and tribulations we suffer when we are in discord with others hurt us and can bring great sadness. It is through our personal relationship with you, Savior God, that we gain the inner strength to cling to you. When we are close to you, we can live, fearing no one or nothing because you are with us.

(Morning)
I embark on another day seeking to draw nearer to you
for inner strength and courage.
(Prayers of Intercession)

(Evening)
I celebrate your steadfastness today.
As I drew near to you, you were always present.
(Prayers of Intercession)

In God's peace I pray.
(Pray the Prayer of Our Savior.)

(Morning)
God, I will be strong, and my heart will take courage in you. In the light of Christ. Amen.

(Evening)
God, I will be strong, and my heart will take courage in you. In the light of Christ. Amen.

SATURDAY, MARCH 10
(Read Philippians 3:17–4:1)

(Morning)
O God, thank you for the time you granted me
last night to rest my soul in your arms.

(Evening)
O God, today I rejoice in you. Thank you for giving me courage to stand firm with
you. I am comforted by your mercy, which is present when I have failed.

God, there are times when the greatest difficulty in being a Christian is trying
to follow Christ's example. Sometimes we like to forget that we are Christians,
especially when we are forced to be humble or to give someone else the upper
hand. Paul instructed the church at Philippi, "We must stand firm in God." Paul
calls the church to remember that we are citizens of heaven and not of earth.

(Morning)
Help me today, God, to look to my Savior, Jesus Christ,
as a model for how I am to live my Christian life.
(Prayers of Intercession)

(Evening)
I celebrate the life and resurrection of our Savior, Jesus Christ,
whose life I am inspired by and humbly fall short of.
(Prayers of Intercession)

Humbly I pray.
(Pray the Prayer of Our Savior.)

(Morning)
Go with me now, God, as I embrace the
living of this day. Be with me, Jesus, as I
seek to walk closer to you. Fill me, Holy
Spirit, with the courage to live out my
faith today. In the light of Christ. Amen.

(Evening)
As I retire to a time of restful blessing,
O God, inspire me this night to be more
like our Savior. In the light of Christ.
Amen.

SUNDAY, MARCH 11
(Read Luke 9:28–34)

(Morning)
God, be with me as I rise to a new day.

(Evening)
God, thank you for helping me incline my ear in search of your voice.

Merciful God, we can find many distractions to keep us from concentrating and listening to your voice in our lives. You told Peter and his companions not to be distracted by building noble dwellings. At times we, too, become so distracted by our activities that we miss hearing your voice in our lives. Who knows? We may be missing something very important.

(Morning)
Grace me, O God, with the discipline to seek your voice throughout this day.
(Prayers of Intercession)

(Evening)
As the clutter of the day filled my world, thank you, God,
for breaking through with your voice.
(Prayers of Intercession)

With praise I pray.
(Pray the Prayer of Our Savior.)

(Morning)
Be with me now, God, as I go forward with my day. Help me seek your voice where I would otherwise not seek it. Help me to hear when you are blessing me. In the light of Christ. Amen.

(Evening)
I now seek your love as I rest, God. Refresh my soul. Fill me during this time so that tomorrow I can be even closer to your presence in my life. In the light of Christ. Amen.

MONDAY, MARCH 12
(Read Isaiah 55:1–5)

(Morning)
Abundant God, I arise this morning in a spirit of gratitude.
I face the day knowing you are my Provider.

(Evening)
Abundant God, I come to the end of this day in a spirit of gratitude.
I face the night knowing I can find my rest in you.

Too often I forfeit joy, yearning, and searching for the "one thing" that I believe will make me truly happy. I am stressed because my vocation or employment does not provide the comfort for which I strive. I destroy my spirit of gratitude because I just don't seem to have enough. O God, too often I live out of a perception of lack rather than a perception of abundance. The prophet calls us to look to a higher Source, and in these words I receive the promise of abundant life. *¡Aleluya!* Inclining my ears to these words, I want for nothing. Thank you, God, for my wholeness is in you.

(Morning)
I go forth this day with my mind, soul, and heart open to your Word. Israel's Holy
One, I come to you remembering . . .
(Prayers of Intercession)

(Evening)
O God, for the moments I doubted, complained,
or caused pain to another, forgive me.
(Prayers of Intercession)

**Take heed—the enemy despises gratitude because gratitude leads
to a profound sense of sacredness. In all things be grateful.**

(Morning)	(Evening)
Lead me so that I might share of your abundance with all those I meet this day. In the Savior's name. Amen.	For your guidance, protection, and love, thank you! In the Savior's name. Amen.

TUESDAY, MARCH 13
(Read Isaiah 55:6–9)

(Morning)
Merciful God, I arise this morning in a spirit of blessed assurance.
I face the day knowing you are always near.

(Evening)
Merciful God, I come to the end of this day in a spirit of blessed assurance.
I face the night knowing I am never alone.

Too often I seek success and miss my true calling. My competitive edge does not allow me to appreciate the simple. The workplace receives all of my time. My loved ones get what is left over or squeezed in. Busyness is the attitude of the day. I have to do and be all. I spend little time on reflection and renewal. Whose work have I been called to do anyway? The prophet calls us to look to a wiser Source, and in these words I receive the promise of merciful guidance. *¡Aleluya!* Inclining my ears to these words, I find meaning. Thank you, God, for my purpose is in you.

(Morning)
Israel's God of mercy, I come to you remembering . . .
(Prayers of Intercession)

(Evening)
Lead me, guide me, and use me for your will.
(Prayers of Intercession)

Take heed—the enemy despises meditation because it taps into the power of God within. At all times be aware of the great I Am.

(Morning)
I go forth this day with my mind, soul, and heart open to your Word. In the Savior's name. Amen.

(Evening)
O God, for the moments I acted out of self-interest and labored in vain, forgive me. Thank you for your guidance, protection, and love. Thank you! In the Savior's name. Amen.

WEDNESDAY, MARCH 14
(Read Psalm 63:1–4)

(Morning)
Eternal God, I arise this morning in a spirit of praise.
I face the day knowing you are my God.

(Evening)
Eternal God, I come to the end of this day in a spirit of praise.
I face the night knowing you are watching over me.

The psalmist reveals what is in my soul, O God. I seek to know you, to follow your ways, to love as you love. I know my flesh is weak, yet I am created in your divine image. I know my heart is faint, yet Jesus gives me the power to love away sin and sadness. ¡Gloria a Dios! My soul rejoices in you, O God. In an ever-changing world, you are a constant. Thank you, God! My whole being exalts in you.

(Morning)
God of both King David and the woman at the well, I come to you remembering . . .
(Prayers of Intercession)

(Evening)
My whole being shall reveal the joy that is found in you.
(Prayers of Intercession)

**Take heed—the enemy despises praise because praise
creates an opportunity to be a living witness for others.
Praise God in all things and at all times.**

(Morning)
I go forth this day with my mind, soul, and heart open to your Word. In the Savior's name. Amen.

(Evening)
O God, for the moments I reacted out of anger and fear, forgive me. Thank you for your guidance, protection, and love. Thank you! In the Savior's name. Amen.

THURSDAY, MARCH 15
(Read Psalm 63:5–8)

(Morning)
Almighty God, I arise this morning in a spirit of humbleness.
I face the day knowing you are my strength.

(Evening)
Almighty God, I come to the end of this day in a spirit of humbleness.
I face the night knowing my help comes from you.

The psalmist describes an ageless truth: you are a present God. My peace comes in recognizing you are with me in the midst of my pain and you are at the center of my joy. I find strength in knowing that, although I sometimes stray from you, your love for me is unfailing. Bless your name, O steadfast One! Your love endures forever. O God, even in my finitude, your glory is revealed. Thank you, God. I will forever sing your praises!

(Morning)
God of both Job and Mary, the mother of Jesus, I come to you remembering . . .
(Prayers of Intercession)

(Evening)
Almighty God, my life is in your hands.
(Prayers of Intercession)

Take heed—the enemy despises humbleness because in your humbleness is found the strength of God. Remain always humble before God.

(Morning)
I go forth this day with my mind, soul, and heart open to your Word. In the Savior's name. Amen.

(Evening)
O God, for the moments I boasted, scorned another, or chose the spotlight over hard work, forgive me. Thank you for your guidance, protection, and love. Thank you! In the Savior's name. Amen.

FRIDAY, MARCH 16
(Read Luke 13:1–9)

(Morning)
Creator God, I arise this morning in a spirit of agape.
I face the day knowing you are a just God.

(Evening)
Creator God, I come to the end of this day in a spirit of agape.
I face the night knowing your love is unconditional.

Hearing Jesus' words, I realize we are all equal in your sight, O God. As I witness the pain and suffering around me, I claim, "I am blessed." But does this mean those who endure violence, poverty, and oppression are less blessed? No! All are blessed by having been created by your hand. I believe when even one of your creations perishes, you mourn. Creator God, allow me an understanding of the vastness of your unconditional love. Thank you for revealing this love in Jesus.

(Morning)
God of the rich and of the poor, I come to you remembering . . .
(Prayers of Intercession)

(Evening)
I will see the world with the lenses of your love.
(Prayers of Intercession)

**Take heed—the enemy despises unconditional love because
this form of love has the freedom to reach all of God's creation.
Love freely and allow yourself to be loved in return.**

(Morning)
I go forth this day with my mind, soul, and heart open to your Word. In the Savior's name. Amen.

(Evening)
O God, for the moments I deemed myself or another unworthy of your love and blessings, forgive me. Thank you for your guidance, protection, and love. Thank you! In the Savior's name. Amen.

SATURDAY, MARCH 17
(Read 1 Corinthians 10:1–5)

(Morning)
God of my ancestors, I arise this morning in a spirit of faithfulness,
and I face the day knowing you are a God of the second chance.

(Evening)
God of my ancestors, I come to the end of this day in a spirit of faithfulness,
and I face the night knowing you are the same yesterday, today, and tomorrow.

Paul asks us to remember our ancestors and to pay attention to and learn from their experiences. Whose responsibility is it that I know my history and the history of my people? Mine! I need to know where I came from in order to discern who I am and where I am called to be. You, O God, have been present in my life since before I was born. *¡Gracias mi Dios!* Through the growing pains and the joys, you have been the Source of grace and strength for all generations. *¡Aleluya!*

(Morning)
God of Moses and *de mi abuela,* I come to you remembering . . .
(Prayers of Intercession)

(Evening)
God of Moses and *de mi abuela,* I come to you remembering . . .
(Prayers of Intercession)

**Take heed—the enemy despises faithfulness because
at the core of our faithfulness is a God who remains faithful to us.
Remain faithful through all seasons.**

(Morning)
I go forth this day with my mind, soul, and heart open to your Word. I will remember from whom I have come. In the Savior's name. Amen.

(Evening)
O God, for the moments I denied my history and lost faith in my present, forgive me. For your guidance, protection, and love, thank you! In the Savior's name. Amen.

SUNDAY, MARCH 18
(Read 1 Corinthians 10:6–13)

(Morning)
God of grace, I arise this morning in a spirit of righteousness,
and I face the day knowing you are the Rock on which I stand.

(Evening)
God of grace, I come to the end of this day in a spirit of righteousness,
and I face the night knowing my life is in your hands.

Paul teaches us that we are to break the cycles that destroy us as people of God. God, this is not always easy. I want to be better, different, whole, but at times all I know is what I have endured. The cycles of violence, addiction, and oppression are alive and well. It is only by your grace that I have come this far. Thank you, God, for being my Refuge and my Strength. Thank you for the good news revealed in Jesus—I can become a new creation. I can break the cycle. *¡Gloria a Dios!*

(Morning)
God of new beginnings, I come to you remembering . . .
(Prayers of Intercession)

(Evening)
God of new beginnings, I come to you remembering . . .
(Prayers of Intercession)

Take heed—the enemy despises righteousness because righteousness leaves little room for sin. Find your righteousness in God.

(Morning)
I go forth this day with my mind, soul, and heart open to your Word. Give me strength to stop all injustice and hurt I may witness today. In the Savior's name. Amen.

(Evening)
O God, for the moments I turned away in fear or allowed myself to be engaged in wrongful acts, forgive me. For your guidance, protection, and love, thank you! In the Savior's name. Amen.

MONDAY, MARCH 19
(Read Luke 15:11–20)

(Morning)
Seeking and permissive One, help me to recognize
how I have left your household and your care.

(Evening)
Seeking and permissive One, I know where I have been.
Create in me the deep longing to come home.

"How did I get here?" or "Where am I now?" The questions are good ones, especially on a spiritual journey. On occasion, I have asked for my share and proudly walked off to make my own way. I did not realize my share really belongs to you, and my own way lacks fruitful direction. Here is my chance to pause and look around me. Help me to recognize my surroundings for what they are. Am I where you want me to be?

(Morning)
Waiting One, hear my prayers for those who are feeling distant from you today.
Show me how to be your instrument in turning each one toward you.
(Prayers of Intercession)

(Evening)
Receiving One, thank you for revealing that you long for your children's presence.
Bless each of these with the comfort of your embrace.
(Prayers of Intercession)

To find my way home, I need first to recognize where I am now.

(Morning)
Life moves so fast, it's hard to look up and see where I'm actually going. I know I want all my activity to bring me closer to you. Show me the way to take steps toward home. Thanks be to God. Amen.

(Evening)
Grant me rest, O God, and the assurance that today I have been conscious of my need to turn toward home. Thanks be to God. Amen.

TUESDAY, MARCH 20
(Read Luke 15:25–30)

(Morning)
Gracious God, sometimes your graciousness makes me mad.
I'm not always sure that others deserve the good they receive.
Alert me, I pray, to the times when I subtly judge others to be undeserving of your gifts.

(Evening)
Gracious God, thank you for the good news that when I have been unwise,
I am not unwelcome.

I think I believe there is not enough good to go around. Believing your goodness and mercy are scarce tempts me to think that if others received less, I might receive more. Today I want to look, with your help, for opportunities to celebrate lost lives that have been found. Please help me resist the temptation to be jealous of, or insulted by, the forgiveness you lavish on others. There is enough for me, too.

(Morning)
Loving God, turn my heart from competition to compassion. Bless these children of yours, sisters and brothers for whom I have not always hoped for the best.
(Prayers of Intercession)

(Evening)
God of forgiveness, this is hard for me to do.
Soften my heart so I might pray for the people I think have gotten off easy.
(Prayers of Intercession)

**Just because someone else receives a blessing
does not mean I have been cheated out of one.**

(Morning)
Help me to rejoice in the good that happens to others today. Thanks be to God. Amen.

(Evening)
As I go to sleep tonight, let me do so reciting a few of the many blessings I sometimes take for granted. Thanks be to God. Amen.

WEDNESDAY, MARCH 21
(Read Psalm 32:3–4)

(Morning)
Merciful God, today I want to break the silence and talk to you about my sin.
Grant me insight and courage to become transparent before you.

(Evening)
Merciful God, I have told you what I can, and you have not turned away.
Thank you for your mercy.

I sometimes hide my failings as if they are prized possessions. I believe they need to be kept safe deep inside me where not even you, O God, can see. The longer I hide them, the more life-giving energy is sapped from my being. What I am unable to tell you becomes a barrier between us. I can recall the refreshment that comes with confession and the healing that accompanies forgiveness. Nevertheless, I need to be continuously reminded I can trust you with everything.

(Morning)
Be with all those who carry a burden of guilt this day.
Especially I remember before you these sisters and brothers.
(Prayers of Intercession)

(Evening)
You intend for us to be freed from sin and restored to life through forgiveness.
I pray for those who fear your righteousness more than they trust in your mercy.
(Prayers of Intercession)

Acknowledging my sin opens the door to God's forgiveness.

(Morning)
Open my soul and gently expose the failings that have caused my spirit to dry and wither. Thanks be to God. Amen.

(Evening)
Tonight, I confess my imperfection, trusting in your mercy and forgiveness. Grant me the peaceful rest and refreshment that flow from a clear conscience. Thanks be to Christ. Amen.

THURSDAY, MARCH 22
(Read Joshua 5:9–12)

(Morning)
Provider of all, as you delivered your people from disgrace and met their every
need, so you care for me. Thank you for your faithfulness.

(Evening)
Provider of all, how good it is to spend my days in the presence
of One who provides for my every need.

You provided manna for your people when there was no food to be found. You
blessed them in the abundance of the land, which they helped to harvest. God,
you have provided for me, too, in both ordinary and extraordinary ways. Make
me attentive to your provision. Help me, even as I participate in the gathering,
to recognize that these gifts are signs of your loving-kindness.

(Morning)
You fed your hungry people, Israel.
Hear now my prayers for those who hunger in the world around me.
(Prayers of Intercession)

(Evening)
You satisfy the hungers of the heart.
Be with those who need to be satisfied spiritually or emotionally.
(Prayers of Intercession)

God provides in ordinary and extraordinary ways.

(Morning)	(Evening)
As I walk through this day, open my eyes so I might recognize your acts of provision. Thanks be to God. Amen.	God of manna, God of the land, I rest knowing you can provide for tomorrow. Thanks be to God. Amen.

FRIDAY, MARCH 23
(Read Luke 15:20–24; Psalm 32:1–2, 11)

(Morning)
O Keeper of my spiritual home, let my every action today
constitute a step toward you.

(Evening)
O Keeper of my spiritual home, have I come closer to you today?
Thank you for your expectant waiting.

Whether I have been away just a day or on a long trip, it is a relief to come home. Homecomings are, for me, a return to safety, a salve for isolation, a celebration of relationship. You are always waiting for me to return, always beckoning, always there with open arms. Anticipation and excitement build within me. Today I will be on a journey home.

(Morning)
I pray for those whose memories of home are filled with pain and brokenness.
Help each one to catch a vision of home in you, redeeming the image
of a waiting parent through your acts of welcome and forgiveness.
(Prayers of Intercession)

(Evening)
Inviting God, I pray for those who have felt cast out, despised, disowned. By your
Spirit, prompt my words and deeds that they might exemplify your holy hospitality.
(Prayers of Intercession)

While I am still far off, God is filled with compassion.

(Morning)	(Evening)
You are ready to prepare a feast for me. Help me accept your invitation to attend. Thanks be to God. Amen.	Tonight, I know the comfort of lying down in my own bed. I give you heartfelt thanks for offering me a place of spiritual nurture and rest that I can also call home. Thanks be to God. Amen.

SATURDAY, MARCH 24
(Read 2 Corinthians 5:16–17)

(Morning)
Creator God, you are able to make all things new. I seek the gift of spiritual vision
that will enable me to see myself and others through your eyes.

(Evening)
Creator God, have I allowed you to change my mind about anyone today?
Have I seen someone in a new light, the light of your redemptive love?

I judge others so quickly. I am suspicious whenever an individual does not live
up to my prejudices. It takes discipline, practice, and diligence for me to approach each of your children, expecting I might encounter one who has become new. School me in giving others a chance to be someone unexpected.
Break down the equations I have built that make it so easy for me to judge
others.

(Morning)
Around the world people are denied their status as your children. I pray for those
who are viewed through the lenses of prejudice instead of the love of Christ.
(Prayers of Intercession)

(Evening)
I pray for those who have given up on themselves.
Help each one hear the promise that, in Christ, there is a new creation.
(Prayers of Intercession)

"Everything old has passed away; see, everything has become new!"

(Morning)	(Evening)
I enter this day with the confident hope I will meet someone in a way that only your introduction will make possible. Thanks be to God. Amen.	You are an amazing, creative God. I am inspired by the giftedness I witnessed in your children today. Thanks be to God. Amen.

SUNDAY, MARCH 25
(Read 2 Corinthians 5:18–21)

(Morning)
Reconciling God, you have called me to the ministry of reconciliation.
How can I serve you in this call today?

(Evening)
Reconciling God, I come before you seeking reconciliation
as this day comes to an end.

You have made it clear. Reconciliation is not your work alone; I am invited to join you in this ministry. My culture encourages me to fight, to control, to win. Entering each day as a peacemaker makes me feel that I am outside the mainstream, yet I know it's where you want me to be. To remain strong in this resolve, I need confidence that our relationship is deeply rooted in this same reconciliation.

(Morning)
This morning, I pray for those I know who seem to feel separated from you.
I pray for the reconciliation in their lives that will make all things new.
(Prayers of Intercession)

(Evening)
Tonight, I bring those I know who suffer broken relationships with others.
Grant to all a new point of view that makes reconciliation possible.
(Prayers of Intercession)

In the work of reconciliation, I live out the righteousness of God.

(Morning)
Send me forth with confidence to bring your gift of reconciliation to the world. Thanks be to God. Amen.

(Evening)
I give you thanks for your presence with me as I tried to be your ambassador of reconciliation today. Now I rest in the confidence that through Christ, I am reconciled to you. Thanks be to God. Amen.

MONDAY, MARCH 26
(Read John 12:1–8)

(Morning)
Creator God, you have created both this new day and me.
Make clear your purposes for such a match.

(Evening)
Creator God, I praise you for the gift of your Child, Jesus, who allowed others to
fellowship with and minister to him. Keep me open to others.

Loving God, Mary knew the end was near for Jesus. Boldly, she gave him her
very best. Expensive perfume spoke of the value of his life to her own. In the
midst of hostility, she ministered to Jesus. She violated custom to minister to
him. He understood her need to anoint him. It was a blessing to her. May it be
so with me, O God. Empower me with your Holy Spirit so I may be bold in my
service to others. May it be so with me.

(Morning)
Spirit of God, I lift into your holy presence those
who are in special need of your understanding love.
(Prayers of Intercession)

(Evening)
Holy Spirit, I thank you for another day.
Help me to better match my actions to my intentions.
(Prayers of Intercession)

God grants time, but it is not for ourselves alone.

(Morning)
Gracious God, I want to make this a bold day of service for you. Move me, by your Spirit, to make it so. In the name of Jesus. Amen.

(Evening)
Too many excuses get in my way. So many "put off's" to another day. Forgive me, dear God, and let me see you are the One who enables me. Have mercy! In the name of Jesus. Amen.

TUESDAY, MARCH 27
(Read Isaiah 43:16–17)

(Morning)
Dear and mighty God, in the "exit moments" of our lives,
help me to recall that you lead us in hope.

(Evening)
Dear and mighty God, thank you for "making a way"
in the turbulent seas of my life.

God, the Exodus experience for Israel becomes the frame of reference for oppressed people. Your mighty action on behalf of your people reminds us that human beings are not created for entrapment, exploitation, or enslavement. The prophet speaks, for you, O God, are a God who does the impossible. Nothing is impossible for you! Nothing is too big or too small for you to do. The biblical word confirms our faith. I believe in a God of might and power, a God of tenderness and love. How I praise you! Keep speaking to and through my heart, mighty, merciful, able God.

(Morning)
May those for whom I pray this morning, great God,
remember that nothing is beyond your power.
(Prayers of Intercession)

(Evening)
Miraculous God, work great things in the lives of these persons and institutions.
(Prayers of Intercession)

God is no small God!
(Sing "Go Down, Moses" or another familiar hymn.)

(Morning)
Thank you for the hope that comes through your Holy Word. You have made "a way out of no way" in my life, God the Creator; God the Sovereign Son; and God the Holy Spirit. In the name of Jesus. Amen.

(Evening)
Thank you for the courage to go for you.
In the name of Jesus. Amen.

WEDNESDAY, MARCH 28
(Read Isaiah 14:18–21)

(Morning)
Dear God, form me for yourself so I may continually declare your praise.

(Evening)
Dear God, forgive me for resisting your remolding of my life.
Let me become like clay in your hands.

I understand "the new thing" that you, mighty God, were about to do for your chosen ones. You would release them from Babylonian captivity. The "new thing" you did for me was your self-revelation in Jesus Christ. You entered history in human form, showing us not only what you can do, but also who we can be in your image. Jesus has restored my self-confidence. By his teaching model he has shown me your new way for my life. Your protective promise has always been with us. The empowerment of the Holy Spirit enables us to believe in Jesus Christ and to courageously live loving and just lives. My forebears were able to sing in slavery not "Were You There When They Crucified *Their* Lord?" but "Were You There When They Crucified *My* Lord?" Nothing could prevent the import of "the new thing" that you did in Jesus Christ. Praise him!

(Morning)
Dear God, touch by your promise and power those
whom I name before you in the name of Jesus.
(Prayers of Intercession)

(Evening)
This day is ending, saving God. Your blessings are evident.
(Prayers of Intercession)

In a spirit of gratitude and praise, pray the prayer that Jesus taught.
(Pray the Prayer of Our Savior.)

(Morning)
As the potter forms the clay for both
beauty and utility, form me as you will.
In the name of Jesus. Amen.

(Evening)
Thank you, Christ Jesus, for submitting
to God's will for your life so I might
know salvation. In the name of Jesus.
Amen.

THURSDAY, MARCH 29
(Read Psalm 126:1–3)

(Morning)
I praise you, almighty God! You have done great things for me!

(Evening)
I praise you, almighty God! I have experienced the joy of an amazing Savior!

In the midst of troubled times, the joy of an amazing Savior bursts through. Sorrow makes joy appear as a dream. I cherish joy! I taste it! God, I witness to all that you have done for me. I am sure I do not deserve it. God, you are so merciful. I find others to rejoice with me. Family, friends, and neighbors share my blessings. Help me to know, dear God, that you are as present in my tears as you are in my laughter. May those who know me and love me recognize that in my darkest hours, you are my hope. Let me store times of joy in my heart as sustenance for life's bitter days.

(Morning)
O Holy Spirit, lift those who are downhearted into the marvelous power of your joy.
(Prayers of Intercession)

(Evening)
Thank you, gracious God, for using me this day.
Make me an instrument of your joy.
(Prayers of Intercession)

Restore the light of thy face, dear Holy One.
(Sing "O Thou, in Whose Presence" or another familiar hymn.)

(Morning)
I begin this day open to receive whatever joy you send into my life. In the name of Jesus. Amen.

(Evening)
In times of joy I dance through the day; I sing to deep rhythms; I smile all the way. In the name of Jesus. Amen.

FRIDAY, MARCH 30
(Read Psalm 126:4–6)

(Morning)
O Christ, I identify you as the Source of my joy.

(Evening)
O Christ, have I let bitterness rob me of your joy?

When we have experienced joy, gracious God, we know we can expect its return. As the joyous exiles returned home, their joy of restoration was overcome by locusts, drought, and bad harvests. They were at home, but they were a community of poverty. Yet they prayed their joy would be renewed, and bountiful harvests would be restored. They expected to shout with joy again!

(Morning)
Creator God, restore joy to the lives of those for whom I pray.
(Prayers of Intercession)

(Evening)
Thank you, holy God, for your presence that makes a
difference in our lives each day. God is always at work.
(Prayers of Intercession)

We sometimes have to dig deep in faith for joy.

(Morning)
I begin this day with gratitude that you are with me, dear God. You know the heights of my joy and the depths of my sorrow. I learn to wait on you. In the name of Jesus. Amen.

(Evening)
We learn to wait until change comes in our conflicted lives. Waiting for your direction is an act of faith. We do not wait for what we do not expect. Grant us strength. In the name of Jesus. Amen.

SATURDAY, MARCH 31
(Read Philippians 3:4–11)

(Morning)
Creator God, the words of Paul reflect your ability
to refocus and renew us through Christ Jesus.

(Evening)
Creator God, even when we list our "accomplishments," help us
"regard them as rubbish in order that we may gain" you!

In his life experiences, Paul was qualified to be many things to many persons. Thanks be to you, God, that he understood the significance of being found in Christ rather than boasting of righteousness that comes from the law. May I yearn to know Christ so I recognize true righteousness as rooted in him. Like Paul, "I want to know your Child and the power of his resurrection and the sharing of his sufferings by becoming like him in his death." Christ still loved, still forgave, still trusted.

(Morning)
O holy Savior, there are those who are in need of deeper faith.
Deepen my faith so I may serve them better.
(Prayers of Intercession)

(Evening)
Dear saving Friend, you prove your love so deeply and so clearly.
(Prayers of Intercession)

Christ still loved, still forgave, still trusted.
(Sing "Lord, I Want to Be a Christian" or another familiar hymn.)

(Morning)
If need be, dear God, turn me completely around so that my choices day by day will be yours for me rather than those of impressing others. In the name of Jesus. Amen.

(Evening)
Whenever the day ends, I find myself praying for more time and more faith to live out my intentions. Thank you for your grace, forgiving God. Grant peaceful rest. In the name of Jesus. Amen.

SUNDAY, APRIL 1
(Read Philippians 3:12–14)

(Morning)
Creator God, grant strength, courage, and power for this new day.

(Evening)
Creator God, in gratitude I lift my voice in praise of you—almighty God,
Sovereign Son, Holy Spirit.

God, how clearly the scriptures teach that we will not reach the goal of Christian perfection easily. Our faith is risky business in this world. Our yearning to be like Christ Jesus demands "pressing," "forgetting what lies behind and straining forward to what lies ahead." I know I cannot make it on my own, but I am willing to "strain forward." In the witness of my elderly friend, Sister Brown, "I don't feel no ways tired. I just want to press on to see what the end will be." Charles Albert Tindley testifies to such in his hymn, "We'll Understand It Better By and By."

(Morning)
Lift these, Christ Jesus, who are enmeshed in troubles and trials.
(Prayers of Intercession)

(Evening)
Thank you, Creator, Sovereign Son, Holy Spirit. Your powerful unity sustains me.
(Prayers of Intercession)

God will provide us with understanding.
(Sing a hymn that empowers and lifts you.)

(Morning)
I recognize the distance I must run in a single day. Be with me, Christ Jesus. In the name of Jesus. Amen.

(Evening)
Dear Holy Spirit, in the press of this day, I have felt your presence and power. I stand amazed! Praise God. In the name of Jesus. Amen.

MONDAY, APRIL 2
(Read Psalm 118:1–2)

(Morning)
God is good, all the time! All the time, God is good!
Praise to you, almighty and ever-loving Creator!

(Evening)
God is good, all the time! All the time, God is good!
Praise to you, almighty and ever-loving Creator!

Every human situation is portrayed in the Hebrew and Christian Scriptures. When we think, "No one understands me!" When we cry out in anguish and anger, "Why, God? Why did you let this happen?" When pain and tragedy overcome health and joy, someone has been in our place—ages and ages ago, as told in a Bible story.

(Morning)
You are the Creator, God of the cosmos. You expand the universe beyond our
knowledge. On this planet, you cry with us and laugh with us
beyond our imaginations. Today, caring God, let me see you represented
in a tear on a cheek and a smile on a face.
(Prayers of Intercession)

(Evening)
Sovereign Creator, who made everything from nothing,
have I experienced you today in tears or laughter, in grass or sky?
(Prayers of Intercession)

**"O give thanks to God, for God is good.
God's steadfast love endures forever!"**

(Morning)	(Evening)
Today, where there are joy and laughter, let me pause to say, "Thank you, God!" Where there are pain and tragedy, remind me of your tears and sorrow. In the matchless name of the Christ. Amen.	So now, O God, you have given me breath for another day—a day like no other before. Thank you. Give me rest now for tomorrow's new creation. In the matchless name of the Christ. Amen.

TUESDAY, APRIL 3
(Read Psalm 118:19–29)

(Morning)
This is the day God has made; let us rejoice and be glad in it.

(Evening)
This is the night God has made; let us rest and be glad in it.

God, in this psalm, we do not know the tragedy or disappointment or who overcame it. We do not know who was like a rejected stone, later to become a cornerstone. But we know that early Christians found meaning in this ancient image for the death and resurrection of Jesus. Like the psalmist, I must reflect on the sorrows or disappointments I have overcome in my life for which to give you thanks.

(Morning)
I thank you that you have answered me, O God. You have guided me through the obstacles and distresses of life to this new day.
(Prayers of Intercession)

(Evening)
God is God! Creator of day and night,
I give thanks for the gift of life, yet another day.
(Prayers of Intercession)

**"The stone that the builders rejected has become the chief cornerstone."
This is God's doing in Jesus Christ.**

(Morning)
Whatever danger or difficulty confronts me this day, remind me, O God, that your love lives in me and never dies. In the matchless name of the Christ. Amen.

(Evening)
With Jesus Christ my guide and stay, I have been led with confidence through another day. Thank you, God. In the matchless name of the Christ. Amen.

WEDNESDAY, APRIL 4
(Read Isaiah 50:4–6)

(Morning)
O God, on this day, teach me that I may teach others not to grow weary.

(Evening)
O God, thank you for this day and your sustaining presence in difficult moments.

Caring God, your word is one of several suffering servant songs from Isaiah. We do not know who is suffering or why. We do know that early Christians found meaning in the suffering of Jesus in these ancient songs. The suffering servant's work is to "sustain the weary" by proclaiming the truth. God, you are in charge! For this, the suffering servant incurs hostility, but does not strike back. Is this a day in which I must speak truth and justice against a hostile reaction?

(Morning)
On this day, may God waken me to justice and truth
that I may speak out with courage and conviction.
(Prayers of Intercession)

(Evening)
In your eyes, O God, did I promote your justice and truth this day?
(Prayers of Intercession)

**"God has given me the tongue of a teacher,
that I may know how to sustain the weary with a word."**

(Morning)
Thank you, my Creator, for this day. If it grows too long and I, too weary, sustain me for the journey. In the matchless name of the Christ. Amen.

(Evening)
As I take rest from this day, instill in me a new lesson of your justice and truth for yet another day. In the matchless name of the Christ. Amen.

THURSDAY, APRIL 5
(Read Isaiah 50:7–9)

(Morning)
God of eternal love and peace, make me an instrument
of your love and peace this day.

(Evening)
God of eternal love and peace, where I have been a worthy advocate of love and
peace this day, thank you. Where I have fallen short of your glorious intent for love
and peace—on earth as it is in heaven—forgive me once again, merciful Sustainer.

Sustaining God, again we read from one of Isaiah's suffering servant songs,
which remind me of the suffering of your Child. You sustained both your anony-
mous suffering servant and Jesus in their hard and painful times. If this day
becomes hard and painful, who will sustain me?

(Morning)
Loving Creator, thank you for the breath of life this day.
(Prayers of Intercession)

(Evening)
At the end of this, your day of creation, I breathe in with thanksgiving your love,
and I exhale with thanksgiving the worries that have gathered in me.
(Prayers of Intercession)

God, help me. Who else will stand with me this day?

(Morning)
With your help, O God, I will not be
worn out this day; rather, my troubles
will wear out before me. In the matchless
name of the Christ. Amen.

(Evening)
As I rest my mind from this day, I am
reminded with thanksgiving of the
friend(s) through whom you have
sustained me this day. In the matchless
name of the Christ. Amen.

FRIDAY, APRIL 6
(Read Philippians 2:5–8)

(Morning)
O God, who knows me better than I know myself, I present myself before you this morning with this question, "Will others today see more my humility or my pride?" Guide me, gracious God, in the way of Jesus Christ.

(Evening)
O God, who has been with me this day and whose head
has shaken in exasperation at my self-centered thoughts and actions,
forgive me that I might more fully give tomorrow.

Sustaining God, today's scripture is the first part of probably the oldest recorded Christian song-poem. To follow Jesus means Jesus is our model for relating to other persons. This most ancient of Christian songs tells of your Child's humble, self-giving attitude. Will I follow in the humble and self-giving way of Jesus today?

(Morning)
Thank you, most loving and caring God, for the miraculous mystery of Jesus Christ.
He emptied himself of your divinity to become fully human like me, yet remains
fully divine in you. Help me empty myself of pride today.
(Prayers of Intercession)

(Evening)
So much I cannot understand, God, such as Jesus Christ,
fully human and yet fully divine. Increase my faith and my understanding.
(Prayers of Intercession)

**"He humbled himself and became obedient
to the point of death—even death on a cross."**

(Morning)
Jesus Christ will be my guide and stay this day. My Savior who saves me—mostly from myself. In the matchless name of the Christ. Amen.

(Evening)
Faith leads to understanding, and understanding leads to faith. Thank you for this mysterious, circular miracle in which I rest tonight. In the matchless name of the Christ. Amen.

SATURDAY, APRIL 7
(Read Philippians 2:9–11)

(Morning)
God of the cosmos, who is in my every breath,
if fear comes to me today, remind me who is finally in charge.

(Evening)
God of the cosmos, you love this earth and its inhabitants so much!
I pray I did more good than harm to your creation today!

Creator God, today's scripture is the last part of possibly the very first Christian song-poem. It confirms your promise, given to us in Jesus Christ—that life finally overcomes death. In these verses, I hear your magnificent promise. Jesus Christ is Sovereign over all.

(Morning)
Pain is real. Suffering is real. Death is real. God, remind me this day that healing, joy, and new life are the final realities of your creation.
(Prayers of Intercession)

(Evening)
Tonight I pause to recollect glimpses of heaven on earth I experienced today—
glimpses of healing and joy and new life.
(Prayers of Intercession)

Jesus Christ is Sovereign, to the glory of God the Father. Jesus Christ is sole Head and Sovereign, to the glory of God the Mother.

(Morning)
May the world be a little more joyful today because of the joy made known to me through Jesus Christ. In the matchless name of the Christ. Amen.

(Evening)
Healing, joy, and new life are the final realities of Jesus Christ. Tonight I rest in this wondrous peace from God, which passes all human understanding. In the matchless name of the Christ. Amen.

SUNDAY, APRIL 8
(Read Luke 19:28–40)

(Morning)
Creator God, I am raised once again to a new day!
May I go into this day with your joy, peace, and love.

(Evening)
Creator God, my body and mind are tired from this day.
Grant me rest in your Spirit of peace.

Loving God, the final days of Jesus' life began with a hero's welcome, which lasted for the time it took for the parade to pass. Events led to Jesus' arrest, persecution, suffering, and death. The story, however, ends on an eternally joyful note—Jesus Christ is risen!

(Morning)
Do I live life from one party and celebration to the next, avoiding every unpleasant situation I can? Or do I morbidly seek out and immerse myself in every disaster, so suffering and death will not surprise me? Loving and gentle God, give me the laughter and tears I need for this day.
(Prayers of Intercession)

(Evening)
As I relax in your gentle care for another night, renew my body, mind, and spirit for a fresh, new day tomorrow, a day that will be like no other before it.
(Prayers of Intercession)

"The whole multitude of the disciples began to praise God joyfully with a loud voice for all the deeds of power that they had seen."

(Morning)	(Evening)
This day, may I shout and laugh for the joy of life; and may I whisper soft words and cry for the pain of life. Praise be to you, O God, in life and in death! In the matchless name of the Christ. Amen.	I go to sleep this night counting the stupendously simple miracles of this day, which I have most often taken for granted without due appreciation. Thank you, God. In the matchless name of the Christ. Amen.

MONDAY, APRIL 9
(Read John 20:1–18)

(Morning)
O God, help me as I rise to seek Christ early in my day.

(Evening)
O God, I have met many challenges this day.
Your presence has enabled me to be victorious.

O loving God, the empty tomb reminds us of your resurrection power. Help us, like many, to continue to seek you in all times and places and to know that we, too, may share in your resurrection.

(Morning)
God, this day guide my feet as I walk in the assurance of your strength.
(Prayers of Intercession)

(Evening)
Throughout this day, loving God, your love has been my help and hope.
(Prayers of Intercession)

You can overcome any obstacles.

(Morning)
O God, may I this day tell others that you live. In the Redeemer's name. Amen.

(Evening)
O blessed God, this night I rest in you, knowing that you live for me. In the Redeemer's name. Amen.

TUESDAY, APRIL 10
(Read Acts 10:34–43)

(Morning)
Merciful God, help me this day to hear the good news afresh
and to strive to be a witness for you.

(Evening)
Merciful God, this day, I have tried to be a witness for you.

O eternal God, you indeed are God of all. Help me to allow you to reign in every area of my life so that you may be glorified in all I do.

(Morning)
O God, throughout this day, continue to reveal yourself to me through the spoken word.
(Prayers of Intercession)

(Evening)
Today, Creator God, I have seen you working in all things.
(Prayers of Intercession)

"Make me a witness for you, O God."

(Morning)
Help me, wonderful God, to be an effective witness for you. In the Redeemer's name. Amen.

(Evening)
O God, may I sleep through the night knowing that I have tried to share your Word. In the Redeemer's name. Amen.

WEDNESDAY, APRIL 11
(Read Isaiah 65:17–25)

(Morning)
Dear God, I thank you for the newness of this day
and the fresh opportunity to serve in your vineyard.

(Evening)
Dear God, this evening I reflect on the glimpses of your glorious creation that I have
seen today.

O God, through your prophet Isaiah, you promised us a world where peace
would abide and hope endure. Help us, Divine Teacher, to be the instruments
through which this world may be created. Use us to do your perfect will.

(Morning)
O God, let me focus my attention on those who need an answer from you.
(Prayers of Intercession)

(Evening)
Precious and eternal God, you have moved in mighty ways.
I bring to you now the ones I have encountered today.
(Prayers of Intercession)

The peace of Christ is beyond our understanding.

(Morning)
O God, today let me go into a new world
of possibilities for you. In the
Redeemer's name. Amen.

(Evening)
O God, may I find rest and strength for
tomorrow's journey. In the Redeemer's
name. Amen.

THURSDAY, APRIL 12
(Read Psalm 118:1–2)

(Morning)
Creator God, thank you for this day and for your enduring love.

(Evening)
Creator God, your love has been as real to me as my very being.

O God, you are great and deserving of thanks. When I think of your goodness, I am always overwhelmed by how undeserving I am of all you do. Help me, God, to spread your goodness everywhere I go, so that others may see you in me.

(Morning)
I ask now, O God, for your presence in the lives of others.
(Prayers of Intercession)

(Evening)
For all the goodness I have experienced through your people this day, I give thanks.
(Prayers of Intercession)

"God is good, all the time."

(Morning)
Bless me this day to be a blessing to someone else. In the Redeemer's name. Amen.

(Evening)
As I recline for this evening's repose, let me rest in your goodness. In the Redeemer's name. Amen.

FRIDAY, APRIL 13
(Read Psalm 118:14–25)

(Morning)
Precious God, be a source of strength for the work of this day.

(Evening)
Precious God, your strong hand has upheld me valiantly this day.

Eternal God, I praise you that the rejected One has become the cornerstone of our faith. Enable me, O God, to enter your gates of righteousness and to dwell therein.

(Morning)
O God, I praise you for your salvation and pray for all who need you.
(Prayers of Intercession)

(Evening)
Now, O God, help me to rejoice and be glad in all that you have done this day.
(Prayers of Intercession)

God answers prayer.

(Morning)
I go to this new day with your peace and joy in my heart, dear God. In the Redeemer's name. Amen.

(Evening)
O God, I give you thanks and praise for all the marvelous works that you accomplished this day. In the Redeemer's name. Amen.

SATURDAY, APRIL 14
(Read 1 Corinthians 15:19–26)

(Morning)
Loving God, I rejoice this day that I labor
for an eternal reward prepared by your hand.

(Evening)
Loving God, this evening I celebrate the resurrection power
that has been my source of strength today.

Powerful God, you raised your Child, Jesus Christ, from death to life. And by this, you promise us that we also will be raised. Help me to live in the assurance of your ability to bring renewal in the midst of despair and hope in the midst of sorrow.

(Morning)
God, I offer up to you now all those who need
a resurrection experience within their lives.
(Prayers of Intercession)

(Evening)
Wonderful God, for all whose lives represent your renewing presence,
I give you thanks.
(Prayers of Intercession)

Rise up, O church of God!

(Morning)	(Evening)
I give thanks to you that I am resurrected daily in Christ. In the Redeemer's name. Amen.	I thank you, God, that in my disappointments there is always hope for tomorrow in you. In the Redeemer's name. Amen.

SUNDAY, APRIL 15
(Read Luke 24:1–12)

(Morning)
Dear God, like the women at the empty tomb,
may I run and tell the good news of your resurrection this day.

(Evening)
Dear God, I thank you that this day has been
a celebration of your resurrection from death to life.

God, help me always to handle your truth with fear and trembling. May I never discount a word that comes to me from you, regardless of the source. May I always be amazed by your mighty acts of greatness.

(Morning)
God, I offer to you those who need your renewing touch.
(Prayers of Intercession)

(Evening)
Today, O God, I have touched many lives. For each one, I offer a special prayer.
(Prayers of Intercession)

Christ is risen indeed!

(Morning)	(Evening)
May this day be a day of new life in you, merciful God. In the Redeemer's name. Amen.	Precious God, may I rest my hope in you this night and be restored through sleep. In the Redeemer's name. Amen.

MONDAY, APRIL 16
(Read John 20:10–18)

(Morning)
Creator God, help me to understand what is hard to understand.
Give me a willing spirit to see what seems unbelievable.

(Evening)
Creator God, I have seen the power of your witness in the world through the lives of
others. Have I been a witness this day so that others may know you?

So often in my life, I wonder whether I have been faithful to the power of the
resurrection or have been acting only in my self-interest. Mary thought she
had lost all that she believed and wept over the loss. Yet it was you, God,
through Jesus Christ, who opened her eyes so that she could see life in a new
way. I pray you will open my eyes to see you.

(Morning)
I weep with Mary today because at times I also feel I have lost all hope for the
future. Help me to see what life is challenging me to see today.
(Prayers of Intercession)

(Evening)
You have been a gift to me this day as you have walked with me.
(Prayers of Intercession)

"Woman, why are you weeping? Whom are you looking for?"
(Sing "I Come to the Garden Alone" or another familiar hymn.)

(Morning)
O God, be with me this day so I may
bear witness to your holy name. May
the power of your resurrection give me
new life this day. In the name of Christ
I pray. Amen.

(Evening)
Thank you, God, for this day. You have
given me energy and hope. Give me
peace this night so I may rest to serve
you tomorrow. In the name of Christ
I pray. Amen.

TUESDAY, APRIL 17
(Read John 20:19–23)

(Morning)
O God, help me with my unbelief. Give me faith that I may believe without seeing.

(Evening)
O God, the peace I have received this day comes with the rich blessing
of knowing you have been with me.

The disciples saw Jesus when Jesus entered the room. They believed because they saw the signs of Jesus' suffering and the power of the resurrection. I find that often I also seek to have visible proof before I can truly believe. God, help me to know your presence even at those times I feel alone and lost. I seek your comforting assurance so that I may serve you in faithfulness.

(Morning)
Be with me this day as I seek to live out your presence in my life while I engage in my daily activities. This day I pray particularly for . . .
(Prayers of Intercession)

(Evening)
Thank you, O God, for your presence as I have lived this day. I pray I have been faithful to your will and way. Remember this night . . .
(Prayers of Intercession)

"Receive the Holy Spirit."
(Sing "The Strife Is O'er" or another familiar hymn.)

(Morning)
My hope is in you, O God, as I find my way to witness in your holy name. May my life be a blessing to all that I meet and serve this day. In the name of Christ I pray. Amen.

(Evening)
I sleep this night in the knowledge that you are with me even as I rest. You have been with me throughout this day. May I rise tomorrow with new energy to serve you. In the name of Christ I pray. Amen.

WEDNESDAY, APRIL 18
(Read John 20:24–31)

(Morning)
Comforting God, my doubts seem to overtake my life at times.
Help me this day to see through my doubts and to believe in you.

(Evening)
Comforting God, thank you for being with me
when I have harbored doubts about your presence with me today.

I feel many times like doubting Thomas because I want clear evidence that you are with me. There are many ways in which I want to control other people and even you, O God. I yearn always to believe you are with me, even when doubts seem to overtake me as I see pain and hurt in the world. Thank you, God, for revealing yourself through your Child, Jesus Christ.

(Morning)
Spirit of God, be with me this day as I seek to be a sign of your presence
in the world. Please remember especially this day . . .
(Prayers of Intercession)

(Evening)
Thank you, O God, for being present with me as I have lived this day.
I pray you will forgive the things that I should have done but did not.
Remember this night particularly . . .
(Prayers of Intercession)

"Peace be with you."
(Sing "Peace I Leave with You" or another familiar hymn.)

(Morning)	(Evening)
I begin this day wondering if I am able to do what is required of me. Yet I know all things are possible through you. In the name of Christ I pray. Amen.	I praise your name, O God, for you have given me strength to live this day. Give me rest this night. In the name of Christ I pray. Amen.

THURSDAY, APRIL 19
(Read Acts 5:27–32)

(Morning)
All-knowing God, help me to obey the way you would have me live.
Give me the courage to speak the truth in love.

(Evening)
All-knowing God, have I been the kind of person this day who spoke your Word?
Did I witness as a disciple of Jesus Christ?

I am humbled by the way the disciples were able to stand before others and speak your Word in the midst of danger and disagreement. I want to do the right thing, but so often I lack the courage and slip silently away into the shadows. I yearn to be able to stand for Jesus in my daily living. Help me to have the courage to be a true disciple.

(Morning)
As I face the tasks of this day, give me the courage to speak and live the truth.
Remember this day those who feel weak and afraid.
(Prayers of Intercession)

(Evening)
Thank you for standing with me this day when I lacked the courage
to stand up for you. Remember this night . . .
(Prayers of Intercession)

"We must obey God rather than any human authority."
(Sing "My Shepherd Is the Living God" or another familiar hymn.)

(Morning)
Today I look forward to the hope that I may serve you with faithfulness and speak with courage your word of truth in love. In the name of Christ I pray. Amen.

(Evening)
I give thanks to you, O God, for the gift of strength that you have given to me this day. I ask your presence this night as I rest to serve you tomorrow. In the name of Christ I pray. Amen.

FRIDAY, APRIL 20
(Read Psalm 118:14–29)

(Morning)
O God, help me be one to witness in your name this day.
Help me be a blessing to those who surround me.

(Evening)
O God, thank you for being with me all this day.
Thank you for helping me know that salvation is through you.

I know in my head that your steadfast mercy and love are with me, but there are times when my heart does not feel them. I want to be glad and rejoice in your name, yet many times I feel alone and without hope. The word of the psalmist gives me courage to see each new day as a blessing from you. Help me find the way to your glorious salvation.

(Morning)
Open me, O God, to the gates of righteousness this day.
Remember especially this day . . .
(Prayers of Intercession)

(Evening)
I thank you, O God, that you have come to me and sustained me
so that I may serve you more faithfully. Please remember this night . . .
(Prayers of Intercession)

"God is my strength and my might."
(Sing "Like a Tree Beside the Waters" or another familiar hymn.)

(Morning)
O God, open my heart and eyes to witness in your name this day. I seek your guidance, knowing this is the day you have made. In the name of Christ I pray. Amen.

(Evening)
Thank you for the marvelous way your mercy has been given to me. I know you have made this day, and I rejoice that I have been able to serve you. Give me peaceful rest this night. In the name of Christ I pray. Amen.

SATURDAY, APRIL 21
(Read Psalm 150)

(Morning)
Praise God for the day that is before me!
Help me to praise God by the way I live this day.

(Evening)
Praise God for the night that is before me! I pray that every breath I have taken this
day has been filled by God's Spirit. Let everything within me praise God!

God, this is the day you have made. I seek to serve you with all my being and
energy. The beauty of the day is to be lived as a blessing to your great goodness.
Help me to know the ways of righteousness and justice for all your people. Give
me courage to share the good news of this Eastertide season. Christ has risen!

(Morning)
I sing praises to you, O God, for you have given me life for another day of your creation.
Remember this day those whom I love and those who are hurting . . .
(Prayers of Intercession)

(Evening)
What a glorious day this has been. I have been blessed by your goodness.
Thank you for the signs of your grace and love. Please remember this night . . .
(Prayers of Intercession)

Praise God!
(Sing "I Sing the Mighty Power of God" or another familiar hymn.)

(Morning)
I look with great anticipation for this day because I know you have blessed it by your goodness, O God. Help me be the person of faith who lives as Christ would have me live as a disciple. In the name of Christ I pray. Amen.

(Evening)
Thank you for this gift of another day of your creation. Your love and blessing have given me hope for tomorrow. May I rest well this night by your peace. In the name of Christ I pray. Amen.

SUNDAY, APRIL 22
(Read Revelation 1:4–8)

(Morning)
Holy One, you come to give me life for this day and every day.

(Evening)
Holy One, your grace has been a blessing and the hope for another day.

I have learned from Jesus Christ, the firstborn, that the beginning and end come from you, all-knowing God. I seek to live my life in faithfulness, yet know it is possible only by your grace. We learn about you through Jesus' ministry upon this earth, and we are called to bear witness to that ministry by our own ministry. The resurrection of Christ makes all things possible to those who love you. The new world of your creation was made known by your power and love.

(Morning)
I come to the beginning of this day knowing you will be with me to its very end.
I live with that hope and joy. Please remember this day . . .
(Prayers of Intercession)

(Evening)
Gracious God, your love sustains me even when I feel separated from you and others.
By your grace remember this night . . .
(Prayers of Intercession)

"I am the Alpha and the Omega."
(Sing "Spirit, Spirit of Gentleness" or another familiar hymn.)

(Morning)
I begin this day knowing you are with me from its beginning to its ending. Help me be a witness of the message that Jesus gave to this world. Christ has risen indeed. In the name of Christ I pray. Amen.

(Evening)
Thank you, O Creator God, for fashioning a world where all beginnings and endings are by your grace. Thank you for sustaining me through this day. I offer my praises to you. In the name of Christ I pray. Amen.

MONDAY, APRIL 23
(Read John 21:1–14)

(Morning)
God, I want to be open to your Word and guidance. When I feel like a child in faith, help me grow in understanding and commitment to thoughtful prayer.

(Evening)
God, was I aware of your presence today?
Was I able to fill my net with your great truth?
When I feel vulnerable, help me to listen more closely
and have the courage to stay on board.

"Cast the net to the right side of the boat." Jesus, your guidance was simple and direct. The disciples had no harvest on their own. You called out to them as innocents, "Children, you have no fish, have you?" In response to your words, their nets were filled, and their eyes were opened to recognize you. Today I will remember your great generosity and know your words and ways can nourish me for a lifetime.

(Morning)
God of all, I pray for those whose nets are empty today.
Fill their emptiness with your abiding love.
(Prayers of Intercession)

(Evening)
May those who cannot see you, God, have their eyes opened to your grace.
(Prayers of Intercession)

God, you have nourished me today, and I am grateful!

(Morning)
God, I begin this day in prayer that I will keep my eyes open for your presence in my life. Thanks be to Christ. Amen.

(Evening)
Night is drawing near. I pray I will find a treasure to carry into tomorrow as I reflect on this day. A word of advice, a new idea, a friendship rekindled, a new prayer, what is the gift of today? Thanks be to Christ. Amen.

114

TUESDAY, APRIL 24
(Read John 21:15–19)

(Morning)
Caring God, I wake to a new day and hear an old question, "Do you love me?"
Let my answer be, "Yes." Enlighten me, and inspire
my actions that they may fulfill divine intentions.

(Evening)
Caring God, rest approaches. My day has been full. Have I been at work for you?
Help me see what are and can be your ways at work through my life.

A seventy-five-year-old man named Paul has organized a free Saturday breakfast and bag lunch in my community for eleven years. When asked what motivated him to keep working at this every week, he said, "Read John 21 where Jesus asks Peter three times, 'Do you love me?' " God, your Child sought commitment and faithfulness from Peter and directed him to "feed my sheep." Asking once was not enough. If I love you, what does that mean for my life's choices?

(Morning)
I pray for myself and all those in need of your love and power.
May we open our hearts to you, God.
(Prayers of Intercession)

(Evening)
Loving Leader, I pray for all who need tending today.
(Prayers of Intercession)

God's way is peace and justice for all.

(Morning)
Loving Christ, inspire me today as I seek ways to tend your sheep. Energize my imagination and capacity to care for others. Take away my fears. Thanks be to Christ. Amen.

(Evening)
Loving Spirit, I worship you in grateful praise. Thanks be to Christ. Amen.

WEDNESDAY, APRIL 25
(Read Acts 9:1–9)

(Morning)
God of all that lives and God of my life,
open my eyes that I may know who you are today and every day.

(Evening)
God of all that lives and God of my life, my faith journey has not included
lightning bolts and sudden flashes; it has been quiet and steady.
I pray I will continue to take steps that will bring me closer to you.

Even those who work against you, loving God, can be transformed. In the reading, Saul is a threat to the disciples, yet you chose him to do important work. How many times have I questioned, denied, or doubted the words of faith? Your patience is astounding. God, I know you are open to my growth as a believer. How is it that you seek to grab my attention and pull me closer?

(Morning)
Astonishing and wonderful God, help me see the truth of your message
that I might share your loving Spirit with others.
(Prayers of Intercession)

(Evening)
O spirited God, thank you for the ways that you revealed yourself today.
(Prayers of Intercession)

Our God is forgiving and open to new believers.

(Morning)
Today I pray I will have the courage to recognize my flaws and invite the loving Spirit of God to heal my wounds. Thanks be to Christ. Amen.

(Evening)
God, I will rest tonight, knowing you accept me as a work in progress. Thanks be to Christ. Amen.

THURSDAY, APRIL 26
(Read Acts 9:10–20)

(Morning)
God of yesterday, today, and tomorrow, build a vision for my life.
Guide me in your service.

(Evening)
God of yesterday, today, and tomorrow, have I followed the right path today?
Is there a thoughtful, faithful vision forming for my life?
Be at my side as I rest tonight; fill my dreams with the guidance of your loving Spirit.

Here I am, God. These four words both humble and inspire me. All I have to offer in exchange for the great gift of this life is myself. Here I am. Use me as an instrument for good. I know I will be fearful at times. Like Ananias, I may question what I am asked to do. I may feel unsure. However, my prayer is that you will show me the way!

(Morning)
Powerful and wonderful God, let the scales fall from my eyes today!
(Prayers of Intercession)

(Evening)
Jesus shared the meaning of baptism and was himself baptized.
The grace of God is shown in the gift of baptism.
Today I bring to my prayers an awareness of the grace of our living God.
(Prayers of Intercession)

Be filled with the Holy Spirit!
(Pray the Prayer of Our Savior.)

(Morning)
Loving God, lead me to find the right path today. Show me the way! Thanks be to Christ. Amen.

(Evening)
God of all life, heal my doubt; help me grow in faithfulness. Thanks be to Christ. Amen.

FRIDAY, APRIL 27
(Read Psalm 30:1–5)

(Morning)
Great Comforter. Sunshine. A warm breeze. A day lived in peace.
A hurt forgiven. Interesting work. Music. Rain on parched soil. Remind me today
of all that has been given. I pray with a joyful and thankful spirit.

(Evening)
Great Comforter, I pray in thankfulness and rejoice in life.
Help me to continue to move toward strength.

The loss of someone dear; a severed relationship; a painful experience. How often we carry our burdens in silence. The depths of sorrow can linger, years may pass, and tears still run freely. God, please grant me the freedom to grieve and the opportunity to heal. Through Jesus, I can see joy and hope for a brighter day today.

(Morning)
Weeping may linger for the night, but joy comes with the morning.
Let my prayer work to heal all who linger in the night and hope for the light of a new day.
(Prayers of Intercession)

(Evening)
I cried out for help, and you healed me.
O joyful Spirit, thank you for this glorious day!
(Prayers of Intercession)

Sing praises! Alleluia!

(Morning)
O Ancient One, your wisdom is as fresh as the morning! Bless my day with your renewing presence. Fill me with songs of praise! Thanks be to Christ. Amen.

(Evening)
If I must shed tears, help me transform them into faithful prayers of thankfulness. Thanks be to Christ. Amen.

SATURDAY, APRIL 28
(Read Psalm 30:6–12)

(Morning)
God of wonder and creation, grief is set aside, and praise moves in to take its place!
Today I will dance! I will find strength from a renewed faith in Jesus.

(Evening)
God of wonder and creation, I pray my steps have moved me closer to you today.

From mourning to dancing, the image is clear and optimistic. Faith helps me transform pain into hope. Faith encourages me to find new strength from times when I have fallen or been hurtful. Faith brings creativity and new direction out of my failures. Prayer is the source of new awareness. Caring God, thank you for the gift of prayer!

(Morning)
You have taken off my sackcloth and clothed me with joy.
Hear my prayer that others may join me
in shedding the cloak of sadness and hopelessness.
(Prayers of Intercession)

(Evening)
I give thanks to you for the gift of forgiveness.
Fill me with a spirit of forgiveness for myself and for others.
(Prayers of Intercession)

Let my soul praise you and not be silent! God, I will thank you forever.
(Read Psalm 100.)

(Morning)
God, I am your child. Open my eyes to the needs of all of your children. Thanks be to Christ. Amen.

(Evening)
God of all, you have helped me find my strength by admitting my weaknesses. I am thankful today and always. Thanks be to Christ. Amen.

SUNDAY, APRIL 29
(Read Revelation 5:11–14)

(Morning)
Dear God, day breaks, and I am drawn into prayer. My voice is not alone.
My prayer to you is shared with voices from every corner of the world.
Our voices ask for justice and peace. Our voices praise you and ask for guidance
for our daily lives. As I seek to keep the Sabbath, guide my actions
and words that I may in some small way reflect your love for this world.

(Evening)
Dear God, have I had a day of Sabbath? Is God in the center of my world?
Have my words and choices been a reflection of the truth I seek to live?
Abide with me, Creator; guide me in the week ahead.

Creator God, I have learned and grown as a Christian in community with others. The church has been gloriously imperfect. The challenging history of the church is overshadowed by faith. It is important that we work together to create wonderful, faithful, searching, working faith communities. Together we can heal the scars on the church and reach out with a healing touch at home and throughout the globe.

(Morning)
It is Sunday, and people are gathering for worship.
God, help us to honor you by opening the doors
of our sanctuaries to all in our communities.
(Prayers of Intercession)

(Evening)
Loving God, thank you for the community of faith!
(Prayers of Intercession)

That they may all be one!
(Pray the Prayer of Our Savior.)

(Morning)	(Evening)
Jesus, your presence is more than comfort; it is inspiration! Thanks be to Christ. Amen.	God, your day of rest has been my day of praise! Praise God! Thanks be to Christ. Amen.

MONDAY, APRIL 30
(Read Psalm 23)

(Morning)
Dearest God, Creator of this new day and this new week of life,
thank you for being my Shepherd and for guarding my path.
Lead me in right paths today, that my life may give glory to you.

(Evening)
Dearest God, Creator of this new day and this new week of life,
thank you for being my Shepherd and for guarding my path.

Today I will live in the promise that you are my Shepherd. In my life I have known green pastures; I have also known valleys of death and times when I have stood weak-kneed in the presence of my enemies. Today I choose to feast at the table you set before me in the presence of my enemies—depression, disease, conflicted relationships, disorder in society. I will feast on whatever you provide. I will feast in thankfulness for who you are and who I am to you.

(Morning)
May I begin this day mindful of all the ways you seek to shepherd me.
(Prayers of Intercession)

(Evening)
Good Shepherd, you have led me so lovingly through this day,
being present in times of peace as well as in times of danger.
Lead me just a little farther to the green pastures of renewing sleep.
(Prayers of Intercession)

Thank you for all the ways your care was made evident to me this day.

(Morning)
Today I choose to follow the good Shepherd in the paths that lead to a full life. In the Savior's name. Amen.

(Evening)
Tonight I will sleep in peace, trusting that the Shepherd's eye is upon me. May I rise in the morning, renewed to walk with you through another day of life. In the Savior's name. Amen.

TUESDAY, MAY 1
(Read Psalm 23; John 10:22–30)

(Morning)
Messiah, thank you for revealing yourself to me in so many wondrous ways.
Allow me the grace to see you clearly this day.
Allow me the grace to follow where you lead.

(Evening)
Messiah, thank you for revealing yourself to me in so many wondrous ways.

"How long will you keep us in suspense? If you are the Messiah, tell us plainly."
I am so like the religious leaders who rejected you. I want factual certainty. I am skeptical of the mystery unfolding all around me in your work. I am tempted to close my ears to the sound of your voice in creation. God, thank you for continuing to work in me and in the world, in spite of my doubts, in spite of my troubling disbelief. Thank you for calling to me until I recognize your voice. Thank you for gently prodding me until I willingly follow.

(Morning)
As I begin another day of life, I open my ears and my heart
to the voice of the good Shepherd.
I give myself to the unfolding mystery revealed only
in surrender to you, the One who calls my name.
(Prayers of Intercession)

(Evening)
Loving Shepherd, you have called me to follow you,
to heed your voice throughout this day.
Forgive me for any times when I have refused to listen and follow.
Forgive me if I have in any way thwarted your will.
(Prayers of Intercession)

Thank you for all the ways you lead me through another day of life.

(Morning)
Today I commit myself to being aware of Christ, present and at work in the people and in all of creation around me. In the Savior's name. Amen.

(Evening)
Tonight, loving God, I rest in the mystery of your love for me. May this sleep renew my body, mind, and spirit so that I might walk closer to you. In the Savior's name. Amen.

WEDNESDAY, MAY 2
(Read Acts 9:36–43)

(Morning)
Creator God, Giver of all life, thank you for the birth of another day.
Open me to the power of the resurrection.
Call me out of death to new life in the moments of this new day.

(Evening)
Creator God, Giver of all life, thank you for this day of life,
for calling me out of death to new life in the moments of this past day.

Ever-renewing God, in your love and power you raised Jesus from the dead and worked through Peter to bring life back to your servant Tabitha. I see your resurrecting power in my own life as well as in those around me. You empower me with resurrecting love, that I might be your hands, your feet, your voice, your eyes and ears in this earthly life. O great God, give me the courage to use the power of this love for the good of all.

(Morning)
May I begin this day aware of the power of the resurrection present
in my life and in those around me.
(Prayers of Intercession)

(Evening)
God of all life, you have empowered me this day with your love and grace,
bringing new life to dead places and spaces in my life.
Forgive me for the times when I have chosen death over life.
(Prayers of Intercession)

**Thank you for all the witnesses of new life
I have seen in all of creation this day.**

(Morning)	(Evening)
May I this day be a life-giver, breathing your Spirit into a weary soul. In the Savior's name. Amen.	I surrender myself to restful sleep in Christ, knowing that you will use it for the renewal of my body, mind, and spirit. In the Savior's name. Amen.

THURSDAY, MAY 3
(Read Revelation 7:9–17)

(Morning)
Everlasting, ever-unfolding mystery, you who are both Lamb and Shepherd,
I bow before you at the beginning of another day. I open myself to life in you.

(Evening)
Everlasting, ever-unfolding mystery, you who are both Lamb and Shepherd,
I bow before you at the end of another day.
I pray that I have brought blessings to others and glory to you this day.

With great humility I join the vast multitude before your throne, a multitude so great that it cannot be counted. People from all tribes and lands, all races and languages. I am one of the many who have known your saving power, your loving ways. Today I ponder what it means to be a part of such a diverse people united under one God. Grant me the wisdom to find and accept my particular place in your people and plan.

(Morning)
May I begin this day mindful of the diversity and vast beauty of your people, O God.
(Prayers of Intercession)

(Evening)
Sovereign One, forgive me for the times today when I have seen myself
as too high or too low, when I have isolated myself from the great multitude.
Forgive me for the times I have failed to give you the glory.
(Prayers of Intercession)

**Thank you for surrounding me with such a great multitude
of believers, people of all ages, races, and places.**

(Morning)
I commit myself this day to recognizing your presence in those I perceive as being different from me. In the Savior's name. Amen.

(Evening)
As I come to the end of another day, I thank you for your care and for the rest that you promise me this night and in eternity. In the Savior's name. Amen.

FRIDAY, MAY 4
(Read John 10:22–30; Revelation 7:9–17)

(Morning)
Giver of eternal life, thank you for the gift of another day of life,
a life that holds the promise of eternity within it.
Let me live this day as the beginning of forever.

(Evening)
Giver of eternal life, thank you for the gift of another day of earthly life,
a life that holds the promise of eternity within it.

God, often I feel like one who has come through the "great ordeal"—beaten down, worn out. So many things press upon me that I must admit there are times when I am tempted to give up the faith. I feel like a "Christian at risk." I know the promise, though. If I am one of Christ's sheep, "none will snatch them out of my hand." All this is promised as long as I keep listening for the Shepherd's voice and following, especially in difficult times.

(Morning)
May I live this day not in fear of being lost, but in confidence
of having been found in Christ. I am known to you and am safe in your hands.
(Prayers of Intercession)

(Evening)
Protective, loving God, whose Spirit has held me close this day,
carry me now to a night of peaceful rest.
Forgive me for any times I have turned away from your care and guidance.
(Prayers of Intercession)

**Thank you for holding me in your hands,
not only this day but for all of eternity.**

(Morning)
Today I commit myself to trust the good Shepherd with my entire life. In the Savior's name. Amen.

(Evening)
Tonight I rest in your strong, loving hands and commit my tomorrow to another day of service to you, my sisters, and my brothers. In the Savior's name. Amen.

SATURDAY, MAY 5
(Read Acts 9:36–43; John 10:22–30)

(Morning)
God of all times, thank you for bringing me through another week.
Thank you for shepherding me. As I begin this day and end this week,
I praise you for your power, your wisdom, your protection.

(Evening)
God of all times, thank you for bringing me through
another day and another week of life.
Thank you for shepherding me, for calling me to follow,
for calling me out of death to new life.

God of Tabitha and Peter, I give thanks for the stories of the early church, which give hope and life to me this day. Remind me that what I do today is important, that it has value. As the widows held close the clothing Tabitha had made during her life, so might the works of my life have value to theirs. Give me the grace to use the talents and resources I have been given for your glory.

(Morning)
May I begin this day mindful of the talents and resources I have been given to use
for the building up of your realm and the care of all your creation.
(Prayers of Intercession)

(Evening)
As I come to the end of another day, forgive me, God, for any times I have wasted
or hoarded the gifts you have given me. Forgive me for not sharing.
(Prayers of Intercession)

**Thank you for the many and diverse gifts and abilities
you have given me and all your children.**

(Morning)
At the beginning of this new day,
I ask for the grace to share abundantly
all that I have been given.
In the Savior's name. Amen.

(Evening)
At the end of another day, I am
reminded that whether asleep or awake,
I belong to you, O God. Take my
worries and all my anxieties now, and
let me rest secure in your loving arms.
In the Savior's name. Amen.

SUNDAY, MAY 6
(Read Psalm 23; Acts 9:36–43)

(Morning)
Great God, Lover of my soul, thank you for the beginning
of this new day and this new week. As I celebrate this holy day,
restore and renew in me your resurrecting power.

(Evening)
Great God, Lover of my soul, thank you for the end
of another day and the beginning of another week.

Great God, thank you for continually amazing me with your love and your power, for surprising me by bringing life to places and parts of my life I thought were dead, to relationships, to causes, and to people I had given up on. As I work with you this day for resurrection, remind me of the promise found in Revelation: There will come a time when your realm encompasses all of heaven and earth. Remind me as I work with your plan for the coming of that great day.

(Morning)
May I begin this day aware of all the ways I need the resurrecting power
of you, O God, in my life. May I open myself to your power
so that I might be a conduit of this life for others.
(Prayers of Intercession)

(Evening)
Renewing God, thank you for all the ways you have been present
to me this day, in times of death and resurrection, in times of struggle and peace.
Forgive me for the times I refuse to be a part of your plan for new life, for life eternal.
(Prayers of Intercession)

**Thank you for the promise of a day when pain and death will be no longer.
Thank you for the promise of eternal life with you.**

(Morning)
Today I commit myself to looking for evidence of the in-breaking of your realm all around me. In the Savior's name. Amen.

(Evening)
I now surrender myself to the peace of the night, asking for renewing rest, that I might wake in the morning for another day to serve you. In the Savior's name. Amen.

MONDAY, MAY 7
(Read Psalm 148)

(Morning)
E Kou Makou Makua iloko o Ka Lani, our heavenly God, for the songs of life, voices of birds and animals, wind, the sounds of children and other people, the gurgling of our waterways, the loving embrace of waves upon the shores, all praise you, gracious God. The sounds of praise reflect your majesty and glory, *E Ke Akua* (God).

(Evening)
E Kou Makou Makua iloko o Ka Lani, thank you for creation's sounds
of praise all through the day and as we enter the night hours.
May I also share in the night's praise of you, gracious God.

I hear creation's praise of its source, God. The praising sounds of birds, animals, people, streams, and waterfalls. Trees singing in the wind, waves embracing the shore. Even the sounds of technology have their own sounds of life and praise. I share in these varied songs of praise. I love you, God, and I lift my voice to praise you.

(Morning)
Source of my life, may my sounds today bring only praise
to you and add to the praises from creation. Praise God.
(Prayers of Intercession)

(Evening)
Evening has come; the day has been spent praising you.
Thank you for accepting sounds. May my praises be included with the praises
throughout the night, for the world is truly yours, O gracious One.
(Prayers of Intercession)

The wondrous voices of the universe praise God—
I, too, lift my voice in praise to you.

(Morning)
May my life be filled with praises to you,
gracious God. In Jesus' name. Amen.

(Evening)
May all of the sounds of life praise you
always. In Jesus' name. Amen.

TUESDAY, MAY 8
(Read Psalm 148; Acts 11:1–8)

(Morning)
To you, the Source of all creation, the *Ha* (breath) of all life,
your glory is revealed in the goodness of creation and all the universe.

(Evening)
To you, the Source of all creation, I thank you for sharing with me the purity of life.
As I praise and reflect on this day, may I also prepare to share in the specialness
of the voices of praise throughout the night.

I am very much a part of the family of creation. Part of my responsibility is to share in recognizing, honoring, and praising you, O God. It is a joy to praise you; it is a joy to lift my voice with the other voices of creation, praising you, the Source of all life.

(Morning)
Praise God, from whom all blessings flow; praise God,
all creatures here below; praise God, all you heavenly host; praise God.
(Prayers of Intercession)

(Evening)
May my sounds and actions of praise join the rest of the creation
in praising you, O God, incessantly.
(Prayers of Intercession)

**All of the universe praises God on earth and in the heavens—
and may my voice always be a part of this chorus.**

(Morning)
May my sounds of praise be as honest
and sincere as the sounds of creation
praising you. In Jesus' name. Amen.

(Evening)
May my sounds of praise continue
through the night. In Jesus' name. Amen.

WEDNESDAY, MAY 9
(Read Acts 11:1–9)

(Morning)
E Ke Akua Mauloa, eternal God, thank you for a new morning,
cleansed with the refreshing dew and the cooling breezes
that remind me that each morning brings a fresh day to start anew.

(Evening)
E Ke Akua Mauloa, thank you for your breath *(Ha)* in my being today.
It allows me to share as a special blessing of creation.

I live in a world that attempts to separate everything as good or bad, clean or
unclean. God, as I understand and confess that your breath gives creation its life
energy, I also confess the total acceptance of your creation of which I am a part.
Thank you for your *Ha* in me, for this is a blessed life, filled with blessings.

(Morning)
Gracious God, may I be able to confess the wonderful blessings
of all of creation and your goodness.
(Prayers of Intercession)

(Evening)
E Ke Akua Mauloa, whose *Ha* fills me with all of the goodness of creation and
supports me as I share life with creation, thank you for your *Ha's* cleansing power.
(Prayers of Intercession)

Thank you for the goodness of all parts of creation.

(Morning)	(Evening)
May your *Ha* in me and all of creation be in harmony throughout this day. In Jesus' name. Amen.	May your *Ha* continue to refresh all of creation throughout this night. *Mahalo ia oe, E Ke Akua,* thank you, God. In Jesus' name. Amen.

THURSDAY, MAY 10
(Read Acts 11:1–8; Revelation 21:1–6)

(Morning)
Ever-present God, the *Ha* of our lives, thank you for the completeness of creation and
the continuing love that carries me over my shortcomings to the *lokahi* of creation.

(Evening)
Ever-present God, thank you for your sustaining power this day.
Thank you for sharing in my empowerment to reach the potential
to which you have called me.

Water is very essential for island folk. God, even more important is my foundation based on your love and *Ha*. This reflection allows me to confess your presence from the ever-present beginning to the never-ending completion of my life's journey. God, your *Ha* makes all things possible, for you are my Mother, my Father, my *lokahi* with all of creation. I now need to share this with others.

(Morning)
Good morning, Mother, Father, Grandmother, Grandfather.
All of my relations in creation, how graciously you reflect our God.
May I continue in my journey of faith, leaning on you, the foundation of all life.
(Prayers of Intercession)

(Evening)
Gracious One, the foundation of my life, may I continue to build
on your blessings of life, your breath within me, throughout
the coming night of refreshment and re-creation.
(Prayers of Intercession)

**God is the foundation of my life. Let my life build
on the firm foundation to the glorious heights of serving God,
my Mother, Father, Grandmother, Grandfather.**

(Morning)	(Evening)
How firm a foundation it is to build on your breath in me. In Jesus' name. Amen.	A firm foundation, the comforting coolness and inspiration of your *Ha,* strengthens the building of my life's journey. In Jesus' name. Amen.

FRIDAY, MAY 11
(Read Revelation 21:1–6)

(Morning)
E Ke Akua Mauloa, you are the Alpha and the Omega
in the foundation of my life's journey.
You are also the water of life, *Ka wai ola,* refreshing
and strengthening the growth of my life.
I am thankful for you as the refreshment of my journey—always sustaining.

(Evening)
E Ke Akua Mauloa, through the heat of life's journey, the desert of aloneness, you,
Ka wai ola, have carried me, one step at a time. *Mahalo ia oe, E Ka wai ola.*

As Pacific islanders traveled between islands, their major concerns were a seaworthy canoe (foundation) and water. God, you are thus in my life as I paddle my canoe through life, refreshing myself on *Ka wai ola.*

(Morning)
On my journey today, may my canoe be seaworthy
and the supply of *Ka wai ola* be refreshing and sustaining.
(Prayers of Intercession)

(Evening)
God, today's journey in your canoe, drinking *Ka wai ola,*
has led me to this space in my journey.
May *Ka wai ola* refresh me throughout the night
and prepare me for another day of living.
(Prayers of Intercession)

Sail on, O my soul, with God as my canoe and *Ka wai ola* refreshing my life.

(Morning)
In my canoe, one paddle stroke at a time, refreshed by *Ka wai ola,* God, I will answer your call to witness faithfully. In Jesus' name. Amen.

(Evening)
Evening has come. The table is set with *Ka wai alo* to refresh and strengthen for another day's journey. In Jesus' name. Amen.

SATURDAY, MAY 12
(Read Revelation 21:1–6; John 13:31–35)

(Morning)
E Ka wai ola, you have shared with me the oneness and *lokahi* I have
with all creation as I travel. Thank you for refreshing and strengthening me.

(Evening)
The canoe has been filled with love, *Ke Akua no Aloha*, the God of love.
Thank you for allowing me to share *lokahi*, my firm foundation, and you, *wai ola*,
with others in our canoe. Together, with love, we travel on, supporting one another.

E Ka wai ola, I do not travel alone in the canoe. Continue to teach me how to
love so that I can share your love with others.

(Morning)
God, may your love shared with others, in *lokahi* with creation, continue
to strengthen me as I share a life of loving with others, in your name.
(Prayers of Intercession)

(Evening)
As I pause this evening, I share the refreshing love
with others who have accompanied me.
God, I pray that we will build together on you as our firm foundation
and the fountain of love with no conditions.
(Prayers of Intercession)

**God, as my helm and navigator, fills the journey with all accepting love,
accepting people for who and what they are.**

(Morning)
God, may your *Aloha*, love, be as
refreshing and nourishing as your *Ka
wai ola*. Continue to fill me. In Jesus'
name. Amen.

(Evening)
God, may your love and water of life
shelter and protect me as my body
refreshes itself throughout the night. In
Jesus' name. Amen.

SUNDAY, MAY 13
(Read John 13:31–35)

(Morning)
God, morning has broken, and a new day lies before me.
I thank you for filling me with your love, a love that I can share with all of creation.

(Evening)
God, the coolness and safe rest of the evening give me time
to immerse myself in your love and the love of all of creation.
Thank you for the safety of this foundation of living, *E Ke Akua.*

Sharing life built on love provides a place of safety, a place of rejoicing, a canoe filled with loving people all working toward the same goal. Working together, I am able to share all my potential with the rest of creation.

(Morning)
God, continue to allow me to be filled with your love,
and may I be able to share this love with all
I come into contact with during today's journey.
(Prayers of Intercession)

(Evening)
Thank you, God, for all the love I have been able to share throughout this day.
I pray for your continued guidance.
(Prayers of Intercession)

**Loving is the adhesive that keeps my community of faith together.
This community is part of the foundation that God was, is, and will be.**

(Morning)
Love Divine, all loves excelling, fills all of my life and includes all of creation. Thank you, God. In Jesus' name. Amen.

(Evening)
Love keeps me open to all people and to all of creation. God, thank you for loving and teaching me to love. In Jesus' name. Amen.

MONDAY, MAY 14
(Read Acts 16:9–12)

(Morning)
O God, as we awake, open our ears to the pleadings that arise out of your world.
Let them invite us to deeds of grace and mercy!

(Evening)
O God, remembering those who make claims upon our love,
grant us the rest that strengthens our commitment to care.

Daily the world would have its way with us. Its cries disturb us. Its demands weaken our resolve to walk in ways of hope and healing. Grant us the will to attend to visions that make a difference; the courage to travel in unfamiliar places bearing words that have the power to save us from ourselves. Have we been lured by the hand of Jesus to confront the fears of the world? If so, let us give thanks in the assurance that there is joy amid the very cost of caring. O Spirit of the living God, be with us. Grant us peace.

(Morning)
These prayers we offer on behalf of all who seek wholeness.
(Prayers of Intercession)

(Evening)
Lest we forget those close by who need us most, O God, hear these our prayers.
(Prayers of Intercession)

You are salt for the earth.
(Pray the Prayer of Our Savior.)

(Morning)
If only this once, O God, let me really hear those around me this day. If only this once, let me risk love without any expectation of return. If only this once, let me bear good news amid brokenness. O God, hear my prayer if only this once. In the matchless name of Jesus. Amen.

(Evening)
God, I am tired and in need of rest. But this day, I have not always given in to the ways of the world. This day, I have sought to be an instrument of your peace. Give me peace, that I may have strength to serve tomorrow. In the matchless name of Jesus. Amen.

TUESDAY, MAY 15
(Read Acts 16:13–16)

(Morning)
Inviting God, could it be that you have extended to us an invitation
to dwell in your household? If so, are there obligations?

(Evening)
Inviting God, at your invitation we have returned to be in your presence at the end of this
day. To whom have we spoken? To whom have we listened? Has it made a difference?

Sometimes, O God, when we seek to make the world a place of prayer, it becomes not a place of solace, but a place of surprising conversation. Sometimes entering into prayer is much like entering into dialogue with unexpected partners. Sometimes prayer doesn't seem like prayer because it is interrupted by those who overhear and are intrigued not by the content, but by the very doing of it. Sometimes it's even more remarkable. God, sometimes you use our strange yearnings for transformation. Sometimes at the end of prayer there are invitation and hospitality so amazing, we fear them. O God, intervene; teach us more about prayer.

(Morning)
Hear these prayers we offer on behalf of those who need the open arms of hospitality.
(Prayers of Intercession)

(Evening)
Hear, O God, these our prayers for those who touched our lives this day.
(Prayers of Intercession)

**Hear these prayers we offer on behalf of those who need
the open arms of hospitality.**
(Pray the Prayer of Our Savior.)

(Morning)
Could it be that you have extended to us an invitation to dwell in your household? If so, are there obligations? In the matchless name of Jesus. Amen.

(Evening)
At your invitation we have returned to be in your presence at the end of this day. To whom have we spoken? To whom have we listened? Has it made a difference? In the matchless name of Jesus. Amen.

WEDNESDAY, MAY 16
(Read Psalm 67)

(Morning)
O God, let the peoples praise you. Let all the peoples praise you.

(Evening)
O God, may you continue to bless us; let all the ends of the earth serve you.

How will we know, O God, that you have been gracious to us and made your face to shine upon us? Will it be when we have the things we desire? Will it be when life conforms to our plan for it? Like women and men before us, we are certain about what we want and so unclear about what we need. Forgive us, O God. Then, O God, be gracious to us that your way may be known upon earth, your saving power among all nations.

(Morning)
Hear, O God, our words of praise and thanksgiving.
(Prayers of Intercession)

(Evening)
Hear, O God, our prayers on behalf of the world you love.
(Prayers of Intercession)

Let all the ends of the world praise God.
(Pray the Prayer of Our Savior.)

(Morning)
Grant us the sense of awe and wonder that acknowledges that life is not ours for the taking, but yours for the making. Humble us until our lips can form words of thanksgiving and praise. In the matchless name of Jesus. Amen.

(Evening)
O God, whatever this day has brought—joy or pain, health or hurt, fear or hope, conviction or uncertainty—let us not turn away from it, but lift it up and give thanks for it. This day is your gift to us, O God. Let us find your grace in it and give thanks. In the matchless name of Jesus. Amen.

THURSDAY, MAY 17
(Read Revelation 21:10, 22–27)

(Morning)
Giver of new visions, enliven my imagination at the opening of this day.
Breathe your fresh Spirit within me until my seeing is transformed and life,
once so pedestrian and ordinary, is made new.

(Evening)
Giver of new visions, grant us peace, for we have done our best.
Sustain us by your grace that what we have done wrong is forgiven,
and what we have not done at all still beckons us.

The ways of the world, like deep ruts in a dirt road, restrain and limit us. They make us feel secure, but they are incredibly dangerous. Trapped by them, our energy is consumed in maintenance, and we fear leaving them even as we resent their power over us. O God, supposing we could trust your Spirit to give us wings that would carry us to new heights? What new vision might we see? Would this perspective change everything? Would it invite us to leave the ruts that have their hold on us? Would it reignite our passion for life? Would it call forth deeds of love and mercy? Would it nullify old boundaries? Would it hold out promise for your creation? Would it lead toward peace? Grant us, O God, vision enough to lead into your new future.

(Morning)
This morning I hold in my prayers those who need to see an alternative future . . .
(Prayers of Intercession)

(Evening)
Allow me, by your mercy, the freedom to dream of what might be . . .
(Prayers of Intercession)

Lead me, O God, until I dare sight the future you intend for all humankind.
(Pray the Prayer of Our Savior.)

(Morning)
Let my prayers stretch my soul, O God, for alongside your vision mine is so very small. Extend my love, O God, for it too often seeks only to fulfill itself, when you would use it to extend your reign of peace and justice. In the matchless name of Jesus. Amen.

(Evening)
This day, O God, moves toward its end without a pause. How dangerous that is for me. Let me place this time in your hand, that I may not fail to let your Spirit have its way with me. Let me see as you see. In the matchless name of Jesus. Amen.

FRIDAY, MAY 18
(Read Revelation 22:1–5)

(Morning)
Savior, "then the angel showed me the river of the water of life,
bright as crystal, flowing from the throne of God
and of the Lamb through the middle of the street of the city."

(Evening)
Savior, "the leaves of the tree are for the healing of the nations."

It's not quite the way we think of the city, O God. This is a city where the river runs clean and sparkles like a diamond. A city of promise, of hope, of light. This is a city where you are present, where nations are healed, and where worship is true and faithful. We have given up on our cities; you imagine them as places where life is given. More than self-sufficient, this city produces an abundance to be shared. Could you so transform our imaginations that we might see our cities as holy places, care for them, and allow your water of life to cleanse, renew, and make whole?

(Morning)
Let us pray for our cities.
(Prayers of Intercession)

(Evening)
Let us pray for the healing of the nations.
(Prayers of Intercession)

O God, redeem our cities, and nourish those who live in them.
(Pray the Prayer of Our Savior.)

(Morning)
Teach us, O God, to love our cities, to care for them as much as we ask them to care for us, to believe in their future, to make of them holy places with resources that give life to our souls. In the matchless name of Jesus. Amen.

(Evening)
Sometimes, O God, we act as if we could own you, as if you belong to us alone. What if the whole of creation were yours and you were counting on us to steward it with peace and justice? Make us big enough to embrace all that is yours. In the matchless name of Jesus. Amen.

SATURDAY, MAY 19
(Read John 14:23–29)

(Morning)
Jesus, you said, "Those who love me will keep my word."

(Evening)
Jesus, you said, "Peace I leave with you; my peace I give to you.
I do not give to you as the world gives."

O God, for you, love and promise keeping are inseparable. They are held together by a reciprocal relationship of giving and receiving. Love is fulfilled in covenant. Covenant, in turn, is an invitation to faithfulness. In relationship with you, O God, love and covenant are no longer abstract concepts; they are active realities that require perceiving and embodiment. Love changes everything, for in it, remaining true to self is not enough. In the relationship of love we must be true to another for whom we are responsible. In you, O God, may we be sustained by the deep love that makes its home with us and empowers us to live toward your realm.

(Morning)
Abiding in the embrace of your love, O God, we would fulfill these promises.
(Prayers of Intercession)

(Evening)
Sustained by your deep presence, O Giver of abundant grace,
we would have the courage to pray these prayers that invite us to deeds of mercy.
(Prayers of Intercession)

**Hold us in the strength of your arms, that we may persevere
in our love for the world.**
(Pray the Prayer of Our Savior.)

(Morning)
Keep us close to you, O God. Keep us close that we may not falter in our fidelity to the way of Jesus. When the world seeks to own us, draw us near that our compassion may be fearless and our deeds of justice without compromise. In the matchless name of Jesus. Amen.

(Evening)
Your peace, O God, is enough. It endures where the world's peace fails. It touches the recesses of our inmost being. It is peace mediated through love. It offers strength sufficient to draw us to places where love can make a difference. Be peace to us, O God, this day. In the matchless name of Jesus. Amen.

SUNDAY, MAY 20
(Read John 5:1–9)

(Morning)
Holy One, this is not an ordinary day. This is the sabbath day.
I want to be made well.

(Evening)
Holy One, he took up his mat and began to walk.

It is not hopeless, O God, even for those burdens we have carried for years; even for the encumbrances we cannot imagine ourselves without; even when we have blamed others for lack of compassion and mercy. It is not hopeless. This is a sabbath day, when you take the initiative to do the unexpected and the forbidden. This is a sabbath day. "Stand up, take your mat and walk." The impossible is made possible, not by confession or by pity, but by the intervention of your Spirit. At once the man was made well. It is a sabbath day. God, you seek to do a new thing. Can I believe it? You are not finished yet. It is a sabbath day.

(Morning)
God's mercy is beyond all that we dare imagine.
(Prayers of Intercession)

(Evening)
This day, even this moment, is a gift of God. Let me use it faithfully.
(Prayers of Intercession)

Do not be afraid; I bring you tidings of great joy, which shall come to all people.
(Pray the Prayer of Our Savior.)

(Morning)
It is the first day of the week, O God, and if we use it as but a day of rest, we underestimate your power to transform and make it holy by unconventional workings of your Spirit to heal and make whole. Let us attend to you. In the matchless name of Jesus. Amen.

(Evening)
Grant us, O God, the courage to take actions that allow the entrance of your healing power. In the matchless name of Jesus. Amen.

MONDAY, MAY 21
(Read John 17:20–26)

(Morning)
Most gracious God, always let your Word and wisdom abide in me
so that I am prepared to do your will for your glory.

(Evening)
Most gracious God, I pray that I have been obedient to your will
and that the light you have given me has shone to your glory.

Our Sovereign Savior, I remember your words to King Solomon (2 Chron.
7:14), and my soul yearns to behold a healed world of your children who
have turned from their wicked ways, sought your face, and humbled themselves in prayer. Let us all desire to know you, dear God, and grow closer
to you each day.

(Morning)
Sweet Holy Spirit, I pray for your children that they may unite
in peace and unconditional love for one another.
(Prayers of Intercession)

(Evening)
Almighty God, I thank you for showing me your blessings
of peace in a community united in your love.
(Prayers of Intercession)

**A nation divided cannot stand;
a nation rooted in the Word of God cannot fall.**

(Morning)
Everlasting God, use me for your glory
that others may come to know you and
experience your goodness and mercy. In
your Child's name. Amen.

(Evening)
As I take my rest, I thank you for your
grace, knowing it sees me through each
day. I ask that my soul may find rest in
anticipation of continuing your service.
In your Child's name. Amen.

TUESDAY, MAY 22
(Read Acts 16:16–18)

(Morning)
Most gracious and merciful God, I pray I am ready
to welcome your Holy Spirit today.

(Evening)
Most gracious and merciful God, I pray that I have been open to receive
your Holy Spirit today and that the words of my mouth have been a blessing to you.

I want to be a bold, yet humble servant for you, O most high God. I want to be
used to do your work so your name will be glorified above all others.

(Morning)
Sweet heavenly One, free your people from bondage,
and free their bodies and minds to serve and worship your holy name.
Send your wonder-working power to deliver your children from eternal doom.
(Prayers of Intercession)

(Evening)
Dear God, I thank you for the love and strength you have given
to your people to uplift your name.
May others know you and call upon your name above all others.
(Prayers of Intercession)

**Even a donkey can be used to do God's will. Imagine what God can do
with you once you surrender and allow God to use you.**

(Morning)	(Evening)
Gracious God, make me ready to do your will today. In your Child's name. Amen.	Holy Spirit, thank you for guiding me through this day. Keep me covered in the blood of the Lamb as I take my rest. In your Child's name. Amen.

WEDNESDAY, MAY 23
(Read Acts 16:19–24)

(Morning)
Dear God, as I face a new day, I ask for your almighty strength
to overcome any obstacles that may come my way.

(Evening)
Dear God, I thank you for each battle over which you have given me
the victory throughout this day.

Precious Saving Grace, sometimes I forget I asked to be your servant. I keep forgetting that serving you means I will engage in spiritual warfare. I always seem to turn back from these battles when I asked you to put me there in the first place. If I could just remember to put on my armor, as Paul instructed the Ephesians, I would know I don't have to fight these battles alone. You would see me through to victory.

(Morning)
Holy Creator, I pray for those who shall persecute me for your sake.
(Prayers of Intercession)

(Evening)
Blessed Savior, while others condemn my service to you,
let them receive a blessing that will turn their hearts toward your wondrous light.
(Prayers of Intercession)

**You must experience the rain before you can behold the rainbow
that lines the clear blue sky.**

(Morning)
Precious God, let your glory be manifested in my life so all I encounter shall behold your grace and mercy and know you are God, today and always. In your Child's name. Amen.

(Evening)
Precious God, I know you are here with me. Wrap your loving arms of comfort and care around me as I go to sleep. In your Child's name. Amen.

144

THURSDAY, MAY 24
(Read Acts 16:25–34)

(Morning)
Wonder-working Power, thank you for lifting the cares of yesterday
and blessing me with this day—yet another day to worship your name.

(Evening)
Wonder-working Power, let the heavens rejoice and the people praise
your holy name for the blessings you have given to us this day.

O almighty God, I remember in your Word where it says, "I have never seen
the righteous forsaken." You have truly been a blessing. Even though I am an
unworthy being, you continue to shower me with your grace and deliver me
from the prince of death. Keep me open to do your will.

(Morning)
Glorious God, your presence is here to heal. Let your healing power continue
to touch the lives of those in need, near and far.
(Prayers of Intercession)

(Evening)
Eternal and living God, thank you for your love that touches
the coldest heart and warms it with your sweet grace.
May your love continue to warm the hearts of others.
(Prayers of Intercession)

**The victory is in your praise. We may never know
what blessings God has to bestow upon God's children.**

(Morning)
Living God, may this day bring me the
opportunity to be a witness for you.
Anoint me with your Spirit so I may
help a lost soul find salvation in you. In
your Child's name. Amen.

(Evening)
Eternal and living God, thank you for
using me to do your service. May the
night bring peaceful rest and a growing
desire to serve you to the fullest. In your
Child's name. Amen.

FRIDAY, MAY 25
(Read Revelation 22:12–14)

(Morning)
Sweet Rose of Sharon, prepare me for your return.
Whatever I must do this day, make me ready to be obedient to your will.

(Evening)
Sweet Rose of Sharon, have I been a worker of iniquity,
or have I sown the seed of love by which you are known?

I want a closer walk with you, dear Jesus; I want to be ready when you return. I don't want to be left behind because I had to pack. Day and night, let my soul, body, and mind meditate on you. I am ready and standing with my boarding pass—ready to ride on the wings of the Spirit to your heavenly realm.

(Morning)
So many are in need of your healing. Gracious One,
let them behold your glory that they may be healed and saved by your grace.
(Prayers of Intercession)

(Evening)
Blessed Savior, thank you for your ever-present Holy Spirit
who is all around your people.
May your servants continue to bless your name.
(Prayers of Intercession)

**No one knows the day or the hour when Jesus
will return for God's children.**

(Morning)
O God, as I enter this day, let me remember I am a member of your royal court so that my actions obey your commandments. In your Child's name. Amen.

(Evening)
God, as I lie down to sleep, I pray my slumber consists of visions of the salvation of others who are ready for Jesus' return. In your Child's name. Amen.

SATURDAY, MAY 26
(Read Revelation 22:16–17, 20–21)

(Morning)
Precious Savior, send your Holy Spirit; let the Spirit fall fresh
on me that I might be a testimony for your glory today.

(Evening)
Precious Savior, if you had come today, would I have been ready?

Giver of peace, so many times we have rewritten your commandments to accommodate our own desires. If we could only abide in you and your Word, we would have no need to try to make wrong acceptable. Sovereign One, I want to be your servant. Cleanse the thoughts of my heart and mind so I may be acceptable in your sight.

(Morning)
Bright Morning Star, I pray all who desire eternal life
will come into your holy presence.
(Prayers of Intercession)

(Evening)
Blessed are those who trust in you, O wondrous God.
May you touch their hearts and fill them with your Spirit.
May they be ready for your return.
(Prayers of Intercession)

**No one knows what is on God's mind. Jesus may come at any time.
It is best to be ready, no matter when Jesus returns.**

(Morning)
As I venture out into the day, let the meditation of your Word be in my heart. In your Child's name. Amen.

(Evening)
Thank you for this day and the blessings therein. May your Spirit of peace cover me while I sleep. In the name of your Child. Amen.

SUNDAY, MAY 27
(Read Psalm 97)

(Morning)
Holy and gracious Sovereign God, help me to remember how awesome you are,
lest I forget who and whose I am.

(Evening)
Holy and gracious Sovereign God,
have I been a light unto the people for your glory?

No one else could have made this world and all that resides in it with such an intricate hand. I will bless your name from the grassy plains of the lowest valley to the peaks of the highest mountain. No rock has a need to praise your name in my place.

(Morning)
Let the world know your wonder-working power is manifested through each ray
of sunlight and every drop of rain that comes from your heavenly realm.
May the people be blessed by your righteousness to proclaim and lift up your name.
(Prayers of Intercession)

(Evening)
Almighty and most merciful God, let the hearts of the lost
be turned toward your soul-saving fight;
let them be delivered from their waywardness to serve your glorious name.
(Prayers of Intercession)

"This is the day that God has made. Let us rejoice and be glad in it."

(Morning)
Wondrous One, who can match your wondrous power and glory? Throughout this day, my soul shall rejoice and praise your name. In your Child's name. Amen.

(Evening)
Creator, how excellent is your name! I thank you for closing my day with the beauty of your glorious sunset and the twinkling of millions of scattered stars. Please guard my soul as I lie down to sleep. In the name of your Child. Amen.

MONDAY, MAY 28
(Read Acts 2:1–21)

(Morning)
Spirit of God, were the Holy Spirit to come, how different might my day be today?
Were the Holy Spirit to come, how might the church's ministries differ today?

(Evening)
Spirit of God, how was I receptive to you in my life today?
What signs of the Spirit's presence did I see at work in the world today?

God, birthdays, anniversaries, and milestones reached in life bring us to reflect upon courses of events in which your Spirit has been at work. As I look back upon my journey on this earth, I see the marks of your Comforter upon me throughout my life. Attune my heart and soul that I might be even more open to your presence, through the grace of Jesus Christ.

(Morning)
Spirit of God, fall anew on me this day that I might bear witness
to your loving presence in our world.
(Prayers of Intercession)

(Evening)
Mighty wind of God, I thank you for your movement throughout my life this day.
(Prayers of Intercession)

"All of them were filled with the Holy Spirit."
*(Sing "Holy Spirit, Truth Divine," "Soplo de Dios viviente,"
or another familiar hymn.)*

(Morning)	(Evening)
I open this day with great expectation that throughout its course, I may be afire with the Spirit of the living God and, thereby, bring enthusiasm to all with whom I labor and live. Through Jesus Christ, my Savior. Amen.	Having lived with the vision of peaceful presence this day, now let me dream of that day when all shall see a new heaven and a new earth. Through Jesus Christ, my Savior. Amen.

TUESDAY, MAY 29
(Read Genesis 11:1–9)

(Morning)
God, contemporary technology is so confusing. New terminologies must be learned
so we can communicate electronically in a world in which distance is measured
in milliseconds. Help me not forget, no matter how scattered my life
may become, your presence with me this day.

(Evening)
God, when all circuits are down, hard drives nosedive, and databanks are lost,
there remains One who can be reached in prayer and meditation. Thank you, God,
for keeping that line of communication open in this crazy, mixed-up world!

My first encounter with contemporary technology, via a personal computer, was both scary and awe-inspiring. Since that afternoon, seventeen years ago, I have learned to trust ever more deeply in one-to-one conversation with my spouse, my children, my family, my friends, my colleagues, and you, my God. Technology is tremendous. But nothing replaces a few words spoken in love and the holy silences between them.

(Morning)
Let not the technological attempts to bring the world closer together,
via one kind of computer language or program, mislead me down paths of ease
when it comes to mission and ministry this day, O God.
(Prayers of Intercession)

(Evening)
Where have I remained open to receive what is strange, foreign, and difficult
to understand or accept this day, O God? Improve both my perception
of your presence and my reception of your Spirit in others, I ask this night.
(Prayers of Intercession)

"Now the whole earth had one language and the same words."
(Sing "God Is Truly with Us," "Este es el día," or another familiar hymn.)

(Morning)
May I not seek to make a name for
myself at the expense of your call for
justice, and may your peace roll down
like a mighty stream where all your
people may gather for refreshment.
Through Jesus Christ, my Savior. Amen.

(Evening)
Thank you, God, for being with me
throughout this day so that my heart
has been focused on being your faithful
servant rather than serving myself.
Through Jesus Christ, my Savior.
Amen.

WEDNESDAY, MAY 30
(Read Psalm 104:24–35)

(Morning)
O Star-abiding One, how can I keep from singing this day?
Your works throughout the universe are so wonderfully revealed.
Praised be your name.

(Evening)
O Star-abiding One, have you heard my voice uplifted in praise to you this day?
Receive my evening praise to you for all you have done for us in life today.

Music moves me in so many ways. Whether I sing, play an instrument, or listen to good music, my soul is stretched toward you, my Creator, with praise and thanksgiving by each note and passage. The psalmist invites me to spend all my days in appreciation to you for the gifts of creation, of life. This is not a bad way to spend my days—humming or singing—as the Spirit moves me to utter aloud what I feel in my heart. Thank you, God, for music, the sound of creation at work.

(Morning)
God who has strung the heavens with sounds of praise,
I offer my heart to you in gratitude for this new day.
Attune my soul to the harmonics of your universe this day.
(Prayers of Intercession)

(Evening)
I heard your song today, "Wakantanka Taku Nitawa." It was a mix of winds and words,
pulse and meter, rests and crescendos, all majestically calling my attention to you.
(Prayers of Intercession)

"Bless God, O my soul."
*(Sing "Wakantanka Taku Nitawa," "To You, O God, All Creatures Sing,"
or another familiar hymn.)*

(Morning)
New every morning is my opportunity to thank you, O God, for your abounding love and mercy. May the wonderful sounds that greet me this day devise a symphony of praise and thanksgiving in my soul that will move me, from time to time, to lift up my voice and sing! Through Jesus Christ, my Savior. Amen.

(Evening)
All praise to you, my God, this night! May the last sound I hear before drifting into restful sleep be that of your creation ceaselessly praising you. Through Jesus Christ, my Savior. Amen.

THURSDAY, MAY 31
(Read Romans 8:14–17)

(Morning)
Blessed Redeemer, how will I keep my timidity in check
and share in your suffering this day?
Help me to remember how I have been blessed by you.

(Evening)
Blessed Redeemer, I trust I have shared your blessings this day
with those among whom I live and move and have my being.
Forgive me if I were not as faithful as I intended when this day began.

If only I could always keep in mind how blessed I am by Christ, I would live life more boldly than I do. Where I am anxious and timid, speak to me, Holy Spirit, of my Savior's great gifts to me. Then, God, I will become liberated to serve Christ fully, knowing that nothing that may occur can separate me from your love, through Jesus, my Savior.

(Morning)
Christ, my Shalom, may my service to others this day reflect how blessed
I am to be a member of God's family.
(Prayers of Intercession)

(Evening)
Heavenly Parent, I thank you for teaching me to share in the cost and joy
of walking through life with Christ only as my Savior.
(Prayers of Intercession)

"For all who are led by the Spirit of God are children of God."
(Sing "Blessed Assurance," "Pues si vivimos," or another familiar hymn.)

(Morning)
I believe I can do all things through you, O Christ. Help me with my unbelief this day that the service I give to you throughout the day may reflect your will and not my own. Through Jesus Christ, my Savior. Amen.

(Evening)
Give me peace now, O risen One, my Shalom, that my body may be renewed and refreshed through the gift of slumber, and I may rise to serve you anew come tomorrow. Through Jesus Christ, my Savior. Amen.

FRIDAY, JUNE 1
(Read John 14:8–17)

(Morning)
Jesus, it is easy to be with you and not know you. Your thoughts and ways are so
counter to the culture in which I live. Help me to pay closer attention to you today.

(Evening)
Jesus, by focusing upon you more intentionally today,
I have become more aware of how God is in me. Thank you.

Like a member of the family, the risen One has been present throughout my
life. And like so many with whom I live, Christ is not fully known. Comforting
God, how can I fail so often to note how I am blessed by the Spirit? Help me
increase my attentiveness to your presence with me that I might rejoice in the
awareness of whence you have come, and where I may be, through Jesus Christ,
that joy and peace might flow throughout my life.

(Morning)
God in me, let me greet you in every one of your children this day that,
together, we might do great things in the blessed name of Jesus Christ.
(Prayers of Intercession)

(Evening)
Holy Comforter Spirit, thank you for permitting me to experience
the joy of knowing your presence in my life this day.
(Prayers of Intercession)

"If you love me, you will keep my commandments."
*(Sing "Great Is Your Faithfulness," "Spirit, Spirit of Gentleness,"
or another familiar hymn.)*

(Morning)
Open my eyes this day, Holy Spirit,
Comforter, and Guide, that I may see
the living God in everyone I meet and,
thereby, come to know the meaning of
Christ's promises anew. Through Jesus
Christ, my Savior. Amen.

(Evening)
I thank you, living Savior, for the gift of
this day now ending. I have not lived it
alone, nor have its prayers and deeds in
love been offered in vain. Give me rest
and peace, I ask. Through Jesus Christ,
my Savior. Amen.

SATURDAY, JUNE 2
(Read John 14:25–27)

(Morning)
God, in this world of unending conflict, how am I to know the "peace which passes
understanding"? I need to experience peace in my life, here and now.

(Evening)
God, as I come to the end of my day, I look back to recall glimpses of the presence
of the Comforter and give thanks to you, through Christ, for such a gift as this!

I recall awful things from my childhood, impoverished and hardship-filled as it
was. Depression and war, family struggle and grief, filled those early days. I remember many wonderful persons from my childhood, hopeful and loving were
they. Hope and joy enabled us for the living of those days. I learned then that you,
ever-present God, were with me. I believe that you are with me now. Nothing ever
ultimately severs me from the love that surrounds and upholds every one of us.
"Peace I leave with you" was and is Jesus' eternal promise. Despite this uncertain
journey that has been my life, "Jesus loves me, this I know."

(Morning)
In the mystery that is daybreak, I come to be with you, gentle Spirit,
that you may infuse my new day with confidence in God's never-ending love.
(Prayers of Intercession)

(Evening)
In the uncertainty that is nightfall, I turn to your comforting presence, Holy One,
that my night of rest should be not fitful but rest filled as one of your beloved in sleep.
(Prayers of Intercession)

"I do not give to you as the world gives.
Do not let your hearts be troubled, and do not let them be afraid."
(Sing "There Is a Balm in Gilead," "We Are Often Tossed and Driven,"
or another familiar hymn.)

(Morning)
God of peace and promise, reign in the
world and in my life, that I may abandon
the warfare of my heart and mind. Restore
me and revive me again, O God, to a lively
trust in your gifts of life and love. Thanks
be to Christ, my Savior. Amen.

(Evening)
By your Holy Spirit, give me a night
filled with dreams of your new day of
peace and joy for all, that I might arise
to the glorious presence of Jesus Christ.
Thanks be to Christ, my Savior. Amen.

SUNDAY, JUNE 3
(Read Acts 2:1–21)

(Morning)
Dear Redeemer, as I join others to celebrate the day of Pentecost in worship and praise, give me breath and spirit to worship in word and song while I recall the wonderful deeds of those who have preceded me in this Christian journey.

(Evening)
Dear Redeemer, reflecting on this day of renewal for my soul,
I thank you for the wonderful company of believers among whom
I have found inspiration and hope this day of Pentecost.

The candles upon the birthday cake of the church of Jesus Christ emblazon the world's shadows this holy day. I rejoice in the fact that throughout my life, I have had numerous opportunities to be a participant in the glorious history of apostolic faith. I hope I never lose the sense of love for Christ that came into my life when first I heard those melodious songs of praise and those intriguing words of the pastor interpreting the Scriptures. This is indeed a mighty rush, a powerful force, a compelling vision of the world as it will be one day.

(Morning)
Intoxicate me this day with fervor for the unfulfilled reality promised on the day of Pentecost, almighty God. Give me strength to do my part for the coming of your glorious reign, through Jesus Christ I pray.
(Prayers of Intercession)

(Evening)
Thank you, holy God, for this marvelous day of renewal. May this day's fiery spirit enkindle anew commitment to proclaim your loving deeds, through Jesus Christ.
(Prayers of Intercession)

**"In the last days it will be, God declares,
that I will pour out my Spirit upon all flesh."**
*(Sing "There's a Sweet, Sweet Spirit," "Spirit of God, Descend upon My Heart,"
or another familiar hymn.)*

(Morning)	(Evening)
I am glad to join the gathering of your people this day on which we celebrate the gift of your Holy Spirit. May I be renewed by this morn of praise and worship for the service of Christ in your world. Thanks be to Christ, my Savior. Amen.	I have offered you this day, my God. I trust you have found that upon which I have focused this day pleasing in your sight. And I hope you will watch over me this night that I may rest securely in your peace. Thanks be to Christ, my Savior. Amen.

MONDAY, JUNE 4
(Read Romans 5:1–2)

(Morning)
Good morning, God. Thank you for letting me see another day.
Give me the wisdom and insight I need to remember that I am justified by faith.

(Evening)
Good evening, God. If I have wronged anyone this day,
please allow me another day so that I may seek reconciliation.
Create in me a new heart so that I may be more sensitive to the feelings of others.

Dear God, at times it is easy to forget that my good deeds, solemn prayers, and consistent tithing are not what characterize me as a follower of Christ. I would not do these things were it not for Jesus. Sometimes my faith feels strong; sometimes it seems quite weak. Nonetheless, I do have faith. So I thank you, God, for your Child, Jesus, and the faith and hope that have grown in me as a result of your faithfulness.

(Morning)
I pray now for those who feel they have no faith.
(Prayers of Intercession)

(Evening)
Here is my soul, O God. Please make it more faithful to you alone.
(Prayers of Intercession)

Jesus, lover of my soul, I now pray.
(Pray the Prayer of Our Savior.)

(Morning)
May my faith inspire faith in others this day. In Christ's name. Amen.

(Evening)
Good night, God. May my rest and the rest of my family be peaceful. In Christ's name. Amen.

TUESDAY, JUNE 5
(Read Romans 5:3–5)

(Morning)
God, in addition to hope, I can boast in my suffering.
Help me to understand this truth more completely today.

(Evening)
God, thank you for pouring your love into my heart this day.
May I use this evening to reflect on your Word with even more precision:
"Suffering produces endurance, and endurance produces character,
and character produces hope."

I believe suffering produces character and character produces hope. But sometimes, God, I really think I have enough character and hope. So if it is your will, I don't mind missing any additional suffering. Yet when I look back on all the storms through which you have guided me, I can honestly thank you for them. Your Holy Spirit was there, making me a new person, a stronger person, a wiser person, a more compassionate person. Help me, O God, in difficult times as well as hopeful times to know that you are always pouring out your love.

(Morning)
I pray now for all Christians who suffer and feel they have no hope.
(Prayers of Intercession)

(Evening)
I pray now for those who do not have hope because they do not know you, God.
(Prayers of Intercession)

With hope I pray.
(Pray the Prayer of Our Savior.)

(Morning)	(Evening)
May the words of my mouth and the meditation of my heart be full of hope and inspire hope in all who meet me today. In Christ's name. Amen.	Whatever my lot, it is well with my soul. Good night, God. In Christ's name. Amen.

WEDNESDAY, JUNE 6
(Read Proverbs 8:1–4)

(Morning)
Creator God, when wisdom calls today, I pray that I am ready to listen.

(Evening)
Creator God, may I recognize the wisdom you give to children,
which adults often haughtily overlook.

Like Solomon, I ask for wisdom and understanding. When I am confronted with a disgruntled coworker, make me wise. When my children or others seek my counsel but seem more content to ignore me than to take sound correction, make me wise. When my parents are no longer able to live independently and I must make arrangements for them, please make me wise. O God, whatever the case, I do not want to be a fool who rushes into things and assumes that my years equal wisdom. I want wisdom that comes from being in touch with you. Whatever the circumstance may be, please grant me a portion of your wisdom.

(Morning)
Teach me to find wisdom's lessons wherever I go.
(Prayers of Intercession)

(Evening)
Thank you for granting me wisdom this day.
(Prayers of Intercession)

Humbly I pray.
(Pray the Prayer of Our Savior.)

(Morning)
May my life glorify you today. In Christ's name. Amen.

(Evening)
Another work-filled day has ended. I lay my head to rest now. As I fall asleep, I think of your creation—the earth, the solar system, the universe. In Christ's name. Amen.

THURSDAY, JUNE 7
(Read Proverbs 8:22–31)

(Morning)
Loving God, yesterday I prayed for wisdom, but today I marvel
at the way in which your wisdom precedes all creation.

(Evening)
Loving God, I think of how you have put together all of creation
with perfect understanding and wisdom.
I think of the intricacies of the ecosystem and how
you created us perfectly in your image.

In order to see your wisdom, God, we have to quiet our hearts by going to a quiet place. Perhaps now is a good time to look at the sun as it awakens, or just close our eyes and imagine a sun rising over the ocean. When all is quiet in our hearts, we may listen to Wisdom. What is she telling you about life, family, or creation?

(Morning)
Today I will reflect on the agelessness of wisdom. Wisdom is as old as the universe.
(Prayers of Intercession)

(Evening)
Thank you, God, for letting me enjoy your creation.
Make me aware of my folly so that I will not defeat
the wisdom and understanding that you have given me.
(Prayers of Intercession)

To be wise is to humble oneself to the awesomeness of God.
(Pray the Prayer of Our Savior.)

(Morning)	(Evening)
It is time to spread my light.	It is time to let my light rest.
In Christ's name. Amen.	In Christ's name. Amen.

FRIDAY, JUNE 8
(Read John 16:12–15)

(Morning)
Inspiring God, thank you for waking me up this morning
and allowing me to see a new day.
I wait patiently for the revelation of your mysteries.

(Evening)
Inspiring God, thank you for the rest of this evening.
I wait patiently for the revelation of tomorrow.

God, when Jesus announced his departure to the disciples, they appeared to be anxiety ridden. They wanted to know what was next, and they wanted to follow him. In John 14, Peter knew that Jesus was going somewhere, but Jesus was not clear about his destination. Jesus' words to his disciples may remind us that we, too, will know all that we need to know in due season. Christians need only to wait for the voice of the Holy Spirit. Help me, God, to understand that I do not have to know everything that is to come. It is just as well to trust in you.

(Morning)
I wait patiently for your revelation.
(Prayers of Intercession)

(Evening)
Teach me to wait patiently on the Holy Spirit.
(Prayers of Intercession)

"When the spirit of truth comes, he will guide you into all the truth."
(Sing "Sweet, Sweet Spirit.")

(Morning)
Reveal to me, Holy Spirit, the error in my ways. I know I am not always a loving person. I am not always quick to reconcile. I am not always eager to forgive. I throw myself at your mercy, and I lay before you my transgressions. In Christ's name. Amen.

(Evening)
As I recline, I wait for the gift of sleep and restoration. In Christ's name. Amen.

SATURDAY, JUNE 9
(Read Psalm 8:1–8)

(Morning)
God, I awaken to marvel at your love for me.

(Evening)
God, what am I that you are mindful of me?

When the mundane things that occupy our time threaten to dull our view of the universe, it is time to slow down. How many times have we not noticed the clouds in perfect formation? How often do we fail to notice the beauty of fruits and vegetables? And when was the last time we were overwhelmed by the moonlit stars? If the universe is looking dull and ordinary, it is time for us to slow down and look once more at your work, Creator God.

(Morning)
May I recognize your glory in everything you have created,
especially other human beings, no matter what their state or circumstances.
(Prayers of Intercession)

(Evening)
Help me to remember that I am extraordinarily special to you.
Help me to remember that I am a steward of creation.
I must cherish it and protect it from careless pollution and destruction.
(Prayers of Intercession)

Tonight, spend a few moments enjoying the stars.
(Pray the Prayer of Our Savior.)

(Morning)
I thank you, God, for the birds of the air and the fish of the sea. In Christ's name. Amen.

(Evening)
Nighttime is the work of your hands, O God. You tilted the earth perfectly and spun it on its axis at just the right speed so that now another day has ended. I can finally rest from my labors. In Christ's name. Amen.

SUNDAY, JUNE 10
(Read Psalm 8:9)

(Morning)
God, Creator of the heavens, I commit myself to your service.

(Evening)
God, may I always reflect on your name with joy.

"O God, our Sovereign, how majestic is your name in all the earth!" wrote the psalmist. The psalmist was glorifying God and also distinguishing you from other gods. In short, the psalmist was identifying you as the God of the universe, a God whose magnificence and power surpassed all others. We, too, must remember this. The very reading or utterance of your holy name should move us to deep reverence and humility.

(Morning)
I reflect now on everything your name means to me.
(Prayers of Intercession)

(Evening)
I reflect now on your sovereignty.
(Prayers of Intercession)

In reverence I pray.
(Pray the Prayer of Our Savior.)

(Morning)
When I meet someone in need today, may the mere thought of your name lead me to greater service. In Christ's name. Amen.

(Evening)
In all the earth tonight, you are majestic. In Christ's name. Amen.

MONDAY, JUNE 11
(Read Luke 7:36–8:3)

(Morning)
Loving God, I awake to the fresh grace of a new day.
Let me miss no opportunity to experience and share your love.

(Evening)
Loving God, have I loved today a little or a lot? Which of my sins got in the way?

"Sinners," "demons," "evil spirits"—these words do not often frequent my lips. More prone to notice the sins of others, seldom do I apply such terms to myself. However reluctant I am, the truth remains that the power of sin inhabits even my soul. My life also misses the mark of your divine will, and I stand in need of forgiveness. Gracious God, I confess my sin. Let me experience your grace. I long to be freed by love to live in love.

(Morning)
I pray for those who know not what they do, who know but do not want
to admit their sins, or who are overwhelmed by the debts they carry.
(Prayers of Intercession)

(Evening)
I pray for those who weep tears of joy, and for those
who stand in judgment because of the judging they have done.
(Prayers of Intercession)

"The one to whom little is forgiven, loves little."

(Morning)
God, you have graced my house with your presence. Send me forth by faith, in peace, filled with love. Thanks be to Christ. Amen.

(Evening)
At the close of this day, O God, forgive me my sins, even I have forgiven those who have sinned against me, so that I might awake to love another day. Thanks be to Christ. Amen.

TUESDAY, JUNE 12
(Read 1 Kings 21:1–21)

(Morning)
Bountiful God, you provide more than I need or deserve.
Purge from my soul the longing for even more.

(Evening)
Bountiful God, pronounce your word upon my acts of this day,
so I might be humbled and receive your mercy.

God of the prophets, Ahab coveted Naboth's vineyard. How often have I wanted something belonging to my neighbor—something my money couldn't buy? How often have my thwarted desires deepened into depression? How often have my unfulfilled plans led to scheming plots? O God, keep me from selling out to evil. The Tenth Commandment seems the hardest one to keep. But so long as my heart yearns for what belongs to others, it is not set on you.

(Morning)
I pray for those wise enough to value what they have inherited from your hand, and
for those so foolish as to have not yet learned the meaning of the word "enough."
(Prayers of Intercession)

(Evening)
I pray for those who fell victim to the powerful this day,
and for those who proved to be pawns in the cause of evil.
(Prayers of Intercession)

"You shall not covet . . . anything that belongs to your neighbor."

(Morning)	(Evening)
Focus my thoughts this day not on getting but on giving, not on acquiring but on helping, not on accumulating but on serving. Thanks be to Christ. Amen.	You have answered my prayer for daily bread. Let me live each day dependent on you, grateful for all you provide. Thanks be to Christ. Amen.

WEDNESDAY, JUNE 13
(Read 2 Samuel 11:26–12:7)

(Morning)
Teaching God, justice and righteousness are your nature. Let these traits dwell within me.

(Evening)
Teaching God, whenever my eyes are shut, my ears closed, or my heart grown dull, speak to me in parables, for I seek understanding of your ways and my life.

A little righteous indignation is not all bad. The prophets showed their tempers in the face of wrongdoing. Jesus was displeased with the moneychangers, the scribes, even Peter. So I can understand David's display of anger upon hearing Nathan's sad story. Still I must examine my own behavior and temper with mercy my own demands for justice—lest I be found guilty of doing the very things I condemn and invite greater judgment upon myself.

(Morning)
I pray for those experiencing the reality of grief,
for those without the resources to resist their oppressors,
and for those who would prey upon the vulnerability of others.
(Prayers of Intercession)

(Evening)
I pray for those who hate giving up what they already have,
but think nothing of taking advantage of those with less.
(Prayers of Intercession)

"Nathan said to David, 'You are the one!' "

(Morning)
Am I the one? Where I have yet to perceive how I have displeased God, speak truth to me so I can repent of my deeds. Thanks be to Christ. Amen.

(Evening)
Am I the one? Whomever I have wronged this day, grant me grace to wake tomorrow with another opportunity to set things right. Thanks be to Christ. Amen.

THURSDAY, JUNE 14
(Read 2 Samuel 12:7–10, 13–15)

(Morning)
All-knowing God, you are aware of my every thought, word, and deed.
Be merciful to me in all my humanness, I pray this day.

(Evening)
All-knowing God, far from too little, you heap blessings upon my life.
Tonight I pray you will add one more: forgiveness
for the wrongs I have done this day.

God, you are so good, so gracious, and so giving. How can I be anything except grateful? Yet my behavior too often betrays one who does what is less than good in pursuit of my own delights. I accept there is a price to be paid for my acts. I understand there are natural consequences for my deeds. I regret the pain my transgressions have caused. I know I cannot withstand your wrath. I confess my sin. In your mercy, put it far away from me.

(Morning)
I pray for those who loyally stand in harm's way and for loved ones who wait from afar, that neither shall be overcome by forces beyond their knowledge or control.
(Prayers of Intercession)

(Evening)
I pray for those who suffer though innocent, who are stricken through no cause of their own, victims of my sins and the sins of others.
(Prayers of Intercession)

"David said to Nathan, 'I have sinned against God.' "

(Morning)
Throughout this day, keep me aware of your blessings, attentive to your will, resistant to temptation. Thanks be to Christ. Amen.

(Evening)
I close my eyes praying for the peace that is beyond all understanding. Thanks be to Christ. Amen.

FRIDAY, JUNE 15
(Read Psalm 5:1–8)

(Morning)
O God, my day begins with you, confident that you care enough to hear my voice.

(Evening)
O God, I return to you at the end of this day,
once more pleading for your intervention.

Sometimes my pain is so deep that I cannot find adequate words for my prayers. Sometimes I feel at such a loss that I come before you with nothing more than deep sighs. Sometimes those sighs turn into sobs and a continual crying out, over and over and over again, of your name. I feel free to weep in your arms because I know I am held by your love. Through my tears I watch and wait. And I wonder not "if" or "when" but "how" you will answer my prayers.

(Morning)
I pray for those unwilling to follow your will, for those puffed up
with prideful boasting, and for those deceived by their own lies.
(Prayers of Intercession)

(Evening)
I pray for those who do not pray for themselves, for those
who are engaged in violence, and for those whom I consider hurtful enemies.
(Prayers of Intercession)

"To you I pray."

(Morning)
Lead me in all I do this day, that I may do what is right to the end that your way is followed. Thanks be to Christ. Amen.

(Evening)
Awesome God, who delights not in wickedness, now watch me safely through the night, so I may wake to bow down before you in prayer another day. Thanks be to Christ. Amen.

SATURDAY, JUNE 16
(Read Psalm 32)

(Morning)
Faithful God, as a person of faith, I offer prayer to you now. Remove all stubbornness from within me, so I may learn your ways.

(Evening)
Faithful God, I long to shout the glad cries of deliverance. What secret sin of mine still stands in the way of my rejoicing in you?

People say confession is good for the soul. I believe it. I know from experience that harboring guilt takes its toll on both body and soul. Oh, the sleepless nights when I have tossed and turned; the meals I have left languishing on my plate; the moments I have wished I had just come clean! The fear of being found out leads to much wasted energy; and for what purpose other than to avoid embarrassment or protect ego? How much healthier it is to admit the wrong and discover the happiness of living as one forgiven.

(Morning)
I pray for those burdened by guilt, for those whose strength has withered, for those with groaning souls.
(Prayers of Intercession)

(Evening)
I pray for those who are tormented by the memories of wrongs committed, who have yet to shout for joy in the freedom you offer so freely.
(Prayers of Intercession)

"Happy are those whose transgression is forgiven."

(Morning)
As you protected the psalmist, preserve me from trouble this day. Surround me with love, for I place my trust in you. Thanks be to Christ. Amen.

(Evening)
I will sleep well tonight, refreshed by your grace. Thanks be to Christ. Amen.

SUNDAY, JUNE 17
(Read Galatians 2:15–21)

(Morning)
Almighty God, on the third day you raised the crucified One from the grave.
Lift me as well to the new life you offer through faith.

(Evening)
Almighty God, at the close of this day of rest, I thank you for the reminder that,
no matter what I do, your victory already has been won.

Crime and punishment, arrest and conviction, law and order—such are normal expectations in our world. In contrast you offer law and grace, commandments and forgiveness, "Thus says the Sovereign God" and justification by faith. Sometimes I think and act as if I could accomplish all your expectations by my own sheer efforts. But a life lived only by the law reveals my deadly sinfulness. I thank you on this resurrection day for the good news of life lived in Christ—life lived by love, life lived both abundantly and eternally.

(Morning)
I pray for those who continue trying to prove their worth and to earn God's love.
(Prayers of Intercession)

(Evening)
I pray for those who use my sins as a justification not to believe in Christ.
(Prayers of Intercession)

"I died to the law, so that I might live to God."
*(Sing "Come, Thou Fount of Every Blessing," "Amazing Grace,"
or another familiar hymn.)*

(Morning)	(Evening)
My spirit soars. Jesus did not die in vain. God's love cannot be defeated. Thanks be to Christ. Amen.	I go to rest now in peace, confident that Christ lives in me. Thanks be to Christ. Amen.

MONDAY, JUNE 18
(Read Psalm 42)

(Morning)
Holy One, as this day begins, my soul thirsts for you.
I yearn for the certainty of your presence, for the fullness of life you bestow.

(Evening)
Holy One, I know you have accompanied me through this day and into this night.
My thirst for you is quenched by my trust, my hope, and my praise!

There are times in my life when I feel so far from you, when my tears have been my food day and night; times when the powers of despair and doubt overwhelm me, when my spirit is cast down and my soul disquieted. I hunger for your life-giving presence. Give me the hope that comes of memory and of trust. Raise me up in praise, song, and prayer!

(Morning)
Thirst-quenching Spirit, I pray that you may grant the life-giving
waters to all for whom I pray . . .
(Prayers of Intercession)

(Evening)
O God, my Rock, in the quiet of these shadows, I ask your holy presence to . . .
(Prayers of Intercession)

Even in times of despair and doubt, God is as near as our yearning.
*(Sing or read aloud "As Pants the Hart for Cooling Streams"
or another familiar hymn.)*

(Morning)	(Evening)
Now bless me into this day, O God, that I may know your presence with me in all that I do. In the blessed name of Jesus. Amen.	O Holy One, I pray I may rest this night and awaken to a day rich with life with you. In the blessed name of Jesus. Amen.

TUESDAY, JUNE 19
(Read Psalm 43)

(Morning)
O God of light and truth, lead me this day!

(Evening)
O God of light and truth, your light and your truth
have guided me through a challenging day. I give you thanks!

There are days, God, when I wonder where you are, especially when I face injustice, when those around me seem so unfair. I do not understand why I have to face such things. Yet even when I walk about mournfully, I remember you are my refuge, my exceeding joy, and my soul begins to praise you. Lead me to you, O God, by your light and truth, that my understanding may deepen. Help me to set aside my human propensity to wallow in my pain and instead to live in the joy and light you intend.

(Morning)
O God, my God, be a refuge for those for whom I pray . . .
(Prayers of Intercession)

(Evening)
O God, my refuge and my hope, I thank you
for the light and truth that led me today . . .
(Prayers of Intercession)

God leads us with light and truth to be able to face injustice and ungodliness.
(Sing or read aloud "O God, Our Help in Ages Past" or another familiar hymn.)

(Morning)
Be with me all day, O God, and help me to face deceit and injustice by the power of your Holy Spirit. In the blessed name of Jesus. Amen.

(Evening)
Thank you, God, for your light and truth, which have led me this day, and for your joy and hope! In the blessed name of Jesus. Amen.

WEDNESDAY, JUNE 20
(Read Galatians 3:23–29)

(Morning)
Christ, come into my life so fully that I may live entirely by faith!

(Evening)
Christ, I have caught glimmers today of what it means
to live in you, and I give you thanks!

What a vision you have given us, Jesus! A vision of a faith so deep, humanity no longer needs the law; of a baptism so profound, the world's divisions of gender, race, class, and religion no longer function; of a unity so full, we all know we are children of God. May it be so, and may I live my faith and my life according to that vision and promise. Let me remember my baptism into you, O Christ, and enable me to know that I am clothed with your presence.

(Morning)
O good and gracious God, it is a challenge to live according to your hope for us.
Give me strength, and give strength to those for whom I pray . . .
(Prayers of Intercession)

(Evening)
By faith you lead us to be your faithful people.
Lead me and all those for whom I pray . . .
(Prayers of Intercession)

**Baptism in Christ means a profound unity
that sets aside the ways of the world.**
*(Sing or read aloud "In Christ There Is No East or West"
or another familiar hymn.)*

(Morning)
Let me live this day according to your vision and your hope, O Christ. In the blessed name of Jesus. Amen.

(Evening)
How full and rich life is when lived with you, Christ Jesus! I give you thanks. In the blessed name of Jesus. Amen.

THURSDAY, JUNE 21
(Read 1 Kings 19:1–15)

(Morning)
God, you are in the sound of sheer silence, and I seek that holy silence now.

(Evening)
God, in the rush of the day, it is easy to miss you,
and I give thanks for the silences that refresh the human spirit.

When all is falling apart around us, when old loyalties break down and even a wilderness seems safer, it is tempting to look for you in the hard and the harsh, in the earthquake, wind, and fire, in judgment and condemnation. Yet Elijah's experience reminds us that you are more often in simplicity and gentleness. In the sound of sheer silence. A healing, awesome, deep-throated silence. May we listen for you there.

(Morning)
Grant your blessing of rich silence to those for whom I pray . . .
(Prayers of Intercession)

(Evening)
May those for whom I pray know you in the sound of sheer silence,
even in the wildernesses of life.
(Prayers of Intercession)

**God is known to us in simplicity and silence,
especially when we expect otherwise.**
(Sing or read aloud "Spirit, Spirit of Gentleness" or another familiar hymn.)

(Morning)
Help me to listen for you beyond the expected, beyond the loud din of the day. Help me discover the rich, healing silence of your presence, O God. In the blessed name of Jesus. Amen.

(Evening)
You are so powerfully present, God, and I give you thanks! In the blessed name of Jesus. Amen.

FRIDAY, JUNE 22
(Read Psalm 22:19–28)

(Morning)
Faithful Deliverer, I know I can trust you to be with me.

(Evening)
Faithful Deliverer, I give thanks for your faithful presence with me.

Liberating God, when wolves are circling, our prayers become very concrete: Do not be far away! Come quickly to my aid! Deliver my soul from the sword, my life from the power of the dog! O God, help me to know you so deeply that I, too, can call on you in my times of need. Then, like the psalmist, help me to set myself in the midst of your congregation, ready to sing your praises, to testify to your response to prayer. May my vision also reach beyond my own need and embrace the afflicted, the poor, the seekers, the families of all nations in their need to know you. For indeed you reign over everything, and I sing your praise!

(Morning)
Some I know are in need of your deliverance, O God . . .
(Prayers of Intercession)

(Evening)
Grant deliverance from pain, O God, for . . .
(Prayers of Intercession)

Even in times of great suffering, it is possible to praise God.
(Sing or read aloud "I Need You Every Hour" or another familiar hymn.)

(Morning)
Dear God, let this not be one of those days in which the wolves circle, but if it is, be with me and let my life testify to you! In the blessed name of Jesus. Amen.

(Evening)
Ah, God, you have led me through another day, and I give you thanks for it! In the blessed name of Jesus. Amen.

SATURDAY, JUNE 23
(Read Isaiah 65:1–9)

(Morning)
O God, let me not be among the rebellious people who follow their own devices!

(Evening)
O God, I tried to walk in ways that are good this day.

It is tempting, God, to turn to incense and sacrifice and special concoctions when you seem to be far off. Yet you remind me that you are simply waiting for me to call on you. I do not need devices of holiness, only a trusting and genuine spirit. You wait in readiness for me; indeed you seek me, and all I need to do is to ask and seek in return. Can it be that simple? Oh, I pray that it may be so, and that my spirit may be genuine—free of human contrivance and set only on a path that you deem good.

(Morning)
Holy One, may these for whom I pray seek you today . . .
(Prayers of Intercession)

(Evening)
Holy, seeking God, may all these call on your name . . .
(Prayers of Intercession)

God is ready; all you need to do is seek and ask!
(Sing or read aloud "Sweet, Sweet Spirit" or another familiar hymn.)

(Morning)
Thank you, God, for being ready. Now help me be ready. In the blessed name of Jesus. Amen.

(Evening)
Your readiness surprises me, God, and graces me with hope. In the blessed name of Jesus. Amen.

SUNDAY, JUNE 24
(Read Luke 8:26–39)

(Morning)
Christ Jesus, may I be healed as well and sing your praise!

(Evening)
Christ Jesus, your healing presence helped me through this day. Thank you!

It may not be as clear for me as it was for that man in Gerasene, O Christ, yet I know you also work in my life to heal me. I don't see the demons as clearly as you do, yet I know they are there. If not for you, they might take over my life too. I give thanks today for your presence in my life, for your teaching and guidance and healing. Help me to be free of the demons that make me shy about my faith, so I, too, can declare publicly how much God has done for me.

(Morning)
Grant healing to all who are in need . . .
(Prayers of Intercession)

(Evening)
May those who are in need meet you, Jesus.
(Prayers of Intercession)

Christ's healing ministry is for all of us.
(Sing or read aloud "Amazing Grace" or another familiar hymn.)

(Morning)
May I be both healed and healing today, Jesus. In the blessed name of Jesus. Amen.

(Evening)
May the blessing of your healing make me your witness, Jesus. In the blessed name of Jesus. Amen.

MONDAY, JUNE 25
(Read Psalm 16:1–6)

(Morning)
Almighty God, will I act this day as though you are my God
and I have no good apart from you?

(Evening)
Almighty God, have I been a reflection this day of the One in whom I claim to take
refuge, or have I taken upon my lips other gods who will only multiply my sorrows?

Mighty are the idols of the world—idols that promise me wealth, prosperity,
and recognition. In the gong and clang of this Internet world, how easy it is to
be distracted by bread that does not nourish and drink that does not quench my
thirst. Help me to remember that I have no good apart from you.

(Morning)
Ever-present One, may those for whom I pray this day know the mystery
and the power of your presence.
(Prayers of Intercession)

(Evening)
I thank you for all who recognized you, O God, and took refuge in you today.
(Prayers of Intercession)

God is our ever-present strength and help.
(Sing "How Firm a Foundation" or another familiar hymn.)

(Morning)	(Evening)
Help me not be distracted but observant of the presence of your Spirit in all that I do. Thanks be to God. Amen.	I end this day remembering the signs of your presence and ask that you deliver me through sleep to the dawn of a new day. Thanks be to God. Amen.

TUESDAY, JUNE 26
(Read Psalm 16:7–11)

(Morning)
O God, today am I ready for you to show me the path of life that leads to your joy?

(Evening)
O God, how much have I kept you present this day? How much have I experienced
you to be at my right hand? How steadfastly have I not been moved?

How easily I am distracted, O God. You beckon to me, but I can think only of
my plans for the day. You speak to me, but I am smitten by electronic images
and no voices. Help to bring calm to the competing voices of our culture, that
I may hear your voice and follow your path.

(Morning)
O ever-present One, may you be at the right hand of those for whom I pray,
and may they know your presence.
(Prayers of Intercession)

(Evening)
Creator and Inspirer, praise be to you for the joyful moments
of your presence this day.
(Prayers of Intercession)

God is at our right hand; God shall not be moved.
(Sing "Bring Many Names" or another familiar hymn.)

(Morning)
I begin this day to seek in your presence
the path of life that leads to joy. May you
show me the way. Thanks be to God.
Amen.

(Evening)
As I prepare for rest, I remember in the
night you also counsel my heart. May it
be so this night, I pray. Thanks be to
God. Amen.

WEDNESDAY, JUNE 27
(Read Galatians 5:1, 13–18)

(Morning)
O Jesus, our Liberator, will I live today as one who has been set free
or one who is in bondage? Help me to make wise choices.

(Evening)
O Jesus, our Liberator, how well did I use my freedom today?
Did I use it to care for my neighbor or to take care of myself?

How often, O Holy Comforter, do we use your freedom as an escape from our
responsibilities rather than as freedom for the fulfillment of your two greatest
commandments? Instill in us a hunger to exercise our freedom this day as a
sign of your realm blossoming in our midst. Help us to be truly free.

(Morning)
I pray this morning for people I know and people unknown to me who are enslaved
in all manner of ways. O Jesus, may they experience you and the freedom you offer.
(Prayers of Intercession)

(Evening)
O Jesus, our Deliverer, thank you for reminding me of my bondage
to my own prejudices and for offering me an alternative this day.
(Prayers of Intercession)

In Christ Jesus, God has set us free.
(Sing "Jesu, Jesu, Fill Us with Your Love" or another familiar hymn.)

(Morning)
Send me forth today with the courage to make wiser choices than I did yesterday. Thanks be to God. Amen.

(Evening)
For my misuse of freedom today, forgive me. For the choices I must make tomorrow, prepare me. Now, receive me into sleep. Thanks be to God. Amen.

THURSDAY, JUNE 28
(Read Psalm 77:1–2, 11–20)

(Morning)
O God, help me to perceive your footprints before me this day,
and grant that I might follow you in the ways of righteousness.

(Evening)
O God, did I see you today when you beckoned to me to follow you?
When you parted the waters for me, did I recognize you and give you thanks?

You are forever a comfort, almighty God, in times of desolation and grief. As you were to Abraham, Isaac, and Moses, you make yourself available to us—eternally available. As you did with the Hebrew people, you offer to part the seas that enslave us and bring us to that place where our cup runneth over.

(Morning)
Creator and Healer, may all those who cry aloud and stretch out their hands
to you this day know the calm and consolation of your presence.
(Prayers of Intercession)

(Evening)
For all who called upon you and were consoled by your presence, I give you thanks.
(Prayers of Intercession)

God hears our cries and acts to heal us and set us free.
(Sing "God Moves in a Mysterious Way" or another familiar hymn.)

(Morning)
Should I know trouble this day, grant that I might reach out to you for your guiding presence. Thanks be to God. Amen.

(Evening)
As I prepare to sleep, may your unseen footprints be about me and deliver me to a new day. Thanks be to God. Amen.

FRIDAY, JUNE 29
(Read Luke 9:51–62)

(Morning)
Jesus, when you call me to follow you, where will I put you on my agenda?

(Evening)
Jesus, what were my priorities today? In my deeds and in my words was I
a reflection of you, or did I mirror the values of my culture and my own needs?

It is not easy to follow you, Jesus. You keep taking paths we haven't taken. You
don't allow us the comfort of safe places. We keep confronting difficult choices.
You do not let us hesitate, but keep us on the move toward Jerusalem. When we
hesitate, when we look back, call us forward. Do not leave us behind.

(Morning)
I pray this morning, Jesus, for those who have been left behind,
consumed by their own concerns.
(Prayers of Intercession)

(Evening)
I am thankful, Jesus, for those who joined you today
on your ongoing journey to Jerusalem.
(Prayers of Intercession)

Jesus bids us come and join the journey toward Jerusalem.
(Sing "O Jesus, I Have Promised" or another familiar hymn.)

(Morning)
Today, when I tarry on my journey,
absorbed in my own needs and concerns, rebuke me, unsettle me, and set
my eyes toward your realm. Thanks be
to God. Amen.

(Evening)
O Jesus, bid me rest that tomorrow I may
awake refreshed and be prepared anew to
follow you. Thanks be to God. Amen.

SATURDAY, JUNE 30
(Read 1 Kings 2:1–2, 6–14)

(Morning)
O God, what problems and old grudges and old hatreds will I,
like Solomon, inherit this day? Grant that I might respond with wisdom.

(Evening)
O God, did I act responsibly today when confronted with the apathy,
pettiness, or outright greed and hostility of others?

We inherit from those who have gone before us a tangled web of emotions and
aspirations. Lest we should forget, remind us, O God, that sin casts its shadow
upon all of us, whether we are King Davids or only pretenders to the throne.
Grant that while we seek wholeness, we might also confer our contribution to
brokenness this day.

(Morning)
God of saints and of sinners, help me to pray this day for those,
advertently or inadvertently, hurt by my actions.
(Prayers of Intercession)

(Evening)
I thank you, O God, for all who resisted evil and
who knew not vengeance or revenge this day.
(Prayers of Intercession)

Call us in wisdom, O God, that we might not resort to evil.
(Sing "Lord Jesus, Who Through Forty Days" or another familiar hymn.)

(Morning)
Help me today as I inherit the inequities
and injustices of the past, that I may act
with wisdom. Thanks be to God. Amen.

(Evening)
Receive me now in sleep, forgive me
for webs left untangled, and grant that I
may act with justice and kindness in the
new day to come. Thanks be to God.
Amen.

SUNDAY, JULY 1
(Read 1 Kings 19:15–16, 19–21)

(Morning)
O God, how will you cast your mantle upon me today?
What will you call me to do and be?

(Evening)
O God, have I been a reflection this day of one anointed
to proclaim your presence by all that I said and all that I did?

How many are the ways, O God, that you throw your mantle upon us and bid us come? Sometimes we resist; sometimes we hesitate; sometimes we stall, asking to bid our kindred goodbye. But you wait upon us and invite us to follow. Help us to be servants to you this day.

(Morning)
Hear my prayers, O God, for those not conscious of your call.
Grant that they might know you, hear you, and follow you this day.
(Prayers of Intercession)

(Evening)
For all those Elishas who have experienced Elijah's cloak this day, I give you thanks.
(Prayers of Intercession)

God chooses us, calls us, and bids us follow.
(Sing "God the Spirit, Guide and Guardian" or another familiar hymn.)

(Morning)
Lest I become too absorbed in my daily rounds, this day help me to see when you beckon me to follow at moments I do not expect. Thanks be to God. Amen.

(Evening)
Cast your cloak upon me, O God, that I may rest, and call me forth in service in the dawning of the new day. Thanks be to God. Amen.

MONDAY, JULY 2
(Read Isaiah 66:10–14)

(Morning)
Creator God, we rejoice and give thanks for the wonder of your creation.
Awakened afresh to your world and its wonders, we praise your name.
For the gift of life, we thank you and ask your steadfast presence throughout the day.

(Evening)
Creator God, as evening enfolds me, quiet me and make me attentive
to the lessons you offered this day.

In the midst of life's joys and sorrows, God, you are ever present with us and for us. You offer comfort by day and by night. Within the goodness of creation, you have offered us all that we need to sustain life. In your presence, our hearts shall rejoice, certain of the abiding presence and presents of One who comforts us as a mother comforts her child.

(Morning)
For all those this day who seek your comforting
presence, Creator God, we are mindful.
(Prayers of Intercession)

(Evening)
We lift up in prayer those who in this day are bereft and alone.
May they know your comfort.
(Prayers of Intercession)

God's creation is beloved. God will not forsake Jerusalem or us.

(Morning)
To a day of faithful service and discipleship, I commit myself. In Christ's blessed name. Amen.

(Evening)
By your comforting hand, give me rest and refreshment to serve you tomorrow. In Christ's blessed name. Amen.

TUESDAY, JULY 3
(Read 2 Kings 5:1–14)

(Morning)
O God, as I greet the morning sky, I greet you with thanks for the rest and safety
of the night and seek you and your will in this day, which you created.

(Evening)
O God, as shadows lengthen, I turn again to you and seek
in your Word the peace and truth you offer your people.

Why do we modern women and men seek a complex and unfathomable God? Like
Naaman, we do not receive your good gifts with joy and thanksgiving but often
puzzle over your love, O God. In our desire to create you in our own image, we
often seek to thwart your generosity by finding complex approaches to you or even
seeking false gods. Just for today, I will seek your good gifts where I find them.
And without question or doubt, I will receive them with thanksgiving.

(Morning)
God, I lift up to you all those who know brokenness today
and ask your healing touch upon them.
(Prayers of Intercession)

(Evening)
Forgive, O God, our reluctance of heart,
and instill in us the spirit of gratitude and confidence.
(Prayers of Intercession)

I will forsake all false gods and seek the God of creation.

(Morning)
Give me this day an eye for seeing your
wonders, an ear for hearing your call to
faith, and a heart for believing! In
Christ's blessed name. Amen.

(Evening)
For the blessing of this day and its
activities, perfect them by your grace,
and grant me peace. In Christ's blessed
name. Amen.

WEDNESDAY, JULY 4
(Read Psalm 30:1–5)

(Morning)
Strong and present One, "our help in ages past, our hope for years to come,"
we awaken when day is new and draw near to you for strength and guidance.

(Evening)
Strong and present One, as this day runs its course, I look once again to you,
grateful for your promise to be near at hand in waking or in sleeping.

So often life offers up challenges to our minds, our spirits, even our very lives.
God, were it not for your reassuring presence, how would we find the courage to
live? The church in all ages has been sustained in every land and tongue by your
graciousness. Today, may I face the troubles I confront with the confidence that
there will truly be "joy in the morning," for you, O God, are with me.

(Morning)
In this day, there will be those whose concerns and troubles lead them to despair.
I lift all who are struggling for justice, mercy, and peace to your strong embrace.
(Prayers of Intercession)

(Evening)
As the world turns to sleep, I give thanks for this day with its challenges and
your sure promise. Keep this night those who know loneliness, fear, and anxiety.
(Prayers of Intercession)

In life's sorrows and trials I will call upon you alone, O God.

(Morning)
I will find new ways today to sing
praises to your name and witness to the
salvation you offer. In Christ's blessed
name. Amen.

(Evening)
As I grow still and calm in the day's
closing, I take comfort in your promise
that weeping will not linger but that joy
awaits me. In Christ's blessed name.
Amen.

THURSDAY, JULY 5
(Read Psalm 30:6–12)

(Morning)
Precious God, I waken today both calling "God, be my helper"
and praising your wondrous deeds.

(Evening)
Precious God, throughout the day, I have cried out to you,
and you have been there for me in the large ways and the small.

The psalmist sings of crying out to you, precious God, for help. Do you have the capacity to hear all the cries from those who seek help? In every tongue and language? With concerns great and small? The psalmist has no concern for such matters, being certain that you will hear every word of praise or prayer whether whispered alone in a desperate situation or proclaimed from the grandest cathedral. We should be as confident that you will hear us and be gracious.

(Morning)
Ever-present God, hear the cries of all your people.
When they cry out, be their Helper.
(Prayers of Intercession)

(Evening)
As I turn in prayer, I recall others who plead for help and reassurance.
(Prayers of Intercession)

**We give thanks for the gift of prayer
and for the assurance of prayers heard.**

(Morning)
As I go about my day, I will pray in thanksgiving and in times of need, always sure that you hear. In Christ's blessed name. Amen.

(Evening)
At the end of a day filled with prayers both spoken and unspoken, I turn toward slumber with a final prayer of thanksgiving and of praise. In Christ's blessed name. Amen.

FRIDAY, JULY 6
(Read Galatians 6:1–6)

(Morning)
God, this is the day that you have made for your children to rejoice and be glad.
Let me live today conscious of this gift of life.

(Evening)
God, with the close of day, I return to you and wonder if you brood as I do
over the events and missed opportunities of the day.
Attend me as I seek your guidance in reflection and prayer.

Our lives of work, family, neighbors, and strangers bring us often to some conflict or misunderstanding. The letter to the Galatians reminds us of the freedom to be gained not in faulting others but in a spirit of gentleness, restoring those who err. How much we long for that gentle correction but fail to offer it. How quick we are to spot the flaw in another but slow to recognize it in ourselves. How much more fully we would live if truly we recalled this kind word of love to one another.

(Morning)
Forgive me, O God, for my too quick and sharp correction of others and my
slowness to see the ways in which I contribute to the world's woes.
(Prayers of Intercession)

(Evening)
Uphold, loving God, those whom I was quick to fault,
and grant me a gentleness of spirit.
(Prayers of Intercession)

I will study the ways of gently restoring and the art of forgiveness.

(Morning)
Grant me in this day a ready forgiveness and kind spirit. In Christ's blessed name. Amen.

(Evening)
I have sought this day to "carry my own load" in reliance on you. Strengthen me this night to assist others with burdens too heavy to carry. In Christ's blessed name. Amen.

SATURDAY, JULY 7
(Read Galatians 6:7–16)

(Morning)
God in three persons, you attend each of us through the presence of the Spirit
among us. We give thanks for this Companion on life's journey.

(Evening)
God in three persons, weary in good doing and not-so-good doing at day's end,
I turn to your Word looking for guidance and meaning.
By your Spirit, grant me a listening heart.

How it frightens us to recognize that we may indeed reap what we sow. Yet
your promise of mercy sustains us, and your invitation to "sow to the Spirit"
beckons us to another way. In life's busy tumult we are often tempted to ignore
our spiritual formation and spiritual disciplines in favor of activity and enter-
tainment. God, you still call us to the work of the Spirit, prayer, and working
beyond weariness for the good of all.

(Morning)
In company with the Spirit I continue my faith journey,
rededicating myself to work for the common good.
(Prayers of Intercession)

(Evening)
Commending the day's efforts to you, God, through the Spirit,
I now reflect on the good I have left undone this day.
(Prayers of Intercession)

God's will for the good of all is served by women and men of faith.

(Morning)	(Evening)
Empowered by the Spirit of the living God, I approach today in hope and confidence. In Christ's blessed name. Amen.	Lifting today's work to you, O God, with thanksgiving for the calling of all Christians, I seek now peace and renewal and a night's rest to serve all of your children tomorrow. In Christ's blessed name. Amen.

SUNDAY, JULY 8
(Read Luke 10:1–11, 16–20)

(Morning)
Creator God, as morning comes afresh, we give thanks that in every age
you still call people to serve you in love. I give thanks for my baptism today.

(Evening)
Creator God, the demands of the day weigh heavy, but still I hear amid them
you calling us to the faithful Christian life, and I give thanks.

The Gospel of Luke records clearly the message for our day. God, you still call
us in the name of the Christ, not to be a people apart but to go out into the very
midst of life with the message of peace. The great calling for the church and
for all Christians is to find ways to proclaim your peace in a world too busy
and self-absorbed to listen. As people of faith, we need always to remain together in a bond of unity, pronouncing that word of peace even in the least
peaceful settings.

(Morning)
This broken world longs for peace among countries and peoples,
in families and communities. Hear my prayers for peace.
(Prayers of Intercession)

(Evening)
Wars and rumors of war abound today and in all days. Hear my prayers for peace.
(Prayers of Intercession)

Bringer of peace, make me an instrument of your peace.

(Morning)
Answering Christ's call, I will seek to
serve peace this day and in all my days.
In Christ's blessed name. Amen.

(Evening)
O God, I have worked for your peace
and sometimes fallen short. Join my
efforts with others, that all may know
the blessing of your peace. In Christ's
blessed name. Amen.

190

MONDAY, JULY 9
(Read Amos 7:7–17)

(Morning)
O holy God, in the dawning of this new day,
may I know your presence in my life and through my living.

(Evening)
O holy God, in this day, I hope I have both seen and understood you are in the
events of the day and your very Word is the plumb line by which my life is ordered.

How much I believe, O God, that who I am and what I become are primarily
the deeds of my own hand—the growth of my words and deeds. May I know
that true life is your gift and not my going it by myself. Help me to be more
sensitive to the strength of your presence and the power of your Word.

(Morning)
To you, O gracious, loving, and redeeming God,
I lift up the names of those for whom I have special concern.
May they know you are present to care, to heal, and to strengthen.
(Prayers of Intercession)

(Evening)
I give thanks for this day, for the ways
in which others have touched my life for the good.
(Prayers of Intercession)

God is known through our faithfulness and not our fear.
(Sing "Nearer, My God, to You" or another familiar hymn.)

(Morning)
God's Word can be strong and foreboding. It is a Word that calls us from fear to love, from self-serving to other-caring. Thanks be to Christ. Amen.

(Evening)
No matter how well or poorly we have lived, the day must be given to God, for it cannot be changed. May the day be instructive, no matter its occurrences. Thanks be to Christ. Amen.

TUESDAY, JULY 10
(Read Deuteronomy 30:9–14)

(Morning)
O God, may I realize that you find joy in giving to me, so I might live with fullness.

(Evening)
O God, I trust I have not lived this day with either
an ungrateful heart or an ingenuine spirit.

It is so easy to believe my being comes from my having. May I learn growing comes from giving and from loving. May I learn that who I am is best understood in a pure heart and a caring spirit, just like our holy God, who gives us life and guides our living in the first place—through all eternity.

(Morning)
Spirit of the Holy, may your kindness and generosity be known
in the lives of those whom I now name—that you give each of us life.
(Prayers of Intercession)

(Evening)
O gracious God, I thank you for your merciful presence
that guides me in ways of love and peace.
(Prayers of Intercession)

In our mouths and in our hearts, God's presence is as close as breathing.
(Sing "Guide Me, O My Great Redeemer" or another familiar hymn.)

(Morning)
I begin this day wanting to know that
God is with me and that God is fully
giving and loving. May this day be filled
with my good news for God. Thanks be
to Christ. Amen.

(Evening)
I rest now at the end of the day, ever
grateful for the blessings bestowed
upon my life. Thanks be to Christ.
Amen.

WEDNESDAY, JULY 11
(Read Psalm 52)

(Morning)
May this day, O God, be a day in which I praise you through my words and deeds.

(Evening)
May this night, O God, allow me to know your steadfast love prevails over all.

To boast of my achievements is to miss the point. Being righteous does not mean being better. To be righteous is to know the "power to life and living." God, this power comes from your steadfast love and eternal presence. Let us not trust in riches as much as we trust in you and in your delivering power.

(Morning)
O God, I pray for those who cannot pray for themselves;
for those who will not let others do for them what they cannot do for themselves.
(Prayers of Intercession)

(Evening)
Help me, O God, not to hate evil more than I love good,
therefore proving only to be a good hater.
(Prayers of Intercession)

God's name is good; God's Spirit is steadfast love.
(Sing "God, Speak to Me, That I May Speak" or another familiar hymn.)

(Morning)
The new day has dawned! May I not boast I am my own value or resource. May I boast in the goodness of God. Thanks be to Christ. Amen.

(Evening)
As the day closes, the evening comes, and the night's rest is upon me, let me give thanks for God's prevailing love that guides and sustains. Thanks be to Christ. Amen.

THURSDAY, JULY 12
(Read Psalm 15)

(Morning)
O God, it is a new day. Help me to live Psalm 15 not as if it is multiple choice
but as if it is the worthier manner of living!

(Evening)
O God, the day is now turning to night.
Thank you, dear God, for partnering me in this day.

Dear God, sometimes, more often than not, the psalmist chides and fumes and
complains about the ways in which pain hovers upon the human landscape. In
this day I will take Psalm 15 to heart. I will find purpose and strength through
a truth from the heart, a gentleness in the step, and a kindness in the word.

(Morning)
Gracious God, be with those in whom your Word is clearly spoken
and your will is manifest.
(Prayers of Intercession)

(Evening)
To live by your Word and to follow your way bring
my life goodness and gladness. I am grateful!
(Prayers of Intercession)

Who shall abide in God's sanctuary? Can I be there too?
(Sing "Amazing Grace" or another familiar hymn.)

(Morning)
As I read Psalm 15, 1 know the deeper
verity: to be a person of integrity, love,
and kindness is more than a way of life;
it is the very purpose in living by which
strength is known. Thanks be to Christ.
Amen.

(Evening)
As the day concludes, I now realize
that to be good, faithful, and caring
takes focus and energy. The joy I have
experienced in "God's sanctuary" is a
joy beyond measure. Thanks be to
Christ. Amen.

FRIDAY, JULY 13
(Read Colossians 1:1–8)

(Morning)
O God, I want to begin this day knowing your gifts to me of grace and peace.

(Evening)
O God, I ask, "Have I lived this day reflecting grace, peace,
and caring more than complaining?"

I want grace and peace to be more than good ideas, O God. Help me to have them as my manner of living. Help me to be the incarnation of your will so others will have no grounds to deny your presence when they are with me.

(Morning)
I pray now, eternal and ever-present God, for those
who help me know you affirm and care.
(Prayers of Intercession)

(Evening)
Life does not end when the day closes, dear God.
Help me to remember this day, but not be controlled by it.
(Prayers of Intercession)

God's grace and peace are required for purposeful lives.
(Sing "Spirit, Spirit of Gentleness" or another familiar hymn.)

(Morning)	(Evening)
As I take new steps in a new day, may my experiences bear the good fruit of God's grace and peace. Thanks be to Christ. Amen.	I have done my best this day, O God. Help me rest, so the sleep refreshes my body as you strengthen my spirit. Thanks be to Christ. Amen.

SATURDAY, JULY 14
(Read Colossians 1:9–14)

(Morning)
Dear eternal God, help me enjoy this day, knowing my strength comes from you.

(Evening)
Dear eternal God, this day has been your gift for which I am grateful and by which I have deepened bonds with you and those around me.

God, there are times, more times than I will admit to anyone, when my effort becomes holy and your presence gets presumed. On this day, a Saturday, may I think of how your light breaks the darkness into a million pieces and your love is greater than any sin I admit or keep secret.

(Morning)
Gracious and compassionate God, I name those who struggle with life, who believe in their hearts they have to reach up to touch bottom.
(Prayers of Intercession)

(Evening)
I remember in prayer those who have strength; those who grieve but not as those without hope; and those who know their strength brings God joy.
(Prayers of Intercession)

Shadows are evidence of light somewhere.
(Sing "Love Divine, All Loves Excelling" or another familiar hymn.)

(Morning)
As I read Colossians 1:9–14, I am mindful that without God, my life becomes empty, an abyss, not unlike the days before God spoke to bring the creation into being. Thanks be to Christ. Amen.

(Evening)
As I rest from the day, through the night, in preparation for the dawning day, I am grateful for the learnings of this day. Thanks be to Christ. Amen.

SUNDAY, JULY 15
(Read Luke 10:25–37)

(Morning)
Loving God, help me to live fully in this new day, called to recognize
and meet the needs I see in others.

(Evening)
Loving God, I know the lawyer tested Jesus to get an answer.
May it have been this day that I followed Jesus in order to get life.

Caring God, oftentimes my life is like playing in an intellectual volleyball
game, batting ideas back and forth. May this day be known for more than what
I think or reason. May this day be known for how I "went and did likewise."

(Morning)
May I not be blind to the needs of others. May I hear even the cries of silence
from those around me, making the "How are you?" more than a social greeting.
May it be a spiritual inquiry.
(Prayers of Intercession)

(Evening)
I now name everyone I related to today.
May those moments have been reflective of your love.
(Prayers of Intercession)

God needs both talk and walk.
(Sing "O God, Our Help in Ages Past" or another familiar hymn.)

(Morning)
May I listen and understand, see and
recognize, where others have need of
me this day. Thanks be to Christ. Amen.

(Evening)
Grant me, dear and loving God, your
blessing and your grace as I now give
thanks for the day and rest through to the
dawning of your new day. Thanks be to
Christ. Amen.

MONDAY, JULY 16
(Read Amos 8:1–12)

(Morning)
Forgiving God, I awaken to your call.
Lead me this day to do your will and serve your people.

(Evening)
Forgiving God, I come to the end of this day you have given me.
Forgive me if I have trampled on the needy or have turned my back to the poor.

God of grace and glory, let me not be as the ancient believers who could not wait for the Sabbath to be over. Let me carry Sunday worship into Monday living. Let me be in this world but not of it. You call your children to be faithful followers in all we do and say, in all times and places. May how I live this day be worship of you, compassionate God.

(Morning)
Righteous and just God, may your Spirit awaken me to the needs of others.
Strengthen and be with those for whom I pray.
(Prayers of Intercession)

(Evening)
I end this day in thanks to you, O God, for you have been my constant Companion.
Grant peace to those for whom I pray.
(Prayers of Intercession)

"Let justice roll down like waters, and righteousness like an everflowing stream."

(Morning)
As I walk this day, loving Creator, may my hands be outstretched, my eyes ready to see, and my ears alert to hear. Let me be an instrument of your peace. In Christ's name. Amen.

(Evening)
As I rest this night, I close my eyes assured and comforted that your plan for creation will be fulfilled. In Christ's name. Amen.

TUESDAY, JULY 17
(Read Amos 8:1–12)

(Morning)
Giver of all good gifts, thank you for this day! I am excited by all the opportunities
I may have to be a witness to your Word.

(Evening)
Giver of all good gifts, thank you for this night! I am grateful
for all the opportunities you gave me to be a witness to your Word.

You have given us your Logos so we may have life. We live in a world that
constantly bombards us with words—words that tell us how to think, what to
wear, how to look. God of truth, let it be your Word we hear above all others.
You offer us comfort, strength, guidance, peace, wisdom, and love. Renewing
Spirit, never take your Word from us, for we hunger and thirst for its good
news. It is a lamp unto our feet and a light upon our path.

(Morning)
Let me be open to and led by your Word today, my God.
(Prayers of Intercession)

(Evening)
At the end of a day of words, I seek your Word alone.
(Prayers of Intercession)

Let the Word of God dwell within me.

(Morning)
Today I will rejoice in the good news of
Jesus Christ. In Christ's name. Amen.

(Evening)
I am quiet, God, ready to receive your
Word, ready to receive your blessing. In
Christ's name. Amen.

WEDNESDAY, JULY 18
(Read Genesis 18:1–10)

(Morning)
God of surprises, I greet this day with anticipation!
What wonderfulness do you have in store for me?

(Evening)
God of surprises, I welcome this evening that promises rest.
Thank you for this day and the opportunities you gave me to share your love.

Abraham hurried to entertain you and share what he and Sarah had. He seemed to sense something unexpected and important was about to happen. Would I have discerned your presence? In the business of the world, I often do not take note of those I do not know. Awaken me, God of Abraham and Sarah, to be ready for the unexpected. Awaken me to your presence. How often will I meet you today, God of promise, in the faces I see? How often will I entertain angels unaware?

(Morning)
Spirit of wonder, you give me the chance to serve you by serving others.
(Prayers of Intercession)

(Evening)
Spirit of quietness, quiet my soul and renew my spirit.
(Prayers of Intercession)

Show hospitality to strangers, for some have entertained angels unaware.

(Morning)
Let me be mindful, God, when I encounter others, I encounter you. Surprise me, Wonderful One! In Christ's name. Amen.

(Evening)
You kept me on my toes, demanding God. I pray all whom I encountered today were treated as your children. Forgive me if they were not. In Christ's name. Amen.

THURSDAY, JULY 19
(Read Psalm 52)

(Morning)
Faithful God, I rise up rejoicing. Nothing in this world can separate me
from your love in Jesus Christ.

(Evening)
Faithful God, I lie down, finding comfort in the knowledge that nothing
can separate me from your love in Jesus Christ.

Many see themselves as clever, with no need of you, loving God. They use
others to satisfy their desires and ambitions. They rely on themselves. Because
I am your child, you call me to entrust my life and future to you, for you are
faithful to your promises. You know my needs, and you satisfy them. Like
those ancient olive trees planted in the Temple, my life is firmly rooted in your
love, O Source of all life.

(Morning)
Keeper of all souls, I trust in your steadfast love and ask you
to keep close to your heart those for whom I pray.
(Prayers of Intercession)

(Evening)
Hearer of all prayers, I lift up to you and place in your care those for whom I pray.
I will thank you forever because of what you have done.
(Prayers of Intercession)

"In the presence of the faithful, I will proclaim your name, for it is good."

(Morning)
Steadfast God, I entrust my soul to you.
May your Spirit strengthen me and
guide me so I may share your love with
others. In Christ's name. Amen.

(Evening)
Steadfast God, I entrust my soul to you.
May your Spirit quiet me and give me
peace as I rest this night. In Christ's
name. Amen.

FRIDAY, JULY 20
(Read Psalm 15)

(Morning)
God who is above all naming, you kiss me awake with your sunrise.
Let me serve you with love and imagination.

(Evening)
God who is above all naming, rock me to sleep in your loving arms.

The proper gift to bring to you is the gift of one's life. You require your worshipers to live blameless lives, to do what is right, and to speak the truth. Wise and wondrous God, how are we to accomplish this task? We cannot rely on our own understandings. We, who would be called your children, must be open to your instruction. The psalmist reminds us, those who trust in you, O God, have a solid foundation upon which to stand. Once again you promise us life. You promise that those who belong to you shall never be moved. We are secure in your love.

(Morning)
I pray with confidence. You are my God. I belong to you.
(Prayers of Intercession)

(Evening)
I take refuge in you, my God. Hear my prayer.
(Prayers of Intercession)

I trust in the steadfast love of God.

(Morning)
I want to walk in your ways, my God, and speak only your truth. In Christ's name. Amen.

(Evening)
Your promise to hold me fast gives me hope and peace, faithful God. I rest easy this night. In Christ's name. Amen.

SATURDAY, JULY 21
(Read Colossians 2:6–15)

(Morning)
Creator God, I begin this day praising your holy name.
You have given me life so I may serve you.

(Evening)
Creator God, I end this day praising your holy name.
Thank you for this day and the opportunity to serve you.

O dear God, what wonderful promises you give us. Through Jesus Christ, we are given new life. You forgive us for our sinful ways, erasing the record that stands against us. Who is as powerful and wonderful as you? No one. Christ is sufficient for all our needs. In our baptism we died to sin and rose to new life in Christ. We are reminded that the fears of this world do not have a hold on us. We are rooted and built up in Christ, our Savior.

(Morning)
God of new life, I rejoice that I am baptized. Thank you for this new day.
(Prayers of Intercession)

(Evening)
God who never slumbers, watch over me this night.
Keep all your children in the palm of your hand.
(Prayers of Intercession)

We have fullness of life in Christ.

(Morning)
May my thoughts be tuned to you, O God. Do not let me stray from your path. In Christ's name. Amen.

(Evening)
My faith rests in you, O God. Bless me and keep me in your loving care. In Christ's name. Amen.

SUNDAY, JULY 22
(Read Colossians 2:16–19)

(Morning)
Giver of the sabbath, I rejoice in this new day,
a day to rest from my labors and quiet myself with worship of you.

(Evening)
Giver of the sabbath, I thank you for this day. Grant me rest and peace this night.

Too often, my God, we try to make you into our image. We forget we are made in yours. We weaken to the temptations of the flesh and give heed to the things that would become our idols. We pay homage and give allegiance to vanity, power, money, and control. But you claim us as your own, loving God. You bid us to return. Through Christ, you have forgiven us and given us new life. There is none other than you, O Holy One. For you, the one true God, we shed our allegiances to false gods, and we worship only you, the living God.

(Morning)
Rooted in your love, I humbly, yet boldly, offer my prayer.
(Prayers of Intercession)

(Evening)
I pray for your presence to always be with me and with those for whom I pray.
(Prayers of Intercession)

Our God is one. I shall have no other gods.

(Morning)
May I worship you in all I do and say this day, bringing glory to your name. In Christ's name. Amen.

(Evening)
Holy Spirit, grant me a peaceful sleep, so in the morning, I will be renewed, refreshed, and ready to do your will. In Christ's name. Amen.

204

MONDAY, JULY 23
(Read Psalm 85:1–7)

(Morning)
Loving God, I give to you this day, for you are the God of my salvation.

(Evening)
Loving God, as always, you were kind to me as I lived my day.
Thank you for your steadfast love.

Loving God, in times of difficulty I always remember to turn to you for help. But when life is comfortable, I am easily distracted by other pursuits, and I forget you. How foolish I am; but you are full of love, as evident in giving us Jesus Christ, our Savior, to show me the way back to your love. Forgive my ingratitude for your love. Revive me again.

(Morning)
This day will present opportunities to celebrate your steadfast love and salvation.
Open my eyes that I might see signs of your love.
(Prayers of Intercession)

(Evening)
Your steadfast love and salvation graced this day, a day I was privileged
to have lived. I have much for which to be thankful.
(Prayers of Intercession)

We belong to God. Rejoice in God's love.
(Sing "I Am Yours, O Lord" or another familiar hymn.)

(Morning)
It is with eagerness that I look forward to this day, for in it I will experience your restoring presence, which always leads me closer to you. Glory be to Christ. Amen.

(Evening)
Now I can rest in blessed peace, for today I have seen your love, experienced your forgiveness, and been revived by your Spirit. Glory be to Christ. Amen.

TUESDAY, JULY 24
(Read Psalm 85:8–13)

(Morning)
Saving God, I turn my heart to you; I long to hear your voice,
for the words you speak are words of peace.

(Evening)
Good God, you have given to me today what is good:
your steadfast love and faithfulness. Thank you.

Loving God, certain things are important to you: love, faithfulness, righteousness, and peace. They are important to you because they are qualities that describe who you are. Help me to embrace and love these same things, as Jesus Christ, our Savior, showed us to do, that I might live closely with you now and always.

(Morning)
Good God, I look to you to give me this day what is good:
your steadfast love and faithfulness. Hear my prayers.
(Prayers of Intercession)

(Evening)
Your faithfulness sprang up all around me today and is springing up even now.
Hear my prayers, faithful God.
(Prayers of Intercession)

God is a God of justice and peace.
(Sing "O for a World" or another familiar hymn.)

(Morning)
As I walk through my day, help me to look down and notice faithfulness springing from the ground, and to look up and see righteousness looking down upon your creation. Glory be to Christ. Amen.

(Evening)
O God, I end my day with joy, for today I have seen love and faithfulness meet; I have seen righteousness and peace kiss each other; and I have heard your voice of peace. Glory be to Christ. Amen.

WEDNESDAY, JULY 25
(Read Luke 11:1–4)

(Morning)
Providential God, I can pray; I can talk with you.
You desire to hear my voice as I speak with you in prayer. What joy!

(Evening)
Providential God, here I am, thankful for the signs
of your realm I have experienced today.

God in heaven, you have taken care of the details of our lives, even seeing to it that we will have instructions for how to pray. May my life be formed by the prayer our Savior taught. May I learn from that prayer to praise your name, to yearn for your realm, and to trust in your gracious generosity.

(Morning)
Heavenly God, there is no aspect of my life for which you are not concerned.
Hear my prayer for such things as daily bread and strength in temptation.
(Prayers of Intercession)

(Evening)
Giving God, you supply my needs, even the forgiveness of my sins.
I now desire to forgive those who have sinned against me.
(Prayers of Intercession)

God hears us when we pray.
(Sing "Prayer Is the Soul's Sincere Desire" or another familiar hymn.)

(Morning)	(Evening)
God who graces my life with good things, I now set forth on this day you have given, knowing that my daily bread will be provided. Glory be to Christ. Amen.	You have given me signs of your heavenly realm today: food, reconciliation, and strength in trial. I desire nothing but to know the joy of resting in your gracious love. Glory be to Christ. Amen.

THURSDAY, JULY 26
(Read Luke 11:5–8)

(Morning)
God, you are my Friend, and day after day as I come to you in prayer,
you are always willing to listen. Thank you.

(Evening)
God, you have been with me today, listening to my prayers.
What a blessing to have such a Friend as you.

God, what a good Friend you are. I can talk with you anytime, and you will gladly listen to me. If there is any lack of persistence, it is not on your part, for you are always willing to listen. Any lack of persistence is my own for not having taken you up on your offer to talk with you. But now, here I am, and I know you are listening.

(Morning)
I know I am not bothering you, God, for you are always ready to listen.
In your mercy, hear my prayers.
(Prayers of Intercession)

(Evening)
You know my needs better than I do, loving God. As I speak with you,
let me know that you have cared for all my needs.
(Prayers of Intercession)

Jesus is our Friend, always ready to listen.
(Sing "What a Friend We Have in Jesus" or another familiar hymn.)

(Morning)
During this day, help me to remember to talk with you in prayer. Glory be to Christ. Amen.

(Evening)
Even at midnight, I can come to you in prayer, and you are not bothered by my persistence. What love! What grace! Glory be to Christ. Amen.

FRIDAY, JULY 27
(Read Luke 11:9–13)

(Morning)
Generous God, today I will be searching, seeking, and knocking for your blessings.

(Evening)
Generous God, I saw them! I saw blessings all around me.
Some were subtle, others obvious, but all of them were from you!

Heavenly God, help me to ask only for what will lead me to love you more. Guide me to search only for the things that will bring me closer to you. Direct me to inquire only about the things of heaven so that I will better know you. Give me your Holy Spirit. That is all I ask for; I need nothing else.

(Morning)
I am ready to ask, seek, and knock. Help me to trust in your gentle care,
believing in your desire to give me what is good.
(Prayers of Intercession)

(Evening)
I have not finished asking, seeking, and knocking. I desire more of your presence,
for what I have experienced of your presence today has given me life.
Hear my prayers.
(Prayers of Intercession)

In this moment, in this place, God is with me.
(Sing "In Solitude" or another familiar hymn.)

(Morning)
The day ahead of me is filled not with snakes or scorpions, but with the Holy Spirit. How gracious you are, O God! Glory be to Christ. Amen.

(Evening)
Can it be that the Holy Spirit lives within me? Yes, the Holy Spirit dwells within. Grace my night, O God, as you have graced my day with the presence of your Holy Spirit. Glory be to Christ. Amen.

SATURDAY, JULY 28
(Read Hosea 1:2–10)

(Morning)
God of Israel, I humbly come to you this day.
Enable me to hear your voice above all the distracting voices of this world.

(Evening)
God of Israel, here I am, without pretense, trusting only in your unfailing compassion.

God, sometimes you have every right to be upset and angry with your people. We too often think only of ourselves and neglect you and our neighbors. I know I do. But because you are compassionate, you never remain angry; you always offer hope and continue to call us your people, of which I am one by the goodness of your tender mercies.

(Morning)
Hope—I could not live without it. So it is with hope in your unfailing love
that I now make my requests to you. Hear my hope-filled prayers.
(Prayers of Intercession)

(Evening)
Yes, God, I neglected you today. I have sinned. Hear my confession.
And in turn, let me hear your words of acceptance and forgiveness.
(Prayers of Intercession)

I am a child of the living God.
(Sing "Like a Mother Who Has Borne Us" or another familiar hymn.)

(Morning)
Living God, help me to remember you today and to serve you by serving my neighbor. I rejoice in the knowledge that you will not forget me. Glory be to Christ. Amen.

(Evening)
Thank you, living God, for being faithful to me today. Help me to always be faithful to you, even in my dreams. Glory be to Christ. Amen.

SUNDAY, JULY 29
(Read Colossians 2:6–15)

(Morning)
O Savior, I have begun a new day, full of the promise of new life,
awaiting the unfolding of a day filled with the presence of God.

(Evening)
O Savior, there were moments today when I was tempted to trust
in myself and my wisdom. But here I am, trusting in you.

God of life, I thank you for the life you have given me. I do not live this life
alone; I live with you. What a glorious thing it is to have been buried with
Christ in my baptism. And what a wonderful thing, almost too wonderful to
behold, to have been raised to new life with Jesus through that same baptism.
Thank you for life.

(Morning)
Jesus, I am joined to you in faith; you are the Ruler of my life.
Hear the prayers I now offer to you in faith, believing that you will hear them.
(Prayers of Intercession)

(Evening)
Some of this day needs erasing, forgiving God. Forgive all my trespasses,
once again, for I am yours; you have claimed me in baptism.
(Prayers of Intercession)

I am alive; I am baptized.
(Sing "What Ruler Wades through Murky Streams" or another familiar hymn.)

(Morning)
Nothing this day will be able to
separate me from you, for I am alive in
you and you are alive in me. Glory be
to Christ. Amen.

(Evening)
Thank you for this day in which I have
learned to trust even more in your power.
Glory be to Christ. Amen.

MONDAY, JULY 30
(Read Hosea 11:1–7)

(Morning)
Nurturing God, your arms are around me. Teach me to walk with faithfulness today.
Am I ready to trust your caring presence in my life?

(Evening)
Nurturing God, have I turned away from you today? Have I cut the cords
of human kindness toward others and squandered the day in pursuit of idols?

Loving God, when I was least aware of it, you taught me to walk, and you were a healing presence when I stumbled. I am still a spiritual toddler. I career through each day in utter disregard for your hovering nearness. Guide my feet that I might walk with trust and steadiness.

(Morning)
Guide my feet today, God, that I might walk familiar and new paths with courage.
(Prayers of Intercession)

(Evening)
God of my mothers and fathers, today you have held me in your care
and cradled and challenged me. I give you thanks.
(Prayers of Intercession)

"I took them up in my arms."
(Pray the Prayer of Our Savior.)

(Morning)
Today I will most likely do familiar things and walk familiar paths. I will stay in comfortable routines. Give me the courage to take a detour from what is most familiar to what is most faithful. Thanks be to Christ. Amen.

(Evening)
Protecting God, I rest from this day knowing even if I had turned from you, you still hover near. Give me rest that at dawn, I might walk forward trusting in your presence. For Christ in my life I give profound thanks. Thanks be to Christ. Amen.

TUESDAY, JULY 31
(Read Hosea 11:8–11)

(Morning)
Caring God, sometimes I have felt abandoned. Is that because you
have abandoned me, or have I abandoned you? Let me hear your voice in my day.

(Evening)
Caring God, this evening, I have returned to a home
that is a place of safety and a space for rest.
You have kept me through the day and brought me to this place.
I give you thanks.

There are times when I have given up on others and myself. I have let my
anger build walls around me. I have cast others from the circle of my care. I
have felt disappointment in myself and made excuses and apologies. Knowing
God, may I have the courage to trust in Christ's presence, which renews and
reaffirms your covenant with us and our connections with each other.

(Morning)
God, let me show compassion this day for those whom I have alienated from my life.
(Prayers of Intercession)

(Evening)
Holy One, you have been with me today. I am thankful for this time
to give thanks for your not always gentle, yet always nurturing, presence.
(Prayers of Intercession)

My compassion grows warm and tender.
(Hum "Blessed Be the Tie That Binds" or another familiar hymn.)

(Morning)
There is rarely anger in the morning
light. My mind is clear, my body rested.
Keep this patience and freshness with
me through the day. God, let me be
tender with others and with myself.
Thanks be to Christ. Amen.

(Evening)
Once again, I have made it through the
day. God, you have seen my unfaithful-
ness and have had compassion on me.
Let me release any anger I bear toward
others, and let my rest be untroubled.
Thanks be to Christ. Amen.

WEDNESDAY, AUGUST 1
(Read Ecclesiastes 1:2, 12–14; 2:18–23)

(Morning)
God, I know I cannot determine what happens to all for which I have worked
so hard. Today, help me when I am frustrated by not being the one in control.

(Evening)
God, sometimes I feel as though my work is in vain. If I am the focus of my labors,
despair is guaranteed. Let me rest by giving my heart to you.

I have invested myself in things I must release to the care of others. Projects,
congregations, ideas, children, friendships, gardens, even my own body. Sometimes I wonder why I get so involved or care so much. I want to be able to trust
others and not dwell on my need for recognition and power in every situation.

(Morning)
God of all hopefulness, keep me from despairing today. Let me be an agent
of hope for those whom I name before you this morning.
(Prayers of Intercession)

(Evening)
Overcoming One, I have inherited much from the labor of others.
I give thanks for the gifts that were mine to give and receive today.
(Prayers of Intercession)

Work is a vexation.
(Pray the Prayer of Our Savior.)

(Morning)	(Evening)
There are important tasks for me this day. Give me joy in the small tasks and trust, knowing the larger tasks are in your care. Thanks be to Christ. Amen.	Let me lay down my cares for this day and release my frustrations into the night. Give my spirit peace. Thanks be to Christ. Amen.

THURSDAY, AUGUST 2
(Read Psalm 107:1–9, 43)

(Morning)
Guiding God, do I have direction for my life this day, or will I wander aimlessly?
I pray that you will walk with me.

(Evening)
Guiding God, did I follow your direction for my way today?
Did I allow you to redeem me from trouble? Or did I persist in my own ways?

Sometimes it is more comfortable to wander and meander alone than it is to turn our lives over to your direction. All too often, only when we are completely lost, hungry, and parched do we surrender to your guidance. Loving God, how much more creative and effective we could be if we were able to trust your redeeming power.

(Morning)
Spirit of graciousness, let me be one who feeds the hungry, and by your Spirit,
gently help those who seem to struggle for direction.
(Prayers of Intercession)

(Evening)
Today, I will give thanks for the satisfying things in my life.
I will give thanks for the goodness that redeems me from distress.
(Prayers of Intercession)

O give thanks to God.
(Pray the Prayer of Our Savior.)

(Morning)
I give thanks to God for the communities in which I find myself. Grant me the wisdom to help those communities be places of redemption, renewal, and restoration. Thanks be to Christ. Amen.

(Evening)
As this day comes to an end, I give thanks that through the power of God's healing and Holy Spirit, we are nourished. As I lie down to sleep, I entrust myself to God's keeping. Thanks be to Christ. Amen.

FRIDAY, AUGUST 3
(Read Psalm 49:1–12)

(Morning)
God of all days, where do I place my trust? What do I value the most?
Do I cherish this life that I have been so freely given?

(Evening)
God of all days, how have I been a witness for you today?
Has my mouth spoken wisdom and my heart found understanding?

God of all, to the human eye, there are differences among people. The rich and poor, low and high, just and unjust. We all live side by side. But in your eyes we are all your precious children. We are your people, and we are equal in our transience—we all live and die. The "things" of the world are equally transient. We cannot buy eternal life, but you have a claim on our souls. Gracious, giving God, I want to always keep my priorities clear before you.

(Morning)
Enlivening God, let me give thanks for my very breath.
Let me remember before you those who are in peril today.
(Prayers of Intercession)

(Evening)
I give thanks for the gifts of today, for riches that cannot be purchased,
canned, freeze-dried, frozen, or deposited.
(Prayers of Intercession)

Why should I fear?
(Pray the Prayer of Our Savior.)

(Morning)
Let me not fear anyone or any trouble today. Give me the wisdom to see and understand the things that have real value. Let my mouth speak wisdom and my heart meditate on understanding. Thanks be to Christ. Amen.

(Evening)
God, I lie down to rest, entrusting myself to you in my living through the day and sleeping through the night. Thanks be to Christ. Amen.

SATURDAY, AUGUST 4
(Read Colossians 3:1–11)

(Morning)
Gracious God, my mind might be on the things above,
but my daily living is in this world. Today, I pray for perspective.

(Evening)
Gracious God, should I come before you with a contrite spirit?
Have I lost sight of the new self, which comes with Christ?

It sounds idealistic to put aside impurity, passion, greed, anger, and abusive language. If I were to be honest with myself, and with you, God, I would admit I often get pleasure from those things—thus, my human frailty. This is also a sign of my sinful nature. Grant me the power of Christ to rise above my weaknesses to your strength.

(Morning)
God, in Christ Jesus there is a model of One who was raised above
the limitations of human nature. Let me be raised with Christ.
Grant your courage to all who will know temptations today.
(Prayers of Intercession)

(Evening)
Confession does not come easily. I may not lie to others,
but too often I lie to myself, thinking the lie hides my sin from God.
(Prayers of Intercession)

Do not lie.
(Pray the Prayer of Our Savior.)

(Morning)
Just for today, God, let me live as a witness to life lived as a reflection of the risen Christ. Thanks be to Christ. Amen.

(Evening)
In Christ there are forgiveness and encouragement for a new day. Let the rest that comes with night restore my commitment to Christ. Thanks be to Christ. Amen.

SUNDAY, AUGUST 5
(Read Luke 12:13–21)

(Morning)
Generous God, what do I allow to accumulate and clutter my living?
Today will I expend my energies for things that really do not matter?

(Evening)
Generous God, I still feel encumbered by a desire to be visibly successful
and prosperous. Help me, God, to redefine what it means to be a success.

Like the turtle, I carry my possessions on my back. They encumber my soul. I
move slowly and cautiously rather than with spiritual courage. I mistake accu-
mulated goods for faithfulness in living.

(Morning)
God of simplicity, I easily lose sight of what is really important.
Teach me to value richness of spirit rather than the acquisition of goods.
Grant me wisdom in the choices I make and the things I treasure.
(Prayers of Intercession)

(Evening)
God, have I kept appropriate goals in sight today? I confess my taste for the
comforts of the things of the world. Teach me the comforts of faithfulness to you.
(Prayers of Intercession)

Let us be on our guard against all kinds of greed.
(Pray the Prayer of Our Savior.)

(Morning)
God, give me the courage to shed all that
encumbers my spiritual growth in order
to make space for what is truly good and
faithful and just. Thanks be to Christ.
Amen.

(Evening)
God of simplicity, let sleep and rest
from the day restore my commitment to
my spiritual wholeness and health.
Thanks be to Christ. Amen.

MONDAY, AUGUST 6
(Read Hebrews 11:1–3, 8–16)

(Morning)
God, you seem to always find a way to nudge your people into entering where they would not choose to go. Please do so for me this day and nudge me into this new day and this new week.

(Evening)
God, as I close this day, I thank you for drawing me into all that it had to offer and for the way in which it propels me into the days to come. May I enter them willing to do all that you would have me do in Christ's name.

I have a poster that shows an old-fashioned car floating through space with a caption that declares, "I can believe anything as long as it's incredible." I have liked this poster ever since I bought it, even though it has never really made sense to me. But then I must admit, in the same manner, the basis of faith is beyond reason. Through faith, we come to accept even what we can't see. Life is filled with singular events and material variety, each of which is in reality utterly miraculous. When we understand this, we come to understand how the worlds were fashioned by your word. Then faith really becomes possible as the assurance of things hoped for and the conviction of things not seen!

(Morning)
O One who opens our eyes to what we do not see, I pray you will continue to work in my life and will do the same in the lives of those for whom I pray.
(Prayers of Intercession)

(Evening)
Revealer of all that is deep and mysterious and wonderful, I thank you for the subtle ways in which you opened my eyes and enlightened my mind this day.
(Prayers of Intercession)

Through faith, we can even believe in what we cannot see.

(Morning)
I begin this day and this week with an eagerness to see things in new ways. May my eagerness be matched by a willingness to act upon what I see and an openness to discover new truths. In Jesus' name. Amen.

(Evening)
I lie down to sleep, comforted by the ways in which you have sustained my faith through all you have revealed to me: the good news made visible through Christ. In Jesus' name. Amen.

TUESDAY, AUGUST 7
(Read Isaiah 1:1, 10–15)

(Morning)
Holy Presence, the morning headlines seem to scream out the bad news: multiple tragedies of our own making. Guide me to be one who dares speak truth to the multiple powers behind the evils we experience.

(Evening)
Holy Presence, whose will is made clear to us in the midst
of all that is wrong, thank you for giving me the ability to assess
the circumstances that affect me and the lives that intersect with mine.
Thank you for renewed courage to dare to try and make a difference.

When your people sacrificed to you with their upturned hands full of blood, you turned your eyes from them and you closed your ears. So how do our hands look to you? As the rest of the world looks at us, the judgment seems almost universal. We are a nation that prides itself as the continuation of an errand into the wilderness, the New Jerusalem, yet among the nations of the world, we stand out for the violence that permeates our society. We also rank number one as the provider of weapons to the rest of the world. Can it be the case that nothing we do pleases you because of the blood on our hands?

(Morning)
God, may I be an instrument of the peace Christ modeled for all of us,
and may that peace be known in the lives of all of your children.
(Prayers of Intercession)

(Evening)
O One who accepts us even as we are, I thank you for the comfort
and assurance your love and grace grant to all who believe in you.
(Prayers of Intercession)

Any offering is tainted if it is colored by acts of evil.

(Morning)
I struggle with the knowledge that others in the world have a negative view of how our actions impact their lives. Rather than an apologist, help me be one who finds ways to change what does not have to be. In Jesus' name. Amen.

(Evening)
Though I may feel as if I have struggled this day with powers much larger than myself, remind me again, O Protector of all, that my struggles are minor compared to those faced by the majority of your children. Help me to see the world through their eyes and to choose to live my life in solidarity with them. In Jesus' name. Amen.

WEDNESDAY, AUGUST 8
(Read Isaiah 1:16–20)

(Morning)
O God, if I but open my eyes, I will see many who need to be touched
with your love through me. May I touch someone in your name this day.

(Evening)
O God, as I reached out to dare and touch someone who seemed untouchable,
a miraculous thing happened. I may have touched that person, but in the process my
life was touched in a new way as well. Thank you for this unexpected gift!

Your Word contains a constant refrain: your preferential option is for those
who have less; those who are oppressed; those who are victims of discrimina-
tion; those who are hungry; those who are homeless; those who are ill; and
those who are disadvantaged. The list of those whom you favor is so long that
few of us fail to appear on it at some point in our lives. Once a person has been
on your list, that person may begin to see with new eyes and be motivated to
give in new ways. But what if we have never been on your special list? What
will it take to move us to care and share? Is this the reason why you have
inspired us to be the church? Can we name ourselves your church if we fail to
understand and act upon the intent of your good news?

(Morning)
There are so many who need our prayers. Remind us, O God,
how our prayers are only the beginning of your expectations of us.
(Prayers of Intercession)

(Evening)
Sometimes we truly feel that we can make a difference. Don't allow us to stop
with this feeling, O God. Compel us to move beyond good feelings
to renewed prayer, intention, and action to aid others.
(Prayers of Intercession)

If we learn to do good, then we are better equipped to cease to do evil.

(Morning)
I have worked hard to get where I am and
to acquire all I have. Remind me that all I
have comes from you and that your gifts
carry the mandate that I share them with
others. In Jesus' name. Amen.

(Evening)
Thank you for the assurance that you love
me in spite of the blemishes that are mine.
And thank you for the challenge of
expecting me to do good and face evil all
the rest of my days. In Jesus' name. Amen.

THURSDAY, AUGUST 9
(Read Psalm 50:1–8, 22–23)

(Morning)
O God, I have so much for which to be thankful: loving family and friends,
challenging and rewarding work, good health and ample opportunities.
May my sense of thanksgiving truly honor you this day.

(Evening)
O God, my thanksgiving is enlarged by the thanks expressed by those
with whom I have shared. Your Word is lived out: whenever we give, we receive.

An attitude of thanksgiving shifts our focus from self to the other. We begin by
being grateful for what we have received, but the minute we express our gratitude, we move into a frame of mind in which we become ready to step outside
ourselves and encounter you, the One who receives our gratitude. You are honored when we express our thanksgiving in worship. You are the One who first
gave to us, and when we comprehend this, our gratitude becomes the selfless
expression you desire.

(Morning)
O generous God, may my gratitude for what you have given me motivate me
to reach out to others in new ways, not only in acts of giving, but also
in the prayers I lift up on their behalf.
(Prayers of Intercession)

(Evening)
It's so difficult to move beyond concerns for self. May I absorb in a new way
all that has happened to me this day, and may I be moved to think
of the other as Christ would have me do.
(Prayers of Intercession)

Those who bring thanksgiving as their sacrifice honor God.

(Morning)	(Evening)
May the joy that resides within my thanksgiving be apparent to everyone I encounter this day. May my joy be your joy shared with them. In Jesus' name. Amen.	The good feeling of a job well done is the sense of life you wish us to attain, O Giver of all good gifts. May my sense of accomplishment for this day be received by you this evening as my expression of thanksgiving to you. In Jesus' name. Amen.

FRIDAY, AUGUST 10
(Read Luke 12:32–40)

(Morning)
Creator God, help me begin this day without its being colored
by any sense of worry. Help me be open to the unexpected interruptions
and reshaped plans. Broaden my vision.

(Evening)
Creator God, as the day draws to a close and the sun sets in the west, may I set aside all
that distracts me and focus instead on what you would have me see and understand.

Worry gets lifted up to you like a prayer asking for a response. But your Word
reminds us again and again: worry gets us nowhere; there is no treasure we can
bury for a rainy day. You constantly remind us to be ready for the unexpected.
Your realm can and will break into our lives when we least expect it. This is the
treasure we should desire. Help us to understand and believe so we may truly
be worry free!

(Morning)
As I place my thoughts upon the lives of loved ones and those in need,
may my thoughts become the treasure you offer me and those for whom I pray.
(Prayers of Intercession)

(Evening)
O Treasure Giver, may your realm break into our lives this very evening
and in all the days to come. Be present now in the prayers we lift heavenward.
(Prayers of Intercession)

Where we place our hearts defines what we claim as our treasure.

(Morning)
Remind me again, O God, that the
alleged treasures we scramble to
acquire are not the treasures you would
have us seek. Help me be open to the
new life you offer through the One who
was the incarnation of your realm in our
midst. In Jesus' name. Amen.

(Evening)
I can rest easy this night, O God, for now
I know what you promise me and all of
your children is not of this world and is
not bound by the finite nature of the
material things we tend to desire. In
Jesus' name. Amen.

SATURDAY, AUGUST 11
(Read Genesis 15:1–6)

(Morning)
O God, this is a day to do all the things on my list. May what I do be pleasing in your sight, and may it be the proper response to all you have promised me in this new day.

(Evening)
O God, I have once again addressed this list. Things have been scratched off, and new things have been added. Help me keep a proper perspective so my list is your list and my actions enfold the intentions you have for all of life.

"Covenant" is a word that is often only partially heard. It's too easy for us just to hear your promise of descendants as numerous as the stars. It's too easy to interpret descendants as our own offspring and thus get lost in our possessiveness of family and tribe. Is it possible that by descendants, you mean all those whom we have the possibility to impact by what we say and do? If we truly see all people as your children and thus as our brothers and sisters, then our sense of responsibility for our side of the covenant begins to dawn and grow.

(Morning)
I used to pray, "Now I lay me down to sleep . . ." Then I realized the selfishness of my prayer, so I added words for immediate family, extended family, and finally everybody else in the world.
(Prayers of Intercession)

(Evening)
It's still difficult to move beyond friends and family when we think of those for whom we wish to pray. Forgive us for our myopia, and lead us to pray for all your children in such a way that what we pray governs how we reach out to them.
(Prayers of Intercession)

Belief in God's promise is reckoned by God as righteousness.

(Morning)
As we look around the world, we see the results of tribalism, and we know you must be weeping just as Jesus wept when he looked over Jerusalem. Help us gain such sensitivity so we might move beyond such tendencies. In Jesus' name. Amen.

(Evening)
I looked at the stars and was reminded of your promise to Abram that his descendants would be as numerous as the stars in the sky. Please help all of us understand what this means and how you expect us to live in relationship with one another. In Jesus' name. Amen.

SUNDAY, AUGUST 12
(Read Psalm 33:12–22)

(Morning)
Loving God, this is the most special day that you have made. It is a day for all of us to rest, to be renewed, to rejoice and be glad in it. May this day encounter us with your Word, and may your Word refashion us just as it first fashioned all that is.

(Evening)
Loving God, our worship is our attempt to give back to you the love you constantly give to us. It is our attempt to express our gratitude for all that you give.

Our hope is in you, the One who has fashioned our world through the miracle of your Word. Our hope is in you, the One who promises to be in covenant with us. Our hope is in you, the One who expects us to do good and avoid evil. Our hope is in you, the One who chooses our thanksgiving as our sacrifice. Our hope is in you because it is your good pleasure to give us your realm. If we can but believe all of this, then your promise to us becomes abundantly clear: your steadfast love will be upon us!

(Morning)
We place our hope in you, O God, and we lift up others in prayer so they might know as well the hope you so graciously offer us.
(Prayers of Intercession)

(Evening)
The hope we have in you, God, is a hope in which we might experience the gift of your realm. May that hope be realized by all human beings this evening and in all the days to come.
(Prayers of Intercession)

God's love is upon those who hope.
(Recite Psalm 23.)

(Morning)
Your Word became known to us in flesh by the life and death of the One who was first with you in the creation of the world. Help us to understand this Word and to be shaped by it in such a way that we are moved to do good. In Jesus' name. Amen.

(Evening)
We have placed our hope in you, O God, and now your promise unfolds in the very midst of our lives: you offer us your realm, and your steadfast love is upon us. Thanks be to you! In Jesus' name. Amen.

MONDAY, AUGUST 13
(Read Psalm 82)

(Morning)
Lover of justice, have I acted justly? Loved mercy? Walked humbly?

(Evening)
Lover of justice, tonight I pray for all people caught
in the snares of violence and injustice.

Great Advocate, I tend to pay more attention to the gods of money, possession, and position than I do to you. I want justice, but I don't always listen unless it is in my own best interests. I know in your household we are to seek justice for all those in need, not just ourselves or our neighbors. You are uncomfortably inclusive, and I cringe at confronting people or systems that oppress. Be with me as I try to walk in someone else's shoes. Help me follow through with right action, lest I be only a clanging cymbal.

(Morning)
Giver of life, I pray for those suffering at the bottom of a hierarchical social system.
(Prayers of Intercession)

(Evening)
As I seek sleep, I am grateful that you are the One who holds us justly
in your strong right hand.
(Prayers of Intercession)

"Your will be done on earth."

(Morning)
Today I remember that you are a refuge for both the high and the lowly. I am thankful that you look after the least of us. In the light of Christ. Amen.

(Evening)
Help me learn to love so that I want for others as much as I have. I rest in the assurance that yours is the ultimate word. In the light of Christ. Amen.

TUESDAY, AUGUST 14
(Read Psalm 80:1–2, 8–19)

(Morning)
Invisible Presence, my fog obscures your sun, and I long for the light of your love.

(Evening)
Invisible Presence, how long before feel your loving hand active in my life again?

The world weighs heavy today. The work pace is hectic. Hearts seem hard. I am quick to judge others and, in the process, myself. I move in shadows of my own making, but I want to touch your shining face. I know your sustaining presence is available to me in any circumstance. I await my own opening, knowing I become the prayer I pray. Holy One, restore me. Teach me to love.

(Morning)
Living Water, refresh my roots in you. Turn your face to all for whom I pray.
(Prayers of Intercession)

(Evening)
As I close my eyes, I remember all the ways you have walked with your people in rain and shine.
(Prayers of Intercession)

"Apart from me you can do nothing."

(Morning)
My day is devoted to faith in your return because I know you never left. May I be ever more open to your loving ways. In the light of Christ. Amen.

(Evening)
I sleep in the peace of your continual presence. I know your love is constant. I feel it, touch it, live it. I joyously surrender to your perfect wholeness. In the light of Christ. Amen.

WEDNESDAY, AUGUST 15
(Read Luke 12:49–56)

(Morning)
Changeless God, with the dawn I remember your wondrous good news.

(Evening)
Changeless God, I am comforted that you are
with me during all the changes of
my life.

Fire of love, you see the hidden places within me that need changing. You know I am assailed by doubt. My heart sometimes feels rent; peace has its price. In these times the world changes quickly. We find strife in our families, our workplaces, and our churches. Even our children are strangers. I want to be part of your new creation; to recommit my life to you. Spirit, purify the motives of my heart. Help me change old patterns so I can follow the Sovereign.

(Morning)
Reconciling God, today I realized the futility of trying to follow the world.
(Prayers of Intercession)

(Evening)
Reconciling God, today I felt misunderstood by others.
I sleep centered in you as I pray for them.
(Prayers of Intercession)

"But strive first for the realm of God."

(Morning)
Today I will try to give up control and trust the Spirit in all things. Help me to be mindful of small changes I can make that will help me get limbered up for larger ones. In the light of Christ. Amen.

(Evening)
I rest in the knowledge of your refreshing Spirit, which washes over me and makes every day new. With this daily baptism, I can reexamine my values and goals in peace. In the light of Christ. Amen.

THURSDAY, AUGUST 16
(Read Jeremiah 23:23–29)

(Morning)
Truthful and Holy One, help me be on guard against accepting
anything that is not of you.

(Evening)
Truthful and Holy One, the world is in need of your truth.
Hear the prayers of all who call on you tonight.

Purifying Potter, I have feet of clay, and I have sometimes unwittingly partici-
pated in systems that oppress the poor. The altar of my heart is not well served
by my chosen idols. I am a part of the problem, the spiritual malaise of these
times. Mold me into a new vessel born of longing for your truth. Help me walk
with those who suffer, offering the hope of your presence at all times through
the grace of the Sovereign.

(Morning)
Inner Knower, help me and those for whom I pray see through
the established dogma of the day.
(Prayers of Intercession)

(Evening)
God, I have been grateful for your gift of spiritual discernment today.
(Prayers of Intercession)

"Beware of the yeast of the Pharisees and the Sadducees."

(Morning)
I start my day in gratitude that you have
made me impatient with any attempt to
put you into a mold. Help me be wary
of "shoulds" and "should nots." Thank
you for good questions. In the light of
Christ. Amen.

(Evening)
Thank you for being available always in
the midst of any and all personal and
social ills. I am grateful that there are
many paths to return to you and that you
are a God of new beginnings. In the light
of Christ. Amen.

FRIDAY, AUGUST 17
(Read Isaiah 5:1–7)

(Morning)
Gracious Giver, have I built barriers in my life that keep me from becoming sweet fruit?

(Evening)
Gracious Giver, did I accept with joy the overflowing abundance you offered me today?

I know you want me to have life abundant, but I seem to dwell more on lack than on plenty. I have closed my eyes to the needs of others in favor of my own wants. I do not always stand for what is just. Let me take my cue from the lavish wastefulness you instilled in nature. Calm my anxieties so I may unclench my hands and free my heart to stake its claim on you, who always sustain and prosper me.

(Morning)
Great Provider, help me keep focused on your abundance,
so I may bear fruit in my life and the lives of those for whom I pray.
(Prayers of Intercession)

(Evening)
Great Provider, thank you for the plenty I found all along my path today.
(Prayers of Intercession)

"The righteous flourish like the palm tree."

(Morning)
Today I desire love. I will give love.
Today I desire peace. I will give peace.
Today I desire abundance. I will give abundantly. In the light of Christ. Amen.

(Evening)
I retire in profound gratitude, knowing you are the answer for every situation. I fall asleep with a smile, eager to share my burden of plenty. In the light of Christ. Amen.

SATURDAY, AUGUST 18
(Read Hebrews 12:1–2)

(Morning)
Holy One, when I open to your power flowing through me, I demonstrate your strength.

(Evening)
Holy One, before I sleep, refresh me with the calm assurance of your presence.
I wait in silence while your Spirit unfolds to turn my burdens into joy.

My soul sings with the remembrance of your promise, and I am grateful for the gift of Christ's supreme example. You know my need before I ask. Help train me with patience so I may stand steadfast in the challenges of daily circumstance. Help me follow the pattern of the Sovereign. I want to do your will.

(Morning)
Sovereign God, help us develop greater awareness of our divine destiny,
that we may persevere with confidence.
(Prayers of Intercession)

(Evening)
Changeless God, thank you for the constancy
of your love, joy, and peace I felt today.
(Prayers of Intercession)

"Put on the whole armor of God."

(Morning)
I start the day eager to be your witness. I look forward to all demonstrations of your loving-kindness and steadfast faith exemplified in those whose paths I cross today. In the light of Christ. Amen.

(Evening)
I am at peace in the knowledge of the One who did your will perfectly. I will remember this act of love, forgiveness, and nonviolence. In the light of Christ. Amen.

SUNDAY, AUGUST 19
(Read Hebrews 11:29–39)

(Morning)
Powerful God, I need to erase the worries and fears of the day with the knowledge
of your presence. Can I believe that you will open new doors?
Will faith be my guide?

(Evening)
Powerful God, is my faith strong enough to trust your greater glories that are at hand?

Strong Deliverer, it is easy to believe when things go well. I have tested my
faith in the crucible of my fear and found it wanting. I forget that when I align
myself with you, I can achieve great things. I want to reinforce my knowing
that you are all that is. Help me let go of negativity and turn to you in total trust
during the difficult times as well.

(Morning)
Those who face pain, poverty, and alienation look to the power
of faith they receive from you for the resolution they seek.
(Prayers of Intercession)

(Evening)
Spirit of justice and righteousness, thank you for being
with those who suffer and are heavy laden.
(Prayers of Intercession)

"The one who believes in me . . . will do greater works than these."

(Morning)
Help me to know beyond any reason to
believe. Help me to be faithful in any
trial that life brings, united with your
will. In the light of Christ. Amen.

(Evening)
I dip into your abundance for the faith I
need, knowing I can be free of dis-
abling fear. I bless the hem of your
garment always available to me. In the
light of Christ. Amen.

MONDAY, AUGUST 20
(Read Hebrews 12:18–29)

(Morning)
Creator God, so terrifying was the sight that Moses said, "I tremble with fear."

(Evening)
Creator God, let us be grateful for receiving your realm, which cannot be shaken.

God, if one as great in your eyes was terrified by what he saw, why should the likes of me wonder at the demonic forces that make my soul tremble? Those "innumerable angels" in festal gathering surrounded Moses and the early church with blessed assurance and a peace that passes all credulity.

(Morning)
Heart of our spiritual ancestors, beat in my shaking frame this day.
When fear laced with sorrow clouds my vision, make my anticipation of trouble a far greater specter than it probably will be in God's grace-filled framing of my life.
(Prayers of Intercession)

(Evening)
Thank you, great God, for all the little assurances
of your sustaining presence throughout this day's events.
(Prayers of Intercession)

God companions God's people always!
(Say the Prayer of Our Savior slowly three times.)

(Morning)
My agenda is before me, long and complicated. I am not quite up to every challenge it includes. One greater than myself companions my every step— even the slippery ones. In the name of our Savior I pray. Amen.

(Evening)
All during this day, when the tiny terrors tried to wrestle my faith to faithlessness in the midst of the struggle, your power lifted me up and over every hurdle. In the name of our Savior I pray. Amen.

TUESDAY, AUGUST 21
(Read Jeremiah 1:4–10)

(Morning)
God, your word came to me!

(Evening)
God, all to whom you send, they shall go, and whatever you command, we shall speak.

God, in our teenage insecurities, we told you the call was not to us, for we were not good enough in looks, brains, attitude, and inclination. Yet you, Creator God, had more faith in us than we had in ourselves. Patiently, you waited out our feeble humanity, and as we were encouraged by others who saw in us what we ourselves preferred to ignore, the glad moment of spiritual self-recognition and church authorization finally dawned.

(Morning)
May that youth of my inner past be emboldened to come forth in spite of wrinkled flesh, bald spot, and arthritic joints. God, encourage me to try to leap tall problems with your bodacious power.
(Prayers of Intercession)

(Evening)
Phew! The sunset of this long day surrounds me with the quiet sense of accomplishments. Accomplishments done well only because you, God of all good surprises, astonished little me once more.
(Prayers of Intercession)

The ageless God leads us always.
(Sing "Now in the Days of Youth" or another familiar hymn.)

(Morning)
I know I will meet people of all ages this day. May I profit from the wealth of age; be visioned by the exuberance of youth; charmed by the innocence of a child; and inspired by the steadiness of middle age. In the name of our Savior I pray. Amen.

(Evening)
Wow! Dear glad God, you showed me what was good and who was best in this wonderful twenty-four hours of so many encounters. I am revived and restored! In the name of our Savior I pray. Amen.

WEDNESDAY, AUGUST 22
(Read Psalm 71:1–6)

(Morning)
O God, in you do I put my trust. Let me never be put to confusion.

(Evening)
O God, in your righteousness deliver me and rescue me;
incline your ear to me; save me!

Loving God, the more your church laments, the less the world cares to be near us. Our lame excuses limp us to the sidelines of life where, wounded, we feel neglected and abandoned. But you, our God, prevail, and the church on earth becomes blessed as the church above!

(Morning)
"Be to me a rock of refuge, a strong fortress to save me,
for you are my rock and my fortress."
(Prayers of Intercession)

(Evening)
"Upon you I have leaned from my birth. My praise is continually of you."
(Prayers of Intercession)

God comes as fire and burns away our excuses.
(Repeat the Nicene Creed.)

(Morning)	(Evening)
"Be to me a rock of refuge, a strong fortress to save me, for you are my rock and my fortress." In the name of our Savior I pray. Amen.	"Upon you I have leaned from my birth. My praise is continually of you." In the name of our Savior I pray. Amen.

THURSDAY, AUGUST 23
(Read Isaiah 58:9–14)

(Morning)
O God, if I delight in you, may I ride on the high places?

(Evening)
O God, if I call the Sabbath joy, will the ruined of my week be repaired?

Promises were made to us as children; some kept, some broken. Incensed, we railed against those who took our trust and blew it away, as a dandelion its seed fluff. Now in our majority, caring God, we invite your Word to be our trust and your vows to be our bond.

(Morning)
Continually guiding God, you satisfy my desire with good things!
(Prayers of Intercession)

(Evening)
My weak bones, you, O God, make strong. Hear my thanks!
(Prayers of Intercession)

God is the repairer of the breach.
(Sing "Love Divine, All Loves Excelling" or another familiar hymn.)

(Morning)
I got up this morning with my heart on Jesus, and lo, I discovered to my delight, he was an earlier riser with the same desire for me! In the name of our Savior I pray. Amen.

(Evening)
Carpenter Child of ancient God, this old house of my believing needed restoration today, and as I retire, I am repaired! In the name of our Savior I pray. Amen.

FRIDAY, AUGUST 24
(Read Luke 13:10–17)

(Morning)
O Great Breaker of shackles, cut a gaping hole in my barbed-wire fence!

(Evening)
O Great Breaker of shackles, I was bound by Satan, freed by Christ.
Is this just an old myth or a sound bite I sing?

God, she lay in the dust of dutiful discouragement, her hope burdened and beaten back when Christ created Sabbath. Hypocrites cried, "Foul, against the grain, not according to religion's rules!" But the healed one laughed and danced. Will I frown or clap?

(Morning)
Jesus of kind manners, unwilling to intrude until I say, "
Come," make my welcome red as a rose.
(Prayers of Intercession)

(Evening)
O Healing Power, my thanks this day for removing the sliver from my eye!
(Prayers of Intercession)

The perfect person prefers pomposity.
(Sing "Jesus Loves Me!" or another familiar hymn.)

(Morning)
On the way to work, the office, the store, the shop, the restaurant, the mall, O God of the daily round, may my ordinary eyes see extraordinary things. Thanks to you! In the name of our Savior I pray. Amen.

(Evening)
So this is the surprise you had in store for me, surreptitious God—to sneak upon me unawares and shower joy to my sad-sack soul. In the name of our Savior I pray. Amen.

SATURDAY, AUGUST 25
(Read Psalm 103:1–21)

(Morning)
Holy God, how shall I bless you today?
And how will all that is within me bless your holy name?

(Evening)
Holy God, as high as the heavens are above this earth,
that is the dimension of your steadfast love for us!

Understanding God, when we are well, we take our health for granted; when well employed, take our paycheck as routine; and when well loved, take our partner in stride. A crisis then creates havoc in our lives, and in sudden desperation, we reach out beyond ourselves for your divine help and blessed assurance.

(Morning)
O ever-relational God, your covenant with this unequal partner
is the super-bonding glue that holds the splinters of my life together.
(Prayers of Intercession)

(Evening)
O God whose strength never diminishes or fades from my inner TV screen,
keep me in the company of angels now and here!
(Prayers of Intercession)

God's steadfast love is from everlasting to everlasting.
(Hum "On Eagle's Wings" or another familiar song.)

(Morning)
As far as the east is from the west, O God, you remove my sin from continuing to pain others and from destroying my peace of mind. In the name of our Savior I pray. Amen.

(Evening)
My soul was blessed, O Mighty One, as I hearkened to your voice through all this day's chatter. *Gracias!* In the name of our Savior I pray. Amen.

SUNDAY, AUGUST 26
(Read Psalm 103:19–22)

(Morning)
Almighty God, ministers do your pleasure! How is my ministry this day?

(Evening)
Almighty God, hearkening to your voice takes concentration
and sacred imagination. Have I honed either today?

God, you deal with us personally—one by one. We prefer to run with the crowd, pace ourselves with peers, and insulate our spiritual curiosity from critical contact with you, "the Mighty One." Dominion and power established their thrones in our personal selfishness until in our limitations we see a loving alternative to preoccupation with you.

(Morning)
O God of tiny things, wake my slumbering spirit
to the gentle giant your passing shadow casts.
(Prayers of Intercession)

(Evening)
O Mighty One, you excel in the strength I need.
(Prayers of Intercession)

We are called to action, not reaction!
(Sing "The Saints of God" or another familiar hymn.)

(Morning)
In the dawn's first light, you open my eyes to my calling, and refreshed by sleep, I take the wings of the morning and dwell in the uttermost parts of the sea! In the name of our Savior I pray. Amen.

(Evening)
How comfortable home seemed to me this night as I turned the key in the lock, dear One. You are like the prodigal son's parent preparing a feast of gladness for me—in spite of all. In the name of our Savior I pray. Amen.

MONDAY, AUGUST 27
(Read Luke 14:1, 7–14)

(Morning)
Creator God, even as we seek to imitate the life of our Savior, so let us remember his word that he "did not come to be served, but to serve." We hear his call: "Follow me."

(Evening)
Creator God, even as we seek to imitate the life of our Savior, so let us remember his word that he "did not come to be served, but to serve." We hear his call: "Follow me."

Gracious God, we read, "The last shall be first." The inverted sense of values proposed by scripture made Jesus unpopular in his day, as the emphasis on winning in our day causes us to ignore some of the basic teachings of our leader. Is our motive to exploit a situation for what it will do for us or to give graciously of ourselves for what we can do for others? "Let the same mind be in you that was in Christ Jesus, who, though he was in the form of God, did not regard equality with God as something to be exploited, but emptied himself, taking the form of a slave, being born in human likeness. And being found in human form, he humbled himself and became obedient to the point of death—even death on a cross."

(Morning)
"The last shall be first."
(Prayers of Intercession)

(Evening)
"The first shall be last."
(Prayers of Intercession)

"Let the same mind be in you that was in Christ Jesus."

(Morning)
Open us today to your incredible unconditional love, that we may become channels for that love going out to others. Thanks be to Christ. Amen.

(Evening)
God of amazing grace, if we have spent this day only in personal concerns and personal interests, forgive us. Open us tomorrow to your incredible unconditional love, that we may become channels for that love going out to others. Come to us again, and renew our strength as we rest and sleep this night. Thanks be to Christ. Amen.

TUESDAY, AUGUST 28
(Read Jeremiah 2:4–13)

(Morning)
Eternal God, on this new day, we would turn our eyes upon Jesus and look fully into that wonderful face. May our focus always be on the Savior and Redeemer of our very lives.

(Evening)
Eternal God, on this evening, we would turn our eyes upon Jesus and look fully into that wonderful face.

Compassionate God, we pray with the assurance that you love us enough to forgive us when we confess our sins, when we acknowledge your direction. We believe that the cross says you love us unconditionally, even when we crucify your way in our world. You have so loved us that we can still call ourselves your children. Sometimes we don't believe this; we don't act upon it; we see ourselves as unrelated to you. We know we need to see again the depth of your mercy and love for us. Help us to grow so your worship is no longer a duty, but a joy; no longer a routine, but a challenge; as ones who are loved and who would serve a caring Creator.

(Morning)
We acknowledge our lack of faith, our failure in the light
of the divine example we know in the life of Jesus the Christ.
(Prayers of Intercession)

(Evening)
We rest in the grateful sense of your acceptance of our lives
as we really are, human beings who are conscious of our need for you.
(Prayers of Intercession)

**We cannot love as you have loved us, but help us to grow
in love until we fear nothing except to grieve your Spirit.**

(Morning)
"We are weak but you are strong."
Grant us a peaceful day. Thanks be to Christ. Amen.

(Evening)
Loving God, as light fades into night to mark the end of your day, we would rest in the grateful sense of your acceptance of our lives as we really are, human beings who are conscious of our need for you. "We are weak but you are strong." Grant us peaceful sleep. Thanks be to Christ. Amen.

WEDNESDAY, AUGUST 29
(Read Psalm 81:1, 10–16)

(Morning)
All-powerful God, we acknowledge your greatness and kneel before your majesty. All glory be to you, our Creator and our Redeemer. We recognize the power of your Spirit, the Spirit of unconditional love, which infuses our lives with strength for the day.

(Evening)
All-powerful God, come to us this day as we turn to you, the Source of all life.

O God, our realization of your strength turns upon our human weakness, our limitations. We are dependent, no longer independent. We accept that in ourselves we cannot face the demands of daily living. So we turn to you, our Maker, our Creator, the Source of all true strength. There is so much we don't know, so much we don't understand about your world and about the meaning of life. Keep us humble, never arrogant, as we relate in caring and concern for others. May we be willing to trust tomorrow to your everlasting power.

(Morning)
We recognize the power of your Spirit, the Spirit of unconditional love, which infuses our lives with strength for the day.
(Prayers of Intercession)

(Evening)
We acknowledge your greatness and kneel before your majesty.
(Prayers of Intercession)

Help us this day never to forget your continuing love and support every moment.

(Morning)
As the day begins, O God, we remember that it will be your day. Thanks be to Christ. Amen.

(Evening)
As the day winds down, we rest in your goodness. Quiet our hearts for the peace of sleep and the restoring of the physical functioning of our bodies. Thanks be to Christ. Amen.

THURSDAY, AUGUST 30
(Read Proverbs 25:6–7)

(Morning)
Gracious God, we would truly find joy in this day that you have given us.
We begin with the thrill of your empowering Spirit.

(Evening)
Gracious God, thank you for helping us to remain
in ecstasy throughout this day's length.

Powerful, sustaining Presence, we would stop to remember you as we go through this day, to wait upon your direction. The psalmist exhorts us to "wait upon God," and we remember that a waitperson is one who serves. As human beings, we recognize our self-centeredness; we know our desire to put self first. Help our concern to be for others, and may our own interests be secondary. May we always remember Jesus' instruction to love you first and then our neighbor. Forgive us when we forget.

(Morning)
Too often we depend upon our own meager powers to decide what we should do.
We pray for your wisdom.
(Prayers of Intercession)

(Evening)
Too often we base decisions on personal pride and self-concern.
We pray for humbleness.
(Prayers of Intercession)

"This is the day that God has made. Let us rejoice and be glad in it."

(Morning)
Forgiving God, let us keep in mind the promises we have made, to you and to ourselves, to live up to the very best we have come to know through Jesus, the true Word. Thanks be to Christ. Amen.

(Evening)
Forgive us when we fail, and give us peace through the knowledge of your love. Thanks be to Christ. Amen.

FRIDAY, AUGUST 31
(Read Psalm 112)

(Morning)
Blessed God and holy Savior, keep from us all apprehension and anxiety
during this time of busy activity. When we forget you, never, never forget us.
Keep us always conscious of your love and support.

(Evening)
Blessed God and holy Savior, we would open our spirits
and our lives to your sustaining presence this evening.

O God of all, never let us be bored with living, and help us to maintain the
enthusiasm of your Spirit. We remember that excitement of earlier days, when
everything was new and fresh. Since then we have tried not to become wrapped
up in our own selfish ways, a pitiful small package. Scripture tells us that
blessedness never comes singly, and that true blessedness is for all who walk
with you.

(Morning)
Keep our thoughts focused outwardly. Caring for others binds us together
and results in benefits for all your children.
(Prayers of Intercession)

(Evening)
Remind us again of the true joy of giving and sharing.
(Prayers of Intercession)

Healthy living comes when we reach out.

(Morning)	(Evening)
Draw us together again in common caring. Bind us as one in love and goodwill for all people. Thanks be to Christ. Amen.	God of quietness and peace, remove all fear from our hearts and minds. Grant us peace and calmness. Thanks be to Christ. Amen.

SATURDAY, SEPTEMBER 1
(Read Hebrews 13:1–8, 15–16)

(Morning)
O Savior, let me walk with you; open me to your Word and help me to be strong.

(Evening)
O Savior, help me to love and teach me to continue on the path of righteousness.

God, we are all guilty together. "Caring for our own need is necessary but must not be dominant. If we would find fulfillment in life our efforts must be directed outwardly toward the needs of others. Our problems come when we forget to turn to you for direction in living. Keep our focus toward you and the world, your world. We are aware of the almost unbearable suffering of so many beyond our kin."

(Morning)
Creator Redeemer, we wake each morning too conscious of how we ourselves feel.
Help us to love as Jesus did, the One who prayed for our sins, because they are shared.
(Prayers of Intercession)

(Evening)
We are too centered in self. Help us to love as did Jesus.
(Prayers of Intercession)

**Let us pray not just "for all people, but also to understand,
to stand alongside and to pray in solidarity
with our fellow Christians around the world."**

(Morning)
Outgoing, giving, loving God, did we reach out this day in concern for others? Did we go beyond our own needs and identify with the problems and pains of friends and neighbors? Thanks be to Christ. Amen.

(Evening)
Did we even participate in the celebrations and joys of other folks? Forgive our self-concern, and grant us serenity for this night of rest in your everlasting arms. Thanks be to Christ. Amen.

SUNDAY, SEPTEMBER 2
(Read Colossians 3:12–17)

(Morning)
Living God, this is a new day; let us be glad in it.
This is the day that you have made; let us rejoice in it.

(Evening)
Living God, whose Spirit breathes throughout the universe,
lift our hearts in thanksgiving for life, for all its challenges and opportunities.

Gracious God, this day is full of thanks for the joy of friendship; the love and support of family; this beautiful world; and this free country of relative equality. Open our eyes to all we have and enjoy. When we are thankful, we really can't blame, complain, and criticize adversely. When we are thankful, everything falls into place, and we are filled with joy. Relationships become positive and supportive.

(Morning)
Gracious God, let this day be filled with thanks, for all our troubles
and problems melt away in the light of gratitude for our many privileges.
(Prayers of Intercession)

(Evening)
Gracious God, let this evening be filled with thanks.
(Prayers of Intercession)

**Thanksgiving keeps us humble and in a right relationship
with you and all human beings.**

(Morning)
Last night was good and we are most grateful. We trust the future to your care. Thanks be to Christ. Amen.

(Evening)
Creator God, this day has been good. In spite of rain and stormy weather, in spite of pain and discomforts, in spite of human failings, you love us. That is what counts. Thanks be to Christ. Amen.

MONDAY, SEPTEMBER 3
(Read Psalm 139:1–6, 13–18)

(Morning)
Spirit of peace, since the beginning, I have been yours, for I am your creation.
Help me to know myself as I have been known.

(Evening)
Spirit of peace, I have come to the end of another day. You are still at my side.
Your Spirit continues to give me life, and in Jesus Christ you make a future for me.

My existence is amazing. Each day I experience a world of marvels: the smell of fresh baked bread; the sound of a child's happy laugh; the feel of warm water; the rich taste of chocolate; and the sight of those I love. I know all these things are your creation, and I have been blessed to share this world with them. I give you thanks for these wonders. Help me develop an even deeper appreciation for everything you have made—myself included. Help me to know the abundance of your grace.

(Morning)
Gracious Creator, Maker of all things, great and small, I remember
in your presence the wonders of your world.
(Prayers of Intercession)

(Evening)
I give you thanks for the gift of this day and for those who have touched my heart.
(Prayers of Intercession)

God has made us and known us. Thanks be to God.
(Sing "For the Beauty of the Earth" or another familiar hymn.)

(Morning)
Each day is a new beginning, a fresh gift from the Creator. May I help make this day a gift for others. In the name of my Redeemer. Amen.

(Evening)
At the end of the day, I see the gift that I have been given. May the gift of the night refresh me and prepare me for new gifts tomorrow. In the name of my Redeemer. Amen.

TUESDAY, SEPTEMBER 4
(Deuteronomy 30:15–20)

(Morning)
Creator God, you have set before us life and death, adversity and prosperity.
Help me to choose the ways that lead to life.

(Evening)
Creator God, I have made choices this day. May your Spirit bless those decisions
so that they lead to life for me and for others.

Your trust in us is humbling. Even though we have often failed to live up to
your expectations, you never stop loving us and offering us the opportunity to
choose your way. You set options before us, some that lead to joy and others
that lead to despair, but you do not choose for us. You treat us with respect and
dignity. May we learn to return that respect, loving you as you have loved us.
May we always choose life and walk in the way of your commandments.

(Morning)
Holy God, each day we make new choices. Help your people to choose wisely.
(Prayers of Intercession)

(Evening)
I give you thanks for all wise choices made this day, and I ask your forgiveness
for every ill-considered decision, both for myself and for others.
(Prayers of Intercession)

God has trusted us to choose life. May we give thanks to God.
(Pray the Prayer of Our Savior.)

(Morning)	(Evening)
May the decisions I make this day serve the glory of God and the welfare of the whole human family. In the name of my Redeemer. Amen.	I give thanks for the love and respect of God that I have had this day and pray for new energy tomorrow. In the name of my Redeemer. Amen.

WEDNESDAY, SEPTEMBER 5
(Read Psalm 1)

(Morning)
Holy God, you have given us Torah to guide us, law to describe our path.
Help me to delight in the law that I may truly prosper.

(Evening)
Holy God, you have watched over me this day. Your Spirit has been with me,
and I have been watered by your love.

It is easy to follow the advice of the wicked. Every day we are bombarded with messages that entice us away from your way. Commercials on television and radio, advertisements in newspapers and magazines, movies, computer games, sometimes even dear friends, tell us that there are easier ways. They tell us that salvation comes through wealth or beauty or strength. Their way seems so easy, your law so restricting. It is easy to turn aside, to become a scoffer. But we know that you are there to bring us back to the right path.

(Morning)
Holy One, temptation will come my way today. Be with me and give me strength.
(Prayers of Intercession)

(Evening)
I give you thanks for your presence at all times. You have been my comfort
and strength. Please remember everyone who has had need of you today.
(Prayers of Intercession)

God does watch over us.
(Pray the Prayer of Our Savior.)

(Morning)
Help me to be your tree today, watered by your Word. Watch over me and help me find the path you have cleared. In the name of my Redeemer. Amen.

(Evening)
May my dreams this evening be meditations on the law and love of God. May I awake tomorrow refreshed and ready for whatever the day may bring. In the name of my Redeemer. Amen.

THURSDAY, SEPTEMBER 6
(Read Philemon 1–7)

(Morning)
Blessed One, I will not be alone this day because, in Christ, I have many brothers and sisters. Help me appreciate their work and give thanks.

(Evening)
Blessed One, I know my brothers and sisters have been engaged in your work. Bless their efforts with your Spirit.

We are not Christians alone. We are part of a community, the church, gathered from every nation on earth. God, your love has overcome the divisions between us and made us one people. Though we do not live out that unity at all times, we do see glimpses of it in the love that Christians have for one another. Thanks to you, God, we are sisters and brothers who care for one another, support one another, celebrate with one another, even cry with one another. Your grace of God has made it so.

(Morning)
Gracious God, I thank you for the gift of my brothers and sisters in faith. May your Spirit be with each of them this day.
(Prayers of Intercession)

(Evening)
Much good has been done in the name of Jesus Christ. I give you thanks for each individual who has made the love of Christ known to another.
(Prayers of Intercession)

Faith and love are present in the church of Jesus Christ.
(Sing "For All the Saints" or another familiar hymn.)

(Morning)
Help me to also be an instrument of your love. Fill me with your Spirit that I may refresh the hearts of others. In the name of my Redeemer. Amen.

(Evening)
Your love has been made known to me through the saints. I rest assured that the work of Jesus Christ has not been in vain. In the name of my Redeemer. Amen.

FRIDAY, SEPTEMBER 7
(Philemon 8–21)

(Morning)
Loving One, in Christ the divisions between people have lost their meaning.
Help me to overcome my prejudices and live from that vision.

(Evening)
Loving One, true companionship is the work of love.
May the Spirit knit us together in one community of grace.

Like Philemon, we all need to grow in faith. Human divisions and prejudices still shape many of our actions and attitudes. We still treat other people as our inferiors, almost as if they were our slaves. But in Christ we have seen a better way. He has shown us how to live, all as servants one to the other, without condescension or falsehood. May the Spirit grant us the grace to treat one another as true sisters and brothers, all together as children—your children.

(Morning)
Holy One, you call us to live our unity in Christ in the way we treat others.
Inspire us with the courage and wisdom to do your will.
(Prayers of Intercession)

(Evening)
You have given me opportunities today to treat others with the respect they are due.
I remember them all as your gift to me.
(Prayers of Intercession)

In Christ there is no slave or free, black or white, male or female.
We are all one in Christ Jesus.
(Sing "In Christ There Is No East or West" or another familiar hymn.)

(Morning)
Help me to share your love with others today. Fill me with your Spirit, and overcome all that divides me from those you love. In the name of my Redeemer. Amen.

(Evening)
Though there are still many divisions in this world, I know that in Jesus Christ, God has brought the promise of unity. In the name of my Redeemer. Amen.

SATURDAY, SEPTEMBER 8
(Jeremiah 18:1–11)

(Morning)
O God, we are the work of your hands. Help us to live as your children.

(Evening)
O God, your hand has shaped another day. Choices have been laid before us.
Bless the Holy One for every assistance in choosing wisely.

The church of Jesus Christ is much like Israel. God, we also are your creation. Like Israel, we are given choices. We can do good, and you will bless us, or we can do evil, and you will curse us. But the choice is not always final. Often, even when we have done great evil, you, Holy One, wait for us to amend our ways and choose good. When we do, once again you are ready to offer us great blessings. May the Spirit inspire us always to do good, that you, loving God, may do good to us.

(Morning)
Holy One, we will have many decisions to make today.
Help us to choose to do good for all our brothers and sisters.
(Prayers of Intercession)

(Evening)
Today I have felt your shaping hand. For all the good I have been able to do,
I give you thanks, and I ask for your patience that I might amend every evil deed.
(Prayers of Intercession)

God has given us the freedom to choose. May we always choose wisely.
(Pray the Prayer of Our Savior.)

(Morning)
May your hand shape my life today. May your Spirit guide me so that every decision I make will be to your glory. In the name of my Redeemer. Amen.

(Evening)
Grant me a night of rest, and shape my dreams that they may prepare me for your service tomorrow. In the name of my Redeemer. Amen.

SUNDAY, SEPTEMBER 9
(Luke 14:25–33)

(Morning)
Creator God, what will be the cost of discipleship today? How will I pay it?

(Evening)
Creator God, I have followed the path of discipleship another day.
The price has not been more than I could bear. Thank you.

It is no easier to take up the cross today than it was two thousand years ago. We still pay a high price to be disciples of Jesus. To be disciples, we must set ourselves apart and at the same time reach out to others. We must live as saints and yet welcome sinners and eat with them without ever feeling superior. We must say unpopular things, even in our own communities, but without being hypocrites. We must do the impossible. Only in the power of the Spirit can we find the courage or wisdom to pay the price of discipleship.

(Morning)
The way before us is difficult, but with the assurance of your presence,
O God, we know we can bear the cost. Help us this day to do your will.
(Prayers of Intercession)

(Evening)
Your Spirit has been with me and given me the power to be a disciple.
May your Spirit also bless the lives of the others I now name.
(Prayers of Intercession)

We must pay the cost of discipleship.
(Sing "O Savior, Let Me Walk with You" or another familiar hymn.)

(Morning)
The cost of discipleship may be high, but with your help I will find joy in your service. In the name of my Redeemer. Amen.

(Evening)
May I face tomorrow fully aware that challenges await me. Be with me all my days that I might give glory to your name. In the name of my Redeemer. Amen.

MONDAY, SEPTEMBER 10
(Read Luke 15:1–10)

(Morning)
Welcoming God, on this new morning, I seek to come near you
and listen to your words of purpose for me today.

(Evening)
Welcoming God, the day is nearly over, and I am grateful you have been with me.
As evening gathers, I rejoice in my homecoming. I pray I have not foolishly set
someone aside or sinned against another. I ask forgiveness for the ways in which I
failed today to see the needs of a neighbor or to rejoice with a friend.

Each day something is lost: by the one whose home no longer stands because
of warring; by the one whose dizzying hunger is not relieved; by the one whose
need for a loving touch is not met; by the one who sees and does not reach out.

(Morning)
Loving God, throughout this day, may I be one who sees and reaches out;
who offers myself for others in ways you make known to me.
(Prayers of Intercession)

(Evening)
Compassionate God, hear my prayer for those who feel lost
and face the night alone. May they sense your embracing presence.
(Prayers of Intercession)

Seek what is missing from your inner household.
(Pray the Prayer of Our Savior.)

(Morning)
Shepherding God, guide me in the ways
of graciousness toward those I meet
before the ending of the day. Thanks be
to Christ. Amen.

(Evening)
May the gift of your peace, O God, fill
my weary spirit as I seek the renewing
rest of night. Thanks be to Christ.
Amen.

TUESDAY, SEPTEMBER 11
(Read Jeremiah 4:11–12)

(Morning)
Companion through the night, I rise today with gratitude for your presence. Guide my thoughts and words this day that they may be full of grace and free from anger.

(Evening)
Companion through the day, if by my careless thoughts and actions I have prevented the good I might have done by wasting your gifts, forgive me.

God, are we, in our ire and divisiveness, undoing your creation? I fear that it is true. It is the strike of a hand or an ugly word spoken by an individual; it is a decision causing deprivation or exclusion by the community that is slowly destroying your people. In what I imagine to be deep sadness for you, how do you see us in these days?

(Morning)
Each day I read the morning news. There is so much destruction and desolation in your world. Of what are your people thinking, O God? Hear my urgent prayers and help my understanding.
(Prayers of Intercession)

(Evening)
It seems I have had only questions tonight. I pray for discernment and guidance for the answers. Help me, strengthening God.
(Prayers of Intercession)

Set aside the anger you hold against someone.
(Pray the Prayer of Our Savior.)

(Morning)
Merciful God, keep me attentive this day to the hurt created by anger. May I not dehumanize anyone by my actions. Thanks be to Christ. Amen.

(Evening)
Embracing God, I am often frightened by the world's chaos and confusion, its attitudes of anger and desperation. Grant me peace for this night and rest, that I may aid the best of tomorrow. Thanks be to Christ. Amen.

WEDNESDAY, SEPTEMBER 12
(Read Jeremiah 4:22–28)

(Morning)
Hospitable God, morning is here, and I rejoice in its possibilities.
A night of peaceful rest has passed, and I give thanks to you.

(Evening)
Hospitable God, as I recall the unexpected glimpses of beauty in this day,
I realize your presence in my life. How grateful I am!

Creator God, I want to understand what is being done for this suffering earth and its people. I am reminded there are those leaders who seek to do justice; nations who take in refugees; organizations who find a way to feed the starving; and people who struggle to save the endangered. O God, give direction to my learning; give vision to my response.

(Morning)
Now the day begins, and I remember there is you, O God,
patiently looking for those of your people who act justly in their lives.
May I this day be one of those whom you seek.
(Prayers of Intercession)

(Evening)
There is hope, for I am reminded that in the wasteland of my life your fruitfulness has emerged, preserving One. You have indeed promised "yet I will not make a full end."
(Prayers of Intercession)

Look to act justly even in the least things.
(Pray the Prayer of Our Savior.)

(Morning)
Purposeful God, help my understanding of the good I might do today, and shield me from foolishness. Thanks be to Christ. Amen.

(Evening)
Ever-present God, stay with me into the night and with those who cry out in anguish or struggle to experience life in wholeness. Thanks be to Christ. Amen.

THURSDAY, SEPTEMBER 13
(Read Psalm 14)

(Morning)
My Protector through the night, I rejoice in your presence
at the beginning of this new day.

(Evening)
My Protector through the day, I reflect upon this day as night closes around me
and I sense the safety of your care, Enveloping Companion.

What is it to do good? Is it more than giving, sharing, and acting in an exterior way on behalf of those in need of physical or spiritual things? God, what of one's interior way, the way of the heart, a profound realization of the restoring goodness of you in us? Doing good is having such wisdom to help restore, to offer safety and refuge for those who are poor in means and spirit.

(Morning)
Often I find myself trying to manage without you, O God, and I become unfocused.
Help me today to order my life through the discernment of your will.
(Prayers of Intercession)

(Evening)
This is a day you have made, O God. I pray I have spent it wisely.
If I have dismissed opportunities to act justly, forgive me.
(Prayers of Intercession.)

Be attentive to another's need.
(Pray the Prayer of Our Savior.)

(Morning)
I awoke this morning rested, renewed, knowing that a life centered in you, eternal One, is one of wholeness. Bless me this day with the wisdom to live in that wholeness. Thanks be to Christ. Amen.

(Evening)
Keep me through this night, protective One. Guard the vulnerable, the poor, those who live on the margins, and those who are at risk. Bless us all. Thanks be to Christ. Amen.

FRIDAY, SEPTEMBER 14
(Read Exodus 32:7–14)

(Morning)
Enduring and nourishing One, bless this day into which I enter.
May I rejoice in its fullness when evening comes.

(Evening)
Enduring and nourishing One, bless this night into which I enter.
May I rise to another day rejoicing in its newness.

O God, I name myself as faithful. But do I grasp who you truly are, or have I made a "useful" and "safe" image in which to believe? I attend to the idols created by human shortsightedness. I forget the mountaintop experiences of your presence in my life. Be patient with me, caring One.

(Morning)
As Moses had the courage to speak to you on behalf of your people Israel,
O God, may I not be too timid to speak up on another's behalf.
(Prayers of Intercession)

(Evening)
I pray for anyone who has been let down by my promises unkept
through mistake or misdeed today.
(Prayers of Intercession)

Recognize the anxiety and impatience in your life.
(Pray the Prayer of Our Savior.)

(Morning)
So often I have sought to listen for a word from you, O God. So often I forget to speak a word to you. I know you will receive my wandering thoughts, even those that are arrogant, doubtful, or foolish. Guide me today with your power to change, listening One. Thanks be to Christ. Amen.

(Evening)
Guardian of my soul, I come to you in the quiet of the evening seeking respite from the day. Give me rest and peace through the night. Thanks be to Christ. Amen.

SATURDAY, SEPTEMBER 15
(Read Psalm 51:1–10)

(Morning)
O God, the stillness of the morning is a gift from you; I am in awe of its beauty.

(Evening)
O God, the hurry of the day is past. Many are in need
of your quieting, calming presence. I, too, wait in gratitude.

Human behavior often alienates us from you, O Author of our being. We contaminate our bodies; we pollute our environment; and we violate one another. We are guilty of many acts that are affronts to you. We have sinned. Reshape and restore us yet again, pardoning One.

(Morning)
As I enter the busyness of today, empowering One, keep me aware
of the importance of joy, truth, and wisdom in my work with others.
(Prayers of Intercession)

(Evening)
"Sin" is such a hard word, gracious God. Surely today I have done things that I
ought not to have done and set aside things that I ought to have done.
Surely tonight I am in need of your cleansing touch.
(Prayers of Intercession)

Release a grudge or regret and seek forgiveness.
(Pray the Prayer of Our Savior.)

(Morning)	(Evening)
With the freshness of this morning, surprising God, create in me a right spirit for new beginnings. Thanks be to Christ. Amen.	Steadfast and loving God, heal me of the pains of today so I might enter sleep this night at peace. Thanks be to Christ. Amen.

SUNDAY, SEPTEMBER 16
(Read 1 Timothy 1:12–17)

(Morning)
Sustaining One, the dawn has revealed the colors of a new day.
May they remind me of the diversity in your creation.

(Evening)
Sustaining One, this sabbath day is over, and I have been filled
with its gifted time. Hear my prayers of thanksgiving.

We human beings are works in process; we journey together, and you, our Creator God, care about what we do. Like Jesus, may we show utmost patience with each other's shortcomings. Like Paul, may our lives be changed so we might share our faith in service to others.

(Morning)
A sabbath day is a reflecting day for me, Most Holy One. I feel joy and sadness as
I think about the health of my relationships with family, friends, and colleagues.
I experience gratitude and regret as I think about the wholeness of my faith.
Help me to see what I must see so I may grow in understanding.
(Prayers of Intercession)

(Evening)
Not everyone has the opportunity to pause a day for rest and renewal.
O God, some must spend every day at work in order to provide for themselves.
May they find sabbath time in other ways.
(Prayers of Intercession)

Reach for a fuller understanding of your faith.
(Pray the Prayer of Our Savior.)

(Morning)
Bless this day with peace and grace, immortal God, for those who labor on behalf of those who rest. Thanks be to Christ. Amen.

(Evening)
This has been a day of tender mercies, gentle God. As the colors of the evening turn to darkness, may your mercies continue as I sleep. Thanks be to Christ. Amen.

MONDAY, SEPTEMBER 17
(Read Jeremiah 8:18–9:1)

(Morning)
Holy God, help me to be open to your word this day
that I might serve you as I am needed.

(Evening)
Holy God, forgive me for the times today when I have failed to be your servant.

Jeremiah has been called the weeping prophet. Much of his prophecy is a lament. These verses are an example of his concern for the people of his day. Holy God, they needed to repent for the sins that they had committed, and strive to get right with you. This is also his call to us. The prophet mourns for those who turn from you, caring God. He cries out, "Is there no balm in Gilead?" The answer for today is yes! The balm is Jesus Christ.

(Morning)
Come into my life, eternal God. Guide me in all that I do this day.
Be with those for whom I pray . . .
(Prayers of Intercession)

(Evening)
Eternal God, at the close of this day, I ask your forgiveness for times when I have failed you. Strengthen me and all those whose names are raised to you in prayer . . .
(Prayers of Intercession)

"Is there no balm in Gilead? Is there no physician there?"
(Pray the Prayer of Our Savior.)

(Morning)
Holy God, help me to be open to your word this day that I might serve you as I am needed. In the name of Jesus. Amen.

(Evening)
Holy God, forgive me for the times today when I have failed to be your servant. In the name of Jesus. Amen.

TUESDAY, SEPTEMBER 18
(Read Psalm 79:1–9)

(Morning)
Open my heart, heavenly Parent, that this day I may be attuned to the needs
of those with whom I come into contact. Grant me the ability to help.

(Evening)
Open my heart, heavenly Parent. As this day comes to a close,
I lay it before you, eternal One. Forgive me for the times when I have fallen short
of doing what you needed me to do.

Like the psalmist, I, too, plead for mercy for Jerusalem; the Holy City had been laid in ruin. Since Israel had a special relationship with you, God, I am sure it was difficult for people to understand why you would permit such destruction to happen. After all, were not the children of Israel your favorite? The cry, "How long, O God?" is a question asked out of anguish. The psalmist could just as well have asked, "How much longer do we have to put up with this?" The answer, of course, is unknown. The children of Israel could only trust that you care and that they will not be forgotten.

(Morning)
God of hope and love, care for all your people this day
and especially for those for whom we pray . . .
(Prayers of Intercession)

(Evening)
We lift up to you, O God, those who need you in some special way . . .
(Prayers of Intercession)

"Help us, O God of our salvation, for the glory of your name; deliver us, and forgive our sins, for your name's sake."

(Morning)
Open my heart, heavenly Parent, that this day I may be attuned to the needs of those with whom I come into contact. Grant me the ability to help. In the name of Jesus. Amen.

(Evening)
Open my heart, heavenly Parent. As this day comes to a close, I lay it before you, eternal One. Forgive me for the times when I have fallen short of doing what you needed me to do. In the name of Jesus. Amen.

WEDNESDAY, SEPTEMBER 19
(Read Amos 8:4–7)

(Morning)
O God, this is a new day! There will be new opportunities to serve you. Grant that all who call upon you might be strengthened to do what you need them to do.

(Evening)
O God, the day is over. Our opportunities to be of service to you have past. Grant me rest this night. I pray I will do better tomorrow.

Today, we often hear folks say, "The more things change, the more they stay the same." These words came to mind reading the lesson from the book of the prophet Amos. Amos was a champion of social justice. He was concerned for the poor and the needy. His message to the "haves" of his day was that they needed to be concerned with the "have-nots." This message continues to be valid, even as we are in the early days of a new millennium. "Let justice roll down like waters, and righteousness like an everflowing stream."

(Morning)
This day, Creator God, help me to see those around me who need my care and concern, especially those whom we lift up to you . . .
(Prayers of Intercession)

(Evening)
We pray, O God, that we will be revitalized by the rest of the night, that on the morrow we might go forward seeking justice for all the oppressed . . .
(Prayers of Intercession)

"This is what God showed me—a basket of summer fruit."

(Morning)
O God, this is a new day! There will be new opportunities to serve you. Grant that all who call upon you might be strengthened to do what you need them to do. In the name of Jesus. Amen.

(Evening)
O God, the day is over. Our opportunities to be of service to you have past. Grant me rest this night. I pray I will do better tomorrow. In the name of Jesus. Amen.

THURSDAY, SEPTEMBER 20
(Read Psalm 113)

(Morning)
God of all people, your name is to be praised above every name. Continue
to care for all of your children as they need you in special ways.

(Evening)
God of all people, in the silence of the night, help us to be mindful that not only are
you a great God who is high above all nations, but One who is near to us all.

All-conquering God, Psalm 113 is really a hymn of praise. It speaks of your
greatness and your nearness to us. When we read this passage with these two
thoughts in mind, we can almost picture early worshipers singing this hymn
with the assurance of their faith that you, their God, live and truly care! This
gives piece of mind and helps to make meeting life a little easier.

(Morning)
We praise your name, O God, and pray that you send your Spirit on us
and all your children, most especially . . .
(Prayers of Intercession)

(Evening)
Because you are the Holy One who created all, we raise our voices to you
at the close of this day, praising you for our lives and for the lives
of your children everywhere. We pray now for your children . . .
(Prayers of Intercession)

"Blessed be the name of God from this time on and forevermore."

(Morning)
God of all people, your name is to be
praised above every name. Continue to
care for all of your children as they need
you in special ways. In the name of
Jesus. Amen.

(Evening)
God of all people, in the silence of the
night, help us to be mindful that not
only are you a great God who is high
above all nations, but One who is near
to us all. In the name of Jesus. Amen.

264

FRIDAY, SEPTEMBER 21
(Read 1 Timothy 2:1–7)

(Morning)
Thank you, eternal Truth, for the night just passed. As this new day dawns, let me
be ever mindful of what you would have me do that will bring souls to you.

(Evening)
Thank you, eternal Truth. I have tried to be faithful to you.
Forgive my shortcomings, and grant me steadfastness in the tomorrows of life.

Timothy was Paul's son in the faith. Paul was his teacher and mentor. His
letters to Timothy were to assist him in his ministry. The words of the text are
Paul's words of instruction about praying. Loving God, the purpose of prayer
is to have the person praying come into a close relationship with you. We pray
through Jesus Christ who is, according to Paul, the one Mediator between you
and humankind. We can be assured that our prayers are heard.

(Morning)
This day, O God, we pray not just for ourselves, but we pray for all people
who need your Spirit working in their lives. Hear us as we pray for . . .
(Prayers of Intercession)

(Evening)
Today, dear God, we have met people who need you in special ways.
We hold them up to you . . .
(Prayers of Intercession)

**"This is right and is acceptable in the sight of God our Savior, who desires
everyone to be saved and to come to the knowledge of the truth."**

(Morning)
Thank you, eternal Truth, for the night
just passed. As this new day dawns, let
me be ever mindful of what you would
have me do that will bring souls to you.
In the name of Jesus. Amen.

(Evening)
Thank you, eternal Truth. I have tried
to be faithful to you. Forgive my
shortcomings, and grant me steadfastness in the tomorrows of life. In the
name of Jesus. Amen.

SATURDAY, SEPTEMBER 22
(Read Luke 16:1–9)

(Morning)
Loving God, a new day has dawned. There is so much to do!
Most of it is busy work. Help me that I might be able
to separate the busy work from what is important for your realm.

(Evening)
Loving God, I hope I acted wisely this day. When I mess up, help me make it right.

Caring God, the manager, while being dishonest, was a smart man. He realized his limitations, and he acted to make the best of a bad situation. And he did! Because he was shrewd in his dealings, he was commended by the owner of the property. This is not an easy parable to understand, except to say that the manager did what he had to do in order to insure his future. We can be received by you, God, by doing what we need to do to be commended by you.

(Morning)
Help us to be alert to ways to glorify you. Save us and all of your children, especially . . .
(Prayers of Intercession)

(Evening)
Only you, God, have the power to save. Save me and those for whom I pray . . .
(Prayers of Intercession)

"So he summoned him and said to him, 'What is this that I hear about you?' "

(Morning)
Loving God, a new day has dawned. There is so much to do! Most of it is busy work. Help me that I might be able to separate the busy work from what is important for your realm. In the name of Jesus. Amen.

(Evening)
Loving God, I hope I acted wisely this day. When I mess up, help me make it right. In the name of Jesus. Amen.

SUNDAY, SEPTEMBER 23
(Read Luke 16:10–13)

(Morning)
O God, help us to choose rightly who we will serve this day.
We need your guidance.

(Evening)
O God, continue to be with us all our days,
even though we do not deserve your care and concern.

God, you demand our all. We need to be one hundred percent honest. Many people try to claim they are your true followers when they are not. They hold back; they do not give their all. We condemn the banker who serves as a church leader but robs from the bank, but many are just like him. We are not what we profess to be. We try to serve two masters. Scripture tells us rather emphatically that we cannot. We serve you, a loving God, but you, the Holy One, require all.

(Morning)
This day, we pray that those for whom we pray may be true to you, O God.
(Prayers of Intercession)

(Evening)
We have all sinned and fallen short of your glory, eternal One.
Cleanse me and all for whom I pray . . .
(Prayers of Intercession)

**"Whoever is faithful in a very little is faithful also in much;
and whoever is dishonest in a very little is dishonest also in much."**

(Morning)
O God, help us to choose rightly who we will serve this day. We need your guidance. In the name of Jesus. Amen.

(Evening)
O God, continue to be with us all our days, even though we do not deserve your care and concern. In the name of Jesus. Amen.

MONDAY, SEPTEMBER 24
(Read 1 Timothy 6:6–19)

(Morning)
Blessed Savior, help me remember that without you, I have nothing.
Help me focus on you so that I may become more like you.

(Evening)
Blessed Savior, thank you for showing me throughout the day how blessed
I truly am. Give me compassion for those who are less fortunate.

It's easy to chase after the riches of this world. Society tells me that without money, a fine home, or fancy cars, I am nothing. Yet the Bible clearly explains that being content with what I have pleases you. You have promised to supply all of my needs. I praise you for all that you have given. Please help me to honor you with a heart of thanksgiving.

(Morning)
Teach me to be content with whatever you give me.
I want to obey and trust your Holy Word.
(Prayers of Intercession)

(Evening)
I always need to depend on you, even when things don't go the way I've planned.
Remind me that you are ultimately in control.
(Prayers of Intercession)

I am so glad that your mercy endures forever.

(Morning)
I am blessed beyond measure. I have a sound mind and a reasonable portion of health and strength. Let me use these gifts to pursue righteousness. In the name of Jesus I pray. Amen.

(Evening)
O God, may my bounty be transformed into gifts for others. May my talents be transformed into tools of service. In the name of Jesus I pray. Amen.

TUESDAY, SEPTEMBER 25
(Read Jeremiah 32:1–3, 6–15)

(Morning)
O God, please let my heart be receptive to your voice.
Don't let me turn away in ignorance from your commands.

(Evening)
O God, speak to me. How well did I obey your voice today?
In what ways can I improve?

Too often I ignore your gentle whisper, Holy Spirit. You call me to pray in the middle of the night, but I roll over because I'm too tired. You encourage me to write a quick note to someone I haven't seen for a while, but I don't because other tasks seem more important. Holy Spirit, I confess that I am not always the best listener. Forgive me and touch me so that I will obey your voice at all times.

(Morning)
Let an attitude of obedience control my actions.
Let a spirit of submission permeate my being.
(Prayers of Intercession)

(Evening)
While I am waiting on you in prayer,
please center my thoughts so that I will not be distracted.
(Prayers of Intercession)

Let this mind be in me, which is also in Christ Jesus.

(Morning)
Please show me today, Jesus, areas in my life that are not fully yielded to you. In the name of Jesus, I pray. Amen.

(Evening)
Ancient of Days, renew my mind. Help me love only you, for you alone are worthy. In the name of Jesus, I pray. Amen.

WEDNESDAY, SEPTEMBER 26
(Read Psalm 91:1–6, 14–16)

(Morning)
Dear God, thank you for your protection and your faithfulness to me.
I praise you because you are God, and there is none other.

(Evening)
Dear God, how wonderful to know you protected me throughout the day
so that I could return home safely.

It's amazing to think that you, the God of the universe, care for me! Always listening and watching, God, you are my refuge and strength in times of trouble. Knowing that you are fully aware of my circumstance brings me peace. You are there to protect me from seen and unseen danger. Jesus has promised never to leave me or forsake me.

(Morning)
There is none like you, and I need never fear since you are my Deliverer.
What a privilege to be hid in the shadow of the Almighty.
(Prayers of Intercession)

(Evening)
Let my love toward others be as generous as you are to me.
(Prayers of Intercession)

I pray for the protection of those whom I love.

(Morning)
I trust you, God, to care for me and others I will see today. I love you. In the name of Jesus I pray. Amen.

(Evening)
I never want to take your faithfulness for granted. Tomorrow is not promised, so let me live each day fully yielded to your call. In the name of Jesus I pray. Amen.

THURSDAY, SEPTEMBER 27
(Read Amos 6:1, 4–7)

(Morning)
Great God, give me wisdom that I might know the things pleasing to you.

(Evening)
Great God, continue to reveal to me areas in my life where I should be more thankful.

At times I am complacent in my relationship with you. It is easy for me not to spend the time with you that I should, or to come to you only when I am in need. I want to change that behavior and to desire you above all else. Give me a passion for devotional time that goes beyond a cursory or superficial exercise. Let an intimacy develop between us. I want to know you.

(Morning)
Please help me not to take for granted all that you have done for me.
(Prayers of Intercession)

(Evening)
Dear God, make me sensitive to the beauty I see in the world that you created.
(Prayers of Intercession)

Restore to me the joy of my salvation, and fill me with your Holy Spirit.

(Morning)
Guide me so that we will have a better relationship. I want to please you and live a life that glorifies you. In the name of Jesus I pray. Amen.

(Evening)
Give me a burning desire to choose you above all else. In the name of Jesus I pray. Amen.

FRIDAY, SEPTEMBER 28
(Read Psalm 146)

(Morning)
O God, you are worthy of all praise. I lift my voice in adoration
for you are holy, righteous, compassionate, and awesome.
Each day is a testimony to both your omnipotence and your omnipresence.

(Evening)
O God, as I come to the end of another day,
bring to mind the sins that distance me from you.

I need to praise you with my heart, my soul, my life. I realize that other human beings can do to me only what you allow. Only you can save me because you are the Creator of all things and you will reign forever. I bow in humble submission before you and will continue to praise you for your mighty acts.

(Morning)
Precious Jesus, I come before you this morning with a willing spirit and a humbled heart. Gird me with your truth so that I might serve you with holy reverence.
(Prayers of Intercession)

(Evening)
Now I pray a prayer of repentance, asking you to forgive me for those sins.
(Prayers of Intercession)

God, I need you.

(Morning)
Thank you for wanting to enter into relationship with me. Your amazing and steadfast love compels me to worship. In the name of Jesus I pray. Amen.

(Evening)
Show me how I can gain victory in the weak areas of my life. Glory be to God. In the name of Jesus I pray. Amen.

SATURDAY, SEPTEMBER 29
(Read Luke 16:19–31)

(Morning)
Wonderful Counselor, help me not be so wrapped up in myself
that I am unable to see another's need.

(Evening)
Wonderful Counselor, bring to mind those who need special prayer at this time.

Never let me forget that my primary goal as a Christian is to lead others to Christ. I don't see myself as an evangelist, but I know that others are watching my life. I may be the only representation of your love that they have. Therefore, show me in your Word how to live my life so that it reflects your holiness. Winning others to you by example and sharing how you have changed my heart may make all the difference in eternity.

(Morning)
Create in me a compassionate spirit so that I will serve others and, in turn, glorify you.
(Prayers of Intercession)

(Evening)
As I approach your throne of grace, give me wisdom to know what I must pray for.
(Prayers of Intercession)

**Place a melody in my heart that I might spend
this moment worshiping you in song.**

(Morning)	(Evening)
Make me a blessing to others. In the name of Jesus I pray. Amen.	Make me an instrument of your peace. In the name of Jesus I pray. Amen.

SUNDAY, SEPTEMBER 30
(Read Psalm 146)

(Morning)
O God, each day you are worthy of all praise.

(Evening)
O God, each evening you are worthy of all praise.

I need to praise you with my heart, my soul, my life. You are the lifter of my head who provides me with all that I have. Like David, I will praise your name forevermore.

(Morning)
Please help me not to take for granted all that you have done for me.
(Prayers of Intercession)

(Evening)
Dear God, make me sensitive to the beauty I see in the world that you created.
(Prayers of Intercession)

I pray for the protection of those whom I love.

(Morning)
I trust you, God, to care for me and others I will see today. I love you. In the name of Jesus I pray. Amen.

(Evening)
I never want to take your faithfulness for granted. Tomorrow is not promised, so let me live each day fully yielded to your call. In the name of Jesus I pray. Amen.

MONDAY, OCTOBER 1
(Read Psalm 137)

(Morning)
Dear God, wherever this day takes me, whatever I experience in lands familiar
or foreign, may I sing with joy songs of praise to your name.

(Evening)
Dear God, let the songs of this day now become a lullaby in this night
as I remember the goodness you sent me this day.

God, geography does not matter, for you are everywhere. You are in my heart.
Whether in Zion or Babylon, all land is your land. Wherever I am, may I live
unto you.

(Morning)
I pray this morning for those who are displaced from their homes.
(Prayers of Intercession)

(Evening)
I pray for those who are unsure where they will lay their heads this night.
(Prayers of Intercession)

**"Even a song sung out of tune, if a sincere song of praise,
is sweet to the ear of God."**

(Morning)
God, as I rise this morning, awaken me
to your holy touch. Bring me to joy and
peace so I may move through this day
in your love. Thanks be to Christ.
Amen.

(Evening)
Calm my spirit with your perfect word
and holy embrace. Good night, sweet
God. Thanks be to Christ. Amen.

TUESDAY, OCTOBER 2
(Read Lamentations 3:19–26)

(Morning)
Dear Elohim, I begin this day by breathing in your holy breath and breathing out stress. Breathing in your holy shalom that passes all understanding, and breathing out bitterness and anger that dwell within me. Let this morning begin anew in your love.

(Evening)
Dear Elohim, in this evening I wait in silence for your sweet and gentle word. It is good to wait in quiet and in thankfulness for this day now becoming night.

Bittersweet, the shrub that grows so prolifically in this season, reminds me on the one hand of the bitterness of grief from loss or even the constant changes that can fill my days. Yet on the other hand it reminds me of your unchanging, everlasting faithfulness. Elohim, you bring me to the sweet potential for new life in each moment.

(Morning)
This morning I place before your compassionate love and mercy so many who feel afflicted by disease, grief, oppression, and violence.
(Prayers of Intercession)

(Evening)
This evening, I give you thanks for the many ways you send your goodness to those in need. I pray again with assurance that you never grow tired of my prayers.
(Prayers of Intercession)

"God is good to those who wait; so good to the seeking soul."
(Sing a stanza of "Great Is Your Faithfulness" or another familiar hymn.)

(Morning)
Place within me your warmth and sunshine that I may share them with all persons I meet this day. Thanks be to Christ. Amen.

(Evening)
I give thanks for how you wrap me in your protective blanket of security. Thanks be to Christ. Amen.

WEDNESDAY, OCTOBER 3
(Read Lamentations 1:1–6)

(Morning)
Dear God, caress my heart with your holy embrace as I walk this new day with
confidence of your divine presence with me in all my experiences.

(Evening)
Dear God, as evening slumber comes upon me, touch my brow
with your holy hand and a gentle kiss of your Spirit.

In truth we are all one in your Spirit. Yet the world creates an illusion of alienation and distance. It leaves me at times feeling fearful and lonely. Remind me
I am neither separate nor alone by bringing me out of myself and into the lives
of all persons I encounter in this day.

(Morning)
There are many around me who are weeping and who are in need
of more comfort than I alone can offer. I lift them to your perfect love.
(Prayers of Intercession)

(Evening)
Where my simple words have fallen short in relieving the affliction of others,
I offer these people to you in your endless wisdom and power, for you
are God most high, yet still you are so close that you feel each beat of our hearts.
(Prayers of Intercession)

"It is my grief that the right hand of the most high has changed."

(Morning)
May I greet this morning with an
adventurous excitement in all that has
been bestowed upon me, and for all you
will place before me in a single day.
Thanks be to Christ. Amen.

(Evening)
I give thanks for one day of life with
you, the Spirit of holy and loving God.
Thanks be to Christ. Amen.

THURSDAY, OCTOBER 4
(Read Psalm 37:1–9)

(Morning)
Everlasting God, let your divine love be a positive force behind all I do this day.

(Evening)
Everlasting God, I hope, in this day now passing, my words
and actions have caused no harm and have been a delight to you.

Ever-present One, help me to rise above all negativity; to live happily by your golden rule. Let me develop insight, calm resolve, and sound judgment in all things.

(Morning)
There are many who feel cast aside. Their lives feel meaningless, devoid of love.
Give them a new vision for their lives as your beloved children.
(Prayers of Intercession)

(Evening)
I give thanks that you pour out your love without ceasing for all creation.
(Prayers of Intercession)

"Be still before God, and wait patiently."

(Morning)
All-seeing God, help me to move among people with your loving eyes. Thanks be to Christ. Amen.

(Evening)
All-seeing God, you know my heart and my intentions. Make me aware of the hurt unknowingly caused. Help me to bring healing tomorrow. Thanks be to Christ. Amen.

FRIDAY, OCTOBER 5
(Read 2 Timothy 1:1–14)

(Morning)
Christ Jesus, fill me with your grace, mercy, and peace as I begin this new day.

(Evening)
Christ Jesus, I hope my actions throughout this day have brought honor
and praise to your holy name.

Many generations of people now past, women and men, youthful and elderly, have nurtured my maturing faith. Help me to seek a way to assist others to grow in faith, to pass on the torchlight that will bring joy to you, caring God.

(Morning)
A suffering world needs a constant reminder that you are always with us.
Help me to be a sign of your presence.
(Prayers of Intercession)

(Evening)
I now focus on your name and form, sweet Jesus,
and feel your warmth and closeness offered to this world, even in a single day.
(Prayers of Intercession)

**"Do not be afraid of testifying to Christ Jesus;
even ready ones need to suffer for the Gospel."**

(Morning)	(Evening)
May this day be a true celebration of rebirth of my life lived through your divine love. Thanks be to Christ. Amen.	I believe I have tried to serve you with a clear conscience. Forgive me where I have fallen short. Thanks be to Christ. Amen.

SATURDAY, OCTOBER 6
(Read Habakkuk 1:1–4; 2:1–4)

(Morning)
All-seeing God, because you are with me, help me to look honestly
at the world this day without fear of what I see.

(Evening)
All-seeing God, thank you for opening my eyes to the needs
of others through this day now ending.

Loving God, help me to be caring; to be as disturbed about the problems and
needs of others as if they were my very own; and to be moved to respond with
actions I would desire for myself.

(Morning)
We pray for all who live in violence. Send your healing and peace.
(Prayers of Intercession)

(Evening)
Send your comfort to your little ones who cry themselves to sleep in fear.
Rescue those who are victimized through misuse of power.
(Prayers of Intercession)

"Let us live by righteousness and faith."

(Morning)
Show me the right way to live. Instill in
me good thoughts, always ready to do
good. Thanks be to Christ. Amen.

(Evening)
Now that my day watch is over, watch
over me this night. Thanks be to Christ.
Amen.

SUNDAY, OCTOBER 7
(Read Luke 17:5–10)

(Morning)
Thank you, Jesus. Keep me faithful as I move through this day.
Let me become your servant.

(Evening)
Thank you, Jesus. I could serve your will in this day now passing.

Loving and Holy Spirit, help me to move closer to you, to spend my time living in your light, to employ your love, to do your work in the life of every person I meet on this and every day.

(Morning)
I pray the world will open ever so much more, even in this day, to your incredible power.
(Prayers of Intercession)

(Evening)
Thank you that every breath of God is a breath of love.
"Breathe on me, Breath of God." Open all people to your Holy Breath.
(Prayers of Intercession)

"Increase my faith daily."

(Morning)	(Evening)
Help me to do all I can today to continue the work Jesus began many years ago. Thanks be to Christ. Amen.	I hope I have invested well in this day all my God-given talents and energies. Tomorrow, help me to increase in your will. Thanks be to Christ. Amen.

MONDAY, OCTOBER 8
(Read Psalm 66:1–12)

(Morning)
Provident God, I greet this day singing the glory of your name,
for you have kept me among the living through yet another night.

(Evening)
Provident God, I welcome this evening, having been tested throughout the day.
I have been tried as silver is tried in the purifying flame of your crucible.

Intimate Friend, for many years of my life I exalted myself in rebellion against you. I pointed to the many burdens people carry, their trials through fire and water, and their oppression by others as proof that you did not exist; or if you existed, that you did not care for us. Yet you never promised freedom from struggle. What you steadfastly promise is to share our burdens; to walk with us through flames and flood; and to give us strength to answer oppression with the power of your love. Forgive my judgment of your ways, and gather me into ever-deepening intimacy with you.

(Morning)
Ever-present God, speak through me this day that I may witness
to your deeds in the lives of those whom I encounter.
(Prayers of Intercession)

(Evening)
Ever-present God, through me you have offered a spacious place for many to lay
their concerns at your feet. I now offer these concerns to you in
trust that something good will be created through the power of your Holy Spirit.
(Prayers of Intercession)

"Come and see what God has done."

(Morning)
Guiding Spirit, order my steps and govern my tongue that I may walk faithfully with those who seek you. Empower me to listen to you and to them, and permit me to know how you would have me respond. In the name of the Giver of peace. Amen.

(Evening)
Guiding Spirit, I gratefully accept your gift of rest, putting behind me the mixed record of today and fearing not the blank slate of tomorrow. In this moment, I am yours completely. In the name of the Giver of peace. Amen.

TUESDAY, OCTOBER 9
(Read Jeremiah 29:1, 4–7)

(Morning)
Brooding Spirit, I awaken this day giving thanks that in you,
I have my citizenship, no matter where I live.

(Evening)
Brooding Spirit, I return to my hearth this evening thankful for the ways
in which you have been present to my communities of family, church,
friends, and neighbors, both familiar and new.

Guiding Shepherd, I am no stranger to exile. Through my own choices and through ostracism by others, I have found myself an outcast in an alien land. In those days, I have sometimes forgotten your presence. In those days, I have refused to make a life for myself that would be pleasing to you, preferring instead to rage against the unfairness of my condition. Forgive me for ignoring your gift of life just because it was not the life I would have chosen for myself. Teach me again to live in the world where I am and, by your grace, to live abundantly in this moment.

(Morning)
Redeeming God, help me to pray and to work for the welfare
of my community and all who live in it this day.
(Prayers of Intercession)

(Evening)
Redeeming God, today you have shown me some persons, situations, and relationships
that are broken and in need of healing. Receive now the prayers of my heart.
(Prayers of Intercession)

Bloom where you are planted.

(Morning)	(Evening)
Guiding Spirit, lead me by the hand throughout this day's journey that I may be a living reminder of Christ to my community. Speak through my voice, work through my hands, and love through my heart to spread the news of your constant presence. In the name of the Giver of peace. Amen.	Guiding Spirit, I could not do all that needed to be done today. I pray I did what I could as faithfully as I could and as you so empowered me. I now release this day to you and your care as I release myself. In the name of the Giver of peace. Amen.

WEDNESDAY, OCTOBER 10
(Read 2 Kings 5:1–3, 7–15)

(Morning)
Compassionate Friend, I greet this day counting my blessings,
for you have entrusted me with responsibilities to discharge in your name.

(Evening)
Compassionate Friend, I bid farewell to this day giving you thanks, for you have
multiplied its blessings even in the midst of absurdity and smallness.
Through your binding of my wounds, you have healed others.

Teacher of patience, like Naaman and Paul, I carry a thorn in my side. Year after
year, I try to overcome it through the force of my will. Then when I surrender my
condition to you, I expect to hear trumpets blow and see lights fill the sky—thinking you will surely remove this thorn in dramatic fashion. Instead, you give me
simple instructions. Go. Wash. Confess. Pray. Ask. Repeat the process. How I resist the simple footwork that living your way requires! Forgive me, God. Open me
to hear your voice, guiding me in the way to healing and wholeness.

(Morning)
Spirit of community, place on my heart this day those
who need to hear a word of hope for healing.
Help me to remember when I reach out to someone else, I open myself to healing.
(Prayers of Intercession)

(Evening)
Spirit of community, you have placed on my heart this evening those whom I have
encountered in their search for wholeness. As you have called me—not in spite of, but
because of, the thorn in my side—so I have tried to minister to your beloved children.
(Prayers of Intercession)

In surrendering to God, you will find healing.

(Morning)
God, grant that I may be an instrument of
your peace this day; an agent of your
healing; a witness to your love. Walk
with me into the hours ahead, and be my
Spiritual Director. In the name of the
Giver of peace. Amen.

(Evening)
God, my earthly temple grows weary,
and I am in need of rest. Grant me your
peace this night, your healing, and your
love. Rest me tonight that I may
awaken tomorrow ready to go out
again, carrying your message of healing
and wholeness. In the name of the
Giver of peace. Amen.

THURSDAY, OCTOBER 11
(Read Psalm 111)

(Morning)
Wonderful God, gracious God, merciful God, I rise up this morning giving
you thanks with my whole heart, for your works delight me.

(Evening)
Wonderful God, gracious God, merciful God, I lie down this evening giving
you thanks with my whole heart, for your works delight me.
As you rested at the end of your creative works, so I welcome your gift of rest.

Holy, awesome God, by you all desires are known, and from you no secrets are
hidden. You know, therefore, how in my secret heart I desire wisdom. I wish to
become a person of consideration, not given to hasty judgments or precipitous
decisions. You know how I have strived for wisdom, thinking its key lay in the right
books, the right teachings, and the right human philosophies. Call me back, O true
Wisdom. Call me back to awe of you and your ways, for that is the beginning of
wisdom. If I would be wise, then show me how to be faithful and just. If I would
live wisely, then teach me to live trustworthily and uprightly. And if I would witness to your wisdom, then direct me to direct others to awe of you.

(Morning)
Faithful God, you work with power in the lives of your people. I now lift these
your children in prayer that they may recognize you at work and give you praise.
(Prayers of Intercession)

(Evening)
Faithful God, it seems there is no end to what needs to be done for us,
your people. As you are ever mindful of your covenant, keep me faithful
to my covenant of ministry, leaving the outcome to you.
(Prayers of Intercession)

Wisdom is a gift gained through practice.

(Morning)
Powerful God, I enter into this day with
my whole heart. Grant me the ability to
recognize and study your delightful
works, in the persons, places, and
events I encounter. In the name of the
Giver of peace. Amen.

(Evening)
Powerful God, as I leave this day behind, I
pray I might have left my mark upon it in
some way for your glory. This was just one
day, but you have established your
precepts forever. In confidence in your
truth, I give myself to you for safekeeping.
In the name of the Giver of peace. Amen.

FRIDAY, OCTOBER 12
(Read 2 Timothy 2:8–15)

(Morning)
God of creative work, I greet this day thankful for the work you have called me to do. Your Word of truth is ever before me, beckoning me to be its witness.

(Evening)
God of creative rest, I greet this night thankful for the work that you placed in my path today. Some of it was known ahead of time; some of it was a surprise. In everything, you were with me, and your truth bore me up.

O Word of Word, you dispersed our understanding at the tower of Babel and brought it together again on the day of Pentecost. Yet it seems we have not sufficiently learned of your power of truth. Even today we drown out your Word with our own quarrels of words. How have I contributed to division and separation when you desire harmony and unity? Search me, O God, and know my most secret pride of intellect and worldly wisdom. Lead me back to being the servant leader you called me to be. Heal me that I may unashamedly become what you intend. Inspire me that I may unapologetically declare your Word.

(Morning)
Uniting God, there are divisions and estrangements among your children. Press your healing touch upon the persons, events, and situations that I now lift to you.
(Prayers of Intercession)

(Evening)
Uniting God, looking back on this day, I see where you were present
in the midst of separation and estrangement.
I pray my thanks for your words of healing and for the unity that is yet to come.
(Prayers of Intercession)

As I am a worker for truth, so I am approved by God.

(Morning)
Father/Mother God, as I step into the day's tasks, the words of many will assail me. Keep me close to your truth. May the words of my mouth and the meditations of my heart be acceptable to you and liberating for your children. In the name of the Giver of peace. Amen.

(Evening)
Mother/Father God, as I loose my hold on the day's tasks, I pray to be released from the many voices that demand my attention. Speak to my dreams with your word alone; a word of truth, of peace, and of rest well earned. In the name of the Giver of peace. Amen.

SATURDAY, OCTOBER 13
(Read Luke 17:11–14)

(Morning)
Revealing God, I awaken this morning with thanks in my heart and on my lips.
I embrace your gifts of the morning—the sunlight, the new day,
the treasure of your Word made flesh.

(Evening)
Revealing God, it has been a long day. I return home to you with a heart full
of the ways in which you have shown mercy to your children.
Thank you, Jesus, that you can cross all distances.

Merciful God, like the people with leprosy, I have walked in that region "between."
I am not quite cast out from my faith in you; but neither am I quite at home with
you. So often have I asked for your mercy while keeping my distance. Am I so
blemished, so unclean, that I fear to place myself boldly in your presence? And yet
you see me as I am and accept me. Moreover, you heal me; then you return me to
the community of those who once thought me unfit. And in this mighty work of
your grace and forgiveness, I am made clean. You have healed me, merciful Christ;
and now you call me to direct others to your powerful, accepting love.

(Morning)
Cleansing Christ, I contemplate the day ahead, aware of some whose burdens
of past or present keep them at a distance from you.
I place them in your presence now, through my prayers.
(Prayers of Intercession)

(Evening)
Cleansing Christ, I reflect upon the day just ended, aware of many
who have not heard or cannot believe that your mercy and grace are meant for them.
Remember with me these your brothers and sisters . . .
(Prayers of Intercession)

By the grace of God in Christ, I am cleansed.

(Morning)
Empowering God, by your love you
make all things new. Help me to bridge
the distance for those in need of your
mercy this day, that they may be
restored to acceptance and community.
In the name of the Giver of peace.
Amen.

(Evening)
Empowering God, I approach my rest with
a grateful heart. I am used up for now.
Take me into your bosom; close my eyes
to the helter-skelter of the world and my
ears to its din. Make me new by your love,
that I may awaken and arise to a new day.
In the name of the Giver of peace. Amen.

SUNDAY, OCTOBER 14
(Read Luke 17:15–19)

(Morning)
Healing God, I greet this day thankful that you have kept me safely through the
night. Hear the praise I lift to you and my joy that in you, I am well.

(Evening)
Healing God, I greet this night thankful that you have guided me safely through the day.
Hear the praise I lift to you and my joy that in coming to the end, I am still with you.

Compassionate Friend, there have been times when I have responded to your
healing the way the nine lepers did. In my haste to show myself to the "priests,"
the individuals or institutions whose approval I desire, I have forgotten to say,
"Thank you." But I also know what it is to be the tenth leper. After giving up
hope of ever being healed, I have been made clean by you. And with no expectation of anyone's approval, I have lain at your feet and given you thanks pri-
vately. Call me always to the humility of the tenth leper. Keep my gratitude
ever before me that I may always remember the true Source of my healing.

(Morning)
Healing Christ, you show your cleansing power in the lives of all who will receive it
in faith. I lift to you now, in faith, the names of these brothers and sisters . . .
(Prayers of Intercession)

(Evening)
Healing Christ, you have shown me your cleansing power in the lives of many
today. Thank you for their faith that opened them to receiving your healing touch.
Thank you for the blessing of witnessing these miracles.
(Prayers of Intercession)

Let my posture be one of gratitude.

(Morning)
Intimate Friend, walk with me into the
day ahead. May I remember to turn back
and praise you for your mighty works of
love and grace. In the name of the Giver
of peace. Amen.

(Evening)
Intimate Friend, carry me into the night
ahead. I commend myself to your
safekeeping, giving you thanks for your
love and grace. In the name of the
Giver of peace. Amen.

MONDAY, OCTOBER 15
(Read Psalm 119:97–104)

(Morning)
God of all life, you have called me into a direct and living relationship with you.
As I begin this day, I pray you will go ahead of me
into each new experience to prepare the next place for me.

(Evening)
God of all life, your living presence has surrounded me this day, even when
I forgot or did not feel it. Now as I prepare for sleep, enfold me in your love;
breathe into me your breath of life and peace.

Great Shepherd, your love is my living law and a lamp for my feet. You have
called me directly into your presence, and your living Word is spoken directly
into my heart. As I rest and quiet myself, let me hear, feel, understand what
you are saying to me and showing me. And even when I cannot clearly sense
your presence and guidance, let me rest in the knowledge of your love and
trust that new clarity and understanding will come to me.

(Morning)
As I prepare to pray for the needs of others, let me inwardly see them enfolded
in your loving, healing light, you who have come through the Healer, Jesus Christ.
(Prayers of Intercession)

(Evening)
I release those for whom I pray trustfully into your hands,
for your care and love for them are far greater than mine.
(Prayers of Intercession)

Lead me beyond words and ideas directly into your presence.

(Morning)
When I feel confused, help me to pause
and wait for your inner guiding love. In
the Savior's name. Amen.

(Evening)
Eternal, unsleeping Love, into your
hands I commit my body and spirit. In
the Savior's name. Amen.

TUESDAY, OCTOBER 16
(Read Jeremiah 31:27–34)

(Morning)
God of love, when I wake to this new day, I wake also to a new covenant with you,
a new way of loving, a new way of living with you as the center of my heart.
You are my great central sun, shining within all that I am and do.

(Evening)
God of love, sometimes I have forgotten my new freedom today,
and I have fallen into old traps and prisons of the spirit.
Though often I have forgotten you, you never have forgotten me.

You, who shine on me through the face of Jesus Christ, this very day you take me by the hand to lead me out of my inner prisons. You have opened your heart to me, and you call me to open my heart to you. You have put your arms around my mistakes and failures, and at this very moment your deep, radical love transforms me.

(Morning)
May all those for whom I pray and all whom I will meet this day be healed
and released from their past pain and inner prisons.
(Prayers of Intercession)

(Evening)
Each day, may I become more released into your life than the day before,
and may those for whom I pray be released more deeply into your love.
(Prayers of Intercession)

Liberating God, when we bond with you, we are released from all bondage.

(Morning)	(Evening)
May each moment of this day be transformed and glorified by your radiance. In the Savior's name. Amen.	As I move into the depth and darkness of sleep, your shining love wraps me in radiance. In the Savior's name. Amen.

THE BOOK OF DAILY PRAYER

2002 order form

CONTACT YOUR LOCAL BOOKSTORE

or call 1-800-537-3394 (9:00 a.m. to 4:30 p.m. ET)

or complete this order form and fax it to 216-736-3713

or mail to: United Church Press
230 Sheldon Road
Berea OH 44017

Date _____

SHIP TO (if different from Bill to):

Name _____

Street Address or P.O. Box _____

City_____ State _____ Zip _____

Phone _____

BILL TO:

Name _____

Street Address or P.O. Box _____

City_____ State _____ Zip _____

Phone _____

TITLE	QTY.	PRICE	TOTAL
The Book of Daily Prayer, 2002	_____	12.95	_____

SUBTOTAL _____

ADD SHIPPING AND HANDLING* _____

TOTAL _____

*Shipping and handling charges: $3.50 for first book, $0.50 for each additional book

Please charge to my credit card: ❏ Visa ❏ MasterCard

Account # _____ Exp. date_____

Signature_____ Daytime phone _____

Prices are subject to change without notice.

CODE BBK02

WEDNESDAY, OCTOBER 17
(Read Genesis 32:22–31)

(Morning)
Faithful God, today there will be difficulties, anxieties, challenges to face.
Help me to discover your angel, your own living presence,
coming to meet and strengthen me in every conflict.

(Evening)
Faithful God, even as your people so long ago were led out of captivity by your
mighty presence, so you have led me this day and will lead me through the night by
the strong light of Jesus Christ within me.

Living God, I am so often in inner conflict; so often I mistrust and resist love, seeing a threat instead of a gift. So often I strive against your presence, resisting your help, release, and empowerment. So often I meet my angel as my enemy, seeing only the painful shadow and not the glowing presence. Thus I exhaust and hurt myself. But you have never abandoned me. You hold me close during my night of inner wars. May I recognize your offered blessing and receive your gift of healing of my self-inflicted pain.

(Morning)
May those for whom I pray feel now the majesty, faithfulness, and tenderness
of your presence, even in the midst of their conflict, fear, and pain.
(Prayers of Intercession)

(Evening)
All that we suffer, all that we feel, you have shared with us.
In all our inner striving and wrestling, you are there to offer your blessing.
(Prayers of Intercession)

**"If I take the wings of the morning and settle at the farthest limits of the
sea, even there . . . your right hand shall hold me fast."**

(Morning)	(Evening)
Through the challenges of this day, may I receive your blessing and bring it to others. In the Savior's name. Amen.	Beloved God, you have embraced my hurts, pain, and resistance. Your blessing fills me. In the Savior's name. Amen.

THURSDAY, OCTOBER 18
(Read Psalm 121)

(Morning)
God, let my first thought this morning be the thought of you,
the central light of my life. Nothing can overwhelm me.
You are my Source, my Shelter, my Strength, my Sustenance.

(Evening)
God, as a full circle joins the end and the beginning, so the end of this day joins
with its beginning, within your heart. As I breathed your breath of morning with all
its challenge, so now I breathe your breath of evening with all its peace.

So often I have forgotten, unsleeping Love, the mighty strength with which
you surround and fill us. We need no lesser strength or source. You are the
ultimate mystery. There is so much we cannot understand. But this we know,
this we are told, the central life of all creation is your heart, which holds us
forever. When we enter into communion with your heart, then our choices, our
actions, our powers and gifts are blessed, guided, and transformed.

(Morning)
May the fears and doubts of those for whom I pray be healed,
melted by your strong and limitless mercy.
(Prayers of Intercession)

(Evening)
As those for whom I pray face the night, help them to sleep in trust,
knowing that you keep them tenderly through the night.
(Prayers of Intercession)

Living Christ, strong Vine of life, help me abide in you as your fruitful branch.

(Morning)
Let my feet be moved only by your
guidance. When I go out, prepare the
way for me. When I return, welcome and
restore me, through Jesus the Shepherd.
In the Savior's name. Amen.

(Evening)
Light of all light, you are more merciful than the sun by day and gentler than
the moon by night. In the Savior's
name. Amen.

FRIDAY, OCTOBER 19
(Read 2 Timothy 3:14–17)

(Morning)
Infinite Mercy, this day I take your offered hand, leading me
into wholeness and completeness and a life drenched in love.
I turn to your living Word, shining on me through Scripture and in the faces
and memories of those who have loved, helped, and guided me in your way.

(Evening)
Infinite Mercy, though so often I am fragmented, not aware
of the wholeness you offer me, I know you believe in it for me and see it in me.
As I enter into sleep, I rest on your tender faith in me.

Not what we learn, but of whom we learn is our Source of life, living Christ.
You have become for us the living Word, the spirit of the Scripture unfolding
in our hearts. When bonded to you, when abiding in you, living Vine, we are
transformed and made complete. Your expanding life in us equips us for a life
of truth, strength, and love. Unfold for me today new light and meaning from
your eternal Word.

(Morning)
I think of those who did not know of your love in childhood and were not taught of your
light and guidance. May special help be given them and loving guides sent them.
(Prayers of Intercession)

(Evening)
Come personally, living Christ, to those for whom I pray. Help all of us
to know that it is not a principle but a person who is our Spring of life.
(Prayers of Intercession)

Living Christ, with you our there is here.

(Morning)
Keep my faith steadfast this day, and
keep me centered in Jesus the Christ. In
the Savior's name. Amen.

(Evening)
Living Christ, breathe on me the healing
of your peace and fire of your spirit. In
the Savior's name. Amen.

SATURDAY, OCTOBER 20
(Read 2 Timothy 4:1–5)

(Morning)
Beloved God, let your Holy Spirit awaken within me. This day, sometimes there will be need to witness to your love and truth: through words, compassionate silence, action, joy, and laughter, and through a look or touch of healing love.

(Evening)
Beloved God, there were times today when I was absent in spirit, but you were always present. Gather up my absences, my dimness, my flickering flame into your hands and heart, and let them be transformed into new, empowered life.

It is not always easy, living God, to be aflame with your love when we so often feel surrounded by the indifference, doubt, and resistance of others. May the sense of your glowing presence waken me when I spiritually sleep, enflame me when I am dim and cold, strengthen me where I am weakest, heal me where I am wounded, and restore me when I am fragmented. Protect me when I feel challenged, and above all, empower me with your fire of love.

(Morning)
So many feel their faith and hope crushed or chilled. Lead them into new hope, strength, and freedom, so they do not fall back into spiritual captivity.
(Prayers of Intercession)

(Evening)
I pray for everyone who longs to know his or her special gifts and calling, and for the joyful strength to fulfill them.
(Prayers of Intercession)

Help me to build my inner altar, so your flame may descend upon it.

(Morning)
This day may I see and understand and fulfill the special ministry to which you call me. In the Savior's name. Amen.

(Evening)
Even in sleep I am in the presence of God and Jesus Christ. Blessed be God! In the Savior's name. Amen.

SUNDAY, OCTOBER 21
(Read Luke 18:1–8)

(Morning)
Faithful God, there will be times today when I do not feel your nearness,
when my prayers seem unanswered. At these times, help me to know that
your love is forever with me and that you heard me before I even spoke to you.

(Evening)
Faithful God, often today I have been like a locked and shuttered house,
closed to your loving light poured upon me. Often you knocked, and I did not
hear you or open my door. As I sleep, open the deep, closed places of my heart.

When I experience the delay of my hopes, when prayer seems unanswered,
when justice seems withheld, help me to trust in your unsleeping love and
justice, God of my life. You have told us that you have heard us before we cry
to you. Eternal Mercy, we do not need to plead with you. Eternal Wisdom, we
do not need to inform you. Your longing to give is far greater than our longing
to receive. The clouds that seem to block your love are not of your making.
From everlasting to everlasting, you are faithful. Enlarge me so that I may
receive all that you long to give me.

(Morning)
May those who feel unloved and unheard find some sign today
that you have been with them forever.
(Prayers of Intercession)

(Evening)
May those for whom I pray be led to you, where all answers are.
Your presence is our answer, our way, truth, and life.
(Prayers of Intercession)

"We love because God first loved us."

(Morning)
As I awaken to this day, may I open all
the cells of my body and the choices of
my heart to your love, which seeks and
guides me. In the Savior's name. Amen.

(Evening)
Even as you welcomed me into
morning, you welcome me into sleep.
But my deep spirit is forever awake,
dancing in your joy. In the Savior's
name. Amen.

MONDAY, OCTOBER 22
(Read Luke 18:9–14)

(Morning)
Dear God, be merciful to me, a sinner. Teach me to pray as you would have me
pray. Teach me to live this day as you would have me live.

(Evening)
Dear God, sometimes I feel like a failure. Help me realize, just because I have
failed, I am not a failure. Grant me your forgiveness, new life, healing, and peace.

Creator God, praying and living "right" are not about fasting, tithing, or praying in public. And "right" praying and living are not reserved only for "holy"
people. Years after spending time with Thomas Merton at the Abbey of
Gethsemani, Frank Tuoti says he wrote the book *Why Not Be a Mystic?* in
order to "make the case that the gift of a contemplative spirituality and the
mystical life is open to all who would seek and desire it—a desire motivated
not by self-serving interests (for our 'self-improvement' or to be able one day
to think of ourselves as 'mystics,' God forbid!) but a response to the first pre-
cept to love God with our entire being and others as ourselves."

(Morning)
Light of the world, may the brightness and warmth of your love shine
on those people and places in need that I now visualize in my mind.
(Prayers of Intercession)

(Evening)
Loving God, my failures remind me of the many ways we human beings fail
to create the kind of world you intend. Let your healing and new life be felt
in the places of suffering highlighted in our evening news.
(Prayers of Intercession)

"The disciples said to him, 'Teach us to pray.'"

(Morning)
God, in your infinite mercy, enable me to
do and be whatever you will for me to do
and be, this day. In Christ I pray. Amen.

(Evening)
Gracious God, have mercy. Help me to
let go of the cares and disappointments of
this day and to resolve, with your help, to
know, love, and serve you more faithfully
tomorrow. In Christ I pray. Amen.

TUESDAY, OCTOBER 23
(Read Psalm 84:1–7)

(Morning)
Ever-present God, today at every moment, give me the joy of being aware
that I am in your house; that I am in your very presence.

(Evening)
Ever-present God from whom all blessings flow, help me now
to remember the many ways I experienced your blessings this day.

God, to really praise you, C. S. Lewis says in *Reflections on the Psalms*, "We must suppose ourselves to be in perfect love with you—drunk with, drowned in, dissolved by, that delight which, far from remaining pent up within ourselves as incommunicable, hence hardly tolerable, bliss, flows out from us incessantly again in effortless and perfect expression, our joy no more separable from the praise in which it liberates and utters itself than the brightness a mirror receives is separable from the brightness it sheds."

(Morning)
Generous God, this day, give me the ability to live with joy; to express appreciation
to those I encounter; to enjoy the simple pleasures of food and laughter;
and to see your beauty in people around me for whom I now pray.
(Prayers of Intercession)

(Evening)
Thank you, merciful God, for loving the persons I encountered today as well as
those whose names I do not know. I place them in the circle of your grace.
(Prayers of Intercession)

"Their life shall become like a watered garden."

(Morning)	(Evening)
Glorious God, help me today to glorify you and to enjoy you at every moment. In Christ I pray. Amen.	Happy are those whose strength is in you. In Christ I pray. Amen.

WEDNESDAY, OCTOBER 24
(Read Psalm 65:1–5)

(Morning)
O God, keep my focus on you today. You are the One who answers prayer;
you are the One who forgives our human failings;
you are the One who delivers us when we most need it and least deserve it.

(Evening)
O God, sometimes I forgot to notice, but you were there.
Sometimes we act as if it's only up to us, but you are really in charge.

The entire universe serves as a container for you, comforting God. You are here, and you are there. God, you are within and around. You are the sea in which we swim, the air we breathe, the reality in which we live. Every person, thing, or idea can speak to us of you, and is a message from you. We only have to pay attention. God, you are the energy for life and goodness and love. You are the One who is.

(Morning)
Strong Deliverer, you are the hope of all the ends of the earth and
of the farthest seas. Give hope to the hopeless in our hospitals and shelters,
in places of starvation and violence. Deliver us all from evil.
(Prayers of Intercession)

(Evening)
Into your hands I place all the cares and concerns of the day.
They are already in your hands anyway. I forgot once again.
(Prayers of Intercession)

"Where can I go from your spirit? Or where can I flee from your presence?"

(Morning)
Help me to grow in my awareness of
your constant presence. In Christ I pray.
Amen.

(Evening)
You give and give and give again.
Thanks be to you, O God. In Christ I
pray. Amen.

THURSDAY, OCTOBER 25
(Read Psalm 65:6–13)

(Morning)
Good morning, God! What a wonderful time of day, when all is fresh
and new again, when birds sing and colors delight.
Remind me throughout the day of the wonders of your creation.

(Evening)
Good evening, God! Have I said thanks often enough today?
Have I said thanks to you for the abundance of your creation?
Have I said thanks to those around me for the kindnesses they have shown me?

God, did you give your children the gift of five senses so we could give thanks
for the joys of nature? C. S. Lewis, in *Letters to Malcolm*, writes, "And but for
our body one whole realm of God's glory—all that we receive through the
senses—would go unpraised. For the beasts can't appreciate it and the angels
are, I suppose, pure intelligences. They understand colors and tastes better
than our greatest scientists; but have they retinas or palates? I fancy the 'beau-
ties of nature' are a secret God has shared with us alone. That may be one of
the reasons why we were made—and why the resurrection of the body is an
important doctrine."

(Morning)
You water the earth and bless its growth, Creator God.
Water now those places and people who thirst for justice.
(Prayers of Intercession)

(Evening)
Thank you, God, for all the people who this day cared gently for your earth,
those who tended gardens as well as those who worked to save the rain forests.
(Prayers of Intercession)

"O taste and see that God is good."

(Morning)
You give us all we need for life and
love. I offer you today all that I think
and say and do. May it be pleasing to
you. In Christ I pray. Amen.

(Evening)
You give us far more than is needed for
life and love. Teach us to share so all
may have enough to live. In Christ I
pray. Amen.

FRIDAY, OCTOBER 26
(Read Jeremiah 14:7–10, 19–22)

(Morning)
Almighty God, keep me mindful of the times I cause someone pain
and of the ways we human beings hurt one another.

(Evening)
Almighty God, I am very sorry for having offended you today.
I regret all the things I have done that I should not have done,
and all the things I failed to do that you would have had me do.

God, like the people in Jeremiah's day, we confess the many occasions when
we have strayed from the ways of goodness and love that you have set before
us. We reap what we sow. We live in the midst of hunger and fear, prejudice
and hate. All-encompassing God, we wish you would just wave a magic wand
and make it all good once again. Stay with the confession for now. Don't move
too quickly to what Bonhoeffer would call "cheap grace."

(Morning)
Wound me today with the suffering of the world.
Fold into your ever-loving arms all the pain of the world, dear God.
(Prayers of Intercession)

(Evening)
Thank you, God, for opening my eyes just a little today. Hear now my prayers for
forgiveness. And hear my prayers for the pain of the world that I have witnessed.
(Prayers of Intercession)

**"They have treated the wound of my people carelessly, saying,
'Peace, peace,' when there is no peace."**

(Morning)
Keep me sensitive to pain today, the pain
that I cause and the pain that I do not
alleviate. In Christ I pray. Amen.

(Evening)
We set our hope on you, O God, for
without you we can do nothing. In
Christ I pray. Amen.

SATURDAY, OCTOBER 27
(Read 2 Timothy 4:6–8, 16–18)

(Morning)
God, some days, life seems too hard to endure.
If this is true for me today, give me a sign that you are with me.
If this is true for others, help me to be a sign of the power of your love to them.

(Evening)
God, we made it through another day.
Take all that has happened today, and use it to your purposes.

This letter to Timothy appears to have been written from prison. Paul interprets his impending death by execution as an offering like a cultic drink; likens his life of faith to an athletic contest; and suggests that even though no one came to his defense at his first trial, he was rescued from death by you. Now, after his second trial, by his own example of endurance in the face of suffering, he hopes to encourage Timothy, and through him all Christians, to similar endurance. God, he expects you to triumph in the end. May we be strengthened in our faith to endure any suffering of our own, and may we help to spread this faith to others.

(Morning)
God, give courage to those who face terrible adversity today. Empower all those who seek to embody your love and forgiveness. Be with refugees and those who minister with them. Welcome new immigrants, and open our hearts to embrace them.
(Prayers of Intercession)

(Evening)
Almighty God, help me to know that your ways may be different from mine.
Help me to pray, for myself and for others, "your will be done."
(Prayers of Intercession)

"For God did not give us a spirit of cowardice, but rather a spirit of power and of love and of self-discipline."

(Morning)
Make me a peacemaker today, O God.
Give me the self-discipline to seek the peaceful way. In Christ I pray. Amen.

(Evening)
Help me to seek the things of lasting value. In Christ I pray. Amen.

SUNDAY, OCTOBER 28
(Read Joel 2:23– 32)

(Morning)
God, this is the day you have made; let us rejoice and be glad in it!

(Evening)
God, you give us all that is needed for life and love. Praise be to you!

"The glory of God," wrote Irenaeus in the second century, "is the human being fully alive!" Flannery O'Connor wrote, eighteen centuries later, "Saints are super-alive people." Loving God, perhaps those whom we call "saints" are those in whom your Spirit is most obviously and visibly present. One day your Spirit will enliven everyone so that all will be "fully alive." Your Spirit will be poured out on all people, irrespective of social status, age, gender, or class (and, quite likely, although this passage doesn't mention it, irrespective of sexual orientation as well). And then we will dream dreams and see visions that will enable your will to become reality on this earth as it is in heaven!

(Morning)
Joy, joy, joy! Wondrous God, may your joy infect my life today
and the lives of those for whom I pray.
(Prayers of Intercession)

(Evening)
Rain to make the flowers grow, food for body and soul, friends and meaningful work to do, for all of this and so much more, make me and those for whom I pray grateful.
(Prayers of Intercession)

"Do you not know that you are God's temple and that God's Spirit dwells in you?"

(Morning)
This day, O God, help me to know you more clearly, love you more dearly, and follow you nearly. In Christ I pray. Amen.

(Evening)
For rest and for worship, for renewal and for inspiration, great God, I give thanks. In Christ I pray. Amen.

MONDAY, OCTOBER 29
(Read Luke 19:1–10)

(Morning)
Seeker and Savior of the lost, I seek your face this morning,
secure in the knowledge that you love me in spite of my shortcomings.

(Evening)
Seeker and Savior of the lost, I thank you for saving me
and welcoming me into your family.

Dear God, I am not so wealthy or so confident in myself that I do not realize I need you. The crowd is not so large that I cannot see you, and I will not be so busy that I cannot hear you calling my name. I will not stray so far away from you that I cannot find my way back to your loving arms. I am happy to welcome you into my heart and my home to dwell forever. Thank you for leaving the door open and the lights on to receive me. I know that you will never leave me or forsake me.

(Morning)
God, give me strength to run the longest race
and climb the highest tree for you today.
(Prayers of Intercession)

(Evening)
Dear Savior, thank you for the strength you continually give me to complete my course.
(Prayers of Intercession)

Is God welcome to dwell in your house today?

(Morning)
My God, it is in you that I live, move, and have my being. Help me stay focused on you today. In Jesus' name I pray. Amen.

(Evening)
What a mighty God you are! You are great and greatly to be praised. Let my praise be a sweet sound in your ear. In Jesus' name I pray. Amen.

TUESDAY, OCTOBER 30
(Read Habakkuk 1:1–4; 2:1–4)

(Morning)
Gracious God, I arise, grateful to you for the dawning of this new day.

(Evening)
Gracious God, I lie down to sleep, grateful to you for guiding my footsteps today.

God, when people ask me, "How are things going today?" my initial response is usually a silly complaint or a negative comment. It seems as though the bad stuff that is going on around me is always magnified. Why do the good die young? Violence, injustices, crime, and cruelty are all around. There are times when I am fearful and confused. Yet I know it's not your will for me to have a spirit of fear. Your will is for me to have a spirit of power, love, and a sound mind. God, I need to trust you and walk by faith, not by sight. Right now I may not understand why there are destruction and violence in this world, but I am sure I will understand better by and by. So today, I will place my hand in your hand as you lead and guide me.

(Morning)
I will stand at my watch post and keep an ear open
to hear what you will speak to my heart today.
(Prayers of Intercession)

(Evening)
I have heard your voice and am confident that you
are faithful to complete the work you've begun in me.
(Prayers of Intercession)

**As the heavens are higher than the earth,
so are God's ways higher than your ways.**
(Sing "Amazing Grace.")

(Morning)
I awaken with a clear vision, secure that I can trust what God has said about my future. Thank you, God. In Jesus' name I pray. Amen.

(Evening)
I lie down with renewed joy and peace because I am holding my Savior's hand. All is well. Thank you, God. In Jesus' name I pray. Amen.

WEDNESDAY, OCTOBER 31
(Read Psalm 119:137–44)

(Morning)
Righteous God, I put all my trust in you today. Help me to practice righteousness.

(Evening)
Righteous God, I have trusted you this day.
Even though trouble came my way, I know your judgments are right.

Great God, you are my righteousness, and I am your humble servant. Instruct me on how to be a person of integrity and character in this sinful world. Even when I feel overlooked and so insignificant in the grand scheme of life, I know you are an ever-present help in times of trouble. I have hidden your words in my heart because your teachings are like pure gold; I treasure what you say through your written Word. Help me to understand your Holy Word and your laws that I may live and serve you all the days of my life.

(Morning)
Holy God, I remember your laws and pray for those who despise me.
(Prayers of Intercession)

(Evening)
Holy God, I have not been all that I could be today. Help me to do better tomorrow.
(Prayers of Intercession)

Your righteousness is an everlasting righteousness.
(Sing "This Little Light of Mine" or another familiar hymn.)

(Morning)
Illuminate my way today, God, that I may see your path and never stray. In Jesus' name I pray. Amen.

(Evening)
Every distress could be handled today when I trusted in you. Thank you, God. In Jesus' name I pray. Amen.

THURSDAY, NOVEMBER 1
(Read Isaiah 1:10–18)

(Morning)
Forgiving God, I come before you this morning offering up the sacrifice of praise.

(Evening)
Forgiving God, thank you for being merciful to the just
and the unjust. I give you all the praise.

God, can we talk? I am not an eloquent speaker and at times I tend to babble, but I really need you to listen to me. I want to learn to live right, worship right, pray right, and give right. I want to see that justice is done and help all those around me who are in need. Renew my mind that I may prove what is your good, acceptable, and perfect will for my life. Help me to conquer the enemies of doubt, fear, and procrastination. I desire to be acceptable in your sight and not succumb to any wrongdoing. This is my prayer request. So now, ever-present God, I wait to hear from you and receive your direction. In the meantime, I will seek your face, your path, and your way every day. Thank you for inviting me into your presence.

(Morning)
God, create in me a clean heart.
(Prayers of Intercession)

(Evening)
God, thank you for looking beyond my faults and seeing my needs.
(Prayers of Intercession)

Seek justice! Defend widows and orphans! Rescue the oppressed!

(Morning)	(Evening)
Wash me cleaner than snow, and remove every scarlet sin. In Jesus' name I pray. Amen.	When I am faced with a hopeless situation, God will see that justice is done. Never fear. In Jesus' name I pray. Amen.

FRIDAY, NOVEMBER 2
(Psalm 32:1–2)

(Morning)
God, I thank you for brand-new mercy this day.
Thank you for waking me up and starting me on my way.

(Evening)
God, I am so happy that you looked past my faults and met my needs.

God, what a blessing it is to know I am forgiven. It is amazing to look back and remember I had ever tried to live my life without your guidance. Yet while I was lost in sin, you saw me and had mercy on me. Like the prodigal son, one day I realized I was starving to death, came to my senses, and returned to you. I didn't feel worthy to be called your child, but I was determined not to look back. I had nothing to lose but everything to gain. And while I was yet stumbling and making my way, you saw me. You had compassion on me and forgave my sins, and a celebration occurred in heaven as you clothed me with your righteousness. Oh, the joy that floods my soul every time I think of your goodness and your forgiveness, wiping my record clean!

(Morning)
I have joy, joy, joy, joy down in my heart. Let my joy be contagious today.
(Prayers of Intercession)

(Evening)
When I confess my sins, I know you are faithful, just, and forgiving.
(Prayers of Intercession)

If we say we have no sin, we deceive ourselves.

(Morning)
Being forgiven gives me a renewed hope that today will be beautiful. Hallelujah. In Jesus' name I pray. Amen.

(Evening)
I may have had some disagreements today, but I choose not to hold a grudge. I will forgive. In Jesus' name I pray. Amen.

SATURDAY, NOVEMBER 3
(Read Psalm 32:3–7)

(Morning)
Forgiving God, I cast all my anxieties upon you this morning
because I know you care for me.

(Evening)
Forgiving God, I lay aside every weight of this day
and anticipate the dawning of a new day.

Like a roaring lion, our adversary prowls about looking for someone to devour. Even though there are times when I actually see the enemy coming, I am not always quick enough to sidestep and get out of the way. I lose my balance. Praise be to you, God, for protecting me from trouble and not letting me fall. God, your Word reminds me that no weapon formed against me shall prosper. If I continually dwell in the secret place of the Most High and rest in the shadow of the Almighty in whom I trust, then no harm will befall me, and no disaster will come near. Give me the strength to resist and stand firm in my faith, even if I have to suffer a little. I know you will restore me. To God be the power and the glory forever and ever.

(Morning)
God, you know my deep need for forgiveness. This morning I forgive . . .
(Prayers of Intercession)

(Evening)
Forgiveness is not an emotion; it is a decision. Tonight I forgive . . .
(Prayers of Intercession)

I will confess my transgressions to God.

(Morning) God, how wonderful it is to know you stand ready to forgive me. In Jesus' name I pray. Amen.	(Evening) God, like David, I hear you say, "Welcome home, [insert your name]." In Jesus' name I pray. Amen.

SUNDAY, NOVEMBER 4
(Read 2 Thessalonians 1:1–4, 11–12)

(Morning)
Holy God, I am encouraged this morning. Your grace is sufficient for me.

(Evening)
Holy God, you have been so kind to me. Thank you for your peace.

Even though this faith journey we travel has its ups and downs, I am determined to endure so that you will get all the glory. Every slight momentary
affliction is preparing me for eternal glory in heaven. Through every trial, my
faith becomes stronger because I have trusted in your promises and you have
shown yourself faithful.

(Morning)
God of peace, sanctify me completely, and preserve me blameless today.
(Prayers of Intercession)

(Evening)
God of peace, sometimes I am tempted to fight back, but I will leave that to you.
(Prayers of Intercession)

No thorns, no throne; no gall, no glory; no cross, no crown.

(Morning)	(Evening)
God, give me a double portion of patience and faith. In Jesus' name I pray. Amen.	God, you have been better to me than I have been to myself. You are so awesome! In Jesus' name I pray. Amen.

MONDAY, NOVEMBER 5
(Read Psalm 98)

(Morning)
Praise you, God. Let me be a new song for this new day you have given us.

(Evening)
Praise you, God. Allow me to rest in your victories you have shown me today.

Parenting God, your steadfast love and your faithfulness have sustained us through all time. Allow us to continue in your victory and be a sweet melody to your ears. As you judge the world with righteousness, let us all praise you together.

(Morning)
As we sing a new song to you, let us praise you with the toil of our hands.
As we sing a new song of praise to you, God, let our song
be pleasant to the ears of those who don't know you.
(Prayers of Intercession)

(Evening)
Thank you, God, for allowing our song of praise to become a sweet melody to your ears.
Thank you for the presence of your Spirit in our song and the song we sing for others.
(Prayers of Intercession)

**"Make a joyful noise to God, all the earth;
break forth into joyous song and sing praises."**

(Morning)
God, today I will sing to you a sweet melody of praise. Guide our steps today as we are sustained by your faithfulness and love. In Jesus' name I pray. Amen.

(Evening)
God, as I lie down to rest, I thank you for the victories I shared with you today. Give us peace, and may we awake to a brighter day. In Jesus' name I pray. Amen.

TUESDAY, NOVEMBER 6
(Read Haggai 1:15–2:9)

(Morning)
Hallelujah, praise you, God, for allowing us another day to feel your presence. We pray today that we will receive your word into our hearts and will be obedient to your will. Let us be your temple.

(Evening)
Hallelujah, thank you, God, for the blessings of today. As I lie down to sleep, give me strength and power to finish the work you have given me.

God, forgive us, your hardheaded, forgetful children, for you have revealed that the time has come for us to do a work that will glorify you. We have grown accustomed to your blessings and neglectful of your work. Remove the fear, empower us with your presence, and allow us to move forward. Let your glory and riches shine through us as we rebuild your house.

(Morning)
Sovereign God, I pray this day for an obedient spirit, to hear you and to do your will. I want to be a temple for your presence.
(Prayers of Intercession)

(Evening)
Thank you for allowing me to be used by you.
As we rebuild our lives to bless others, we will glorify your name.
(Prayers of Intercession)

"Take courage, all you people of the land, says the Sovereign; work, for I am with you, says the Sovereign of hosts."

(Morning)
Sovereign God, I will not fear because I know you are with me. You have promised us your abiding Spirit, and when you shake the nations, I will rest in you because all riches belong to you. In Jesus' name I pray. Amen.

(Evening)
You, O God, have kept your promise. You have shown your children the glory of your splendor. Prosper us as we become your house, a temple for your abiding Spirit. In Jesus' name I pray. Amen.

WEDNESDAY, NOVEMBER 7
(Read Psalm 17:1–9)

(Morning)
O God, hear me as I cry unto you. I have stayed away from the wicked
and kept my lips from deceit. Protect me, this day, from my deadly enemies.

(Evening)
O God, I called to you, and you heard my cry.
You have wondrously shown me your love.

Parent God, I cry unto you to hide me in the shadow of your wings. My enemies
surround me and despoil me. But you guard me as if I were the apple of your eye.
I have kept my lips from deceit; my mouth from transgressions; and my feet
have not slipped. Deliver me in your steadfast love. Vindicate me, O God.

(Morning)
God, unto you I cry, for those who are violent and wicked surround me.
(Prayers of Intercession)

(Evening)
Thank you for vindication and protection from my enemies who surrounded me.
(Prayers of Intercession)

**"I call upon you, for you will answer me, O God;
incline your ear to me, hear my words."**

(Morning)	(Evening)
O God, let the words of my mouth stay free of deceit. Allow my heart to stay free of wickedness as I seek refuge in the shadow of your wings. Wondrously show me your steadfast love. In Jesus' name I pray. Amen.	God, as you have hidden me in the shadow of your wings and guarded me as the apple of your eye, let my adversaries see the glory of your wondrous love for me unfold. In Jesus' name I pray. Amen.

THURSDAY, NOVEMBER 8
(Read Job 19:23–27)

(Morning)
Majesty of the earth, Redeemer of the world,
give this day a special blessing as I praise you. Engrave your words on my heart.

(Evening)
Majesty of the earth, as my skin is destroyed this day
and my words fade to nothing, you, God, will stand forever.

Majestic God, Redeemer of the earth, I pray that my words are engraved in stone. I pray that my words are written in a book so they may last forever. I know you are on my side, even though my skin has been destroyed. My eyes shall see only you, God, and none other.

(Morning)
Majestic God, open my words to the hearts of those who need to hear them.
Allow them to know that you will stand forever.
(Prayers of Intercession)

(Evening)
O God, let this day be a testament and an inscription to you.
I know you will reign forever and ever.
(Prayers of Intercession)

"For I know that my Redeemer lives, and that at the last my Redeemer will stand upon the earth."

(Morning)
Hallelujah, God, you are the Redeemer of the earth. Let this be a day of joy. Let my words of praise be engraved on a rock forever. In Jesus' name I pray. Amen.

(Evening)
Sovereign God, as my skin has been destroyed this day, I see you. O God, I know you are on my side. In Jesus' name I pray. Amen.

FRIDAY, NOVEMBER 9
(Read Psalm 145:1–5, 17–21)

(Morning)
My God and my Ruler, I will bless your name every morning when I arise.
Let your unsearchable greatness be praised today.

(Evening)
My God and my Ruler, on your wondrous majesty I have meditated this day.
Give me sweet peace as I rest.

Mighty God, your wondrous acts are worthy to be praised. I will praise you in the morning. I will praise you in the evening. I will praise you forever more. You are just and kind in all your ways, and when we call to you in truth, you are near to us and hear our cry.

(Morning)
I cry unto you, Sovereign God, and will declare your wondrous,
mighty acts to all generations.
(Prayers of Intercession)

(Evening)
O God, please watch over all who love you, hear their cry, and save them.
(Prayers of Intercession)

"God is just in all God's ways, and kind in all God's doings."

(Morning)
Great are you, God, and greatly to be praised. Your greatness is unsearchable. Give me strength this day to extol you, my Ruler, and tell of your works and mighty acts to the next generation. Allow me to meditate on the splendor of your majesty. In Jesus' name I pray. Amen.

(Evening)
Sovereign God, your justice and mercy have been with me all day. You have been near to me and fulfilled my desires for this day. As I sleep, continue to watch over me because my love for you is unending. In Jesus' name I pray. Amen.

SATURDAY, NOVEMBER 10
(Read Luke 20:27–38)

(Morning)
Good morning, God. Let us come to you with questions for our daily living.
Let us rejoice in the answers you will give to us.

(Evening)
Good evening, God. Thank you for being faithful
to us as you shared your wisdom this day.

Sovereign God, so many cares of today's world plague us. We pray we will not be deceived by our thoughts, but conceived in the resurrection of your Child. We may marry here on earth, but let us remember we shall be married to your Child, Jesus the Christ.

(Morning)
God, this morning, allow me to pray for those
who are married to the world and not to Christ.
(Prayers of Intercession)

(Evening)
Thank you for hearing the words of my prayers
and allowing those for whom I pray to become the children of God.
(Prayers of Intercession)

**"Now God is God not of the dead, but of the living;
for to God all of them are alive."**
(Sing "Sweet, Sweet Spirit" or another familiar hymn.)

(Morning)
God, this morning I pray for those who have not died to this world. I pray asking that they become like angels, the children of God. I pray that they become children of the resurrection and come to know the God of the living, our God—the God of Abraham, Isaac, and Jacob. In Jesus' name I pray. Amen.

(Evening)
Thank you, God, for such a blessed day—a day to walk in the Spirit of resurrection. Thank you for giving us strength to die to the cares of this world and be as angels. In Jesus' name I pray. Amen.

SUNDAY, NOVEMBER 11
(Read 2 Thessalonians 2:1–5, 13–17)

(Morning)
Father God, open our eyes to the deceitful one. Let not any tricks of the enemy
beguile us. Allow us, O God, to see what is good from what is evil.

(Evening)
Mother God, thank you for bringing to our remembrance the things
you have taught us. Let us be prepared for the lawless one's coming.

Sovereign God, you are our mighty oak tree. Thank you for bearing firstfruits
through our lives and choosing us for salvation. Through the sanctification by
your Spirit and belief in the truth, we have obtained the glory of Jesus Christ.
Give us strength to hold fast to the traditions you have taught us, and oppose
the lawless ones whenever we encounter them.

(Morning)
God, I pray for those who have let go of your traditions
and are struggling with the lawless one.
(Prayers of Intercession)

(Evening)
God, I close this day in prayer for those who have been sanctified
by your Spirit and their belief in the truth.
(Prayers of Intercession)

Let us share the good news of salvation today.

(Morning)
Sovereign God, good morning, let this
day be a firstfruit to you. Allow us not to
be deceived by the lawless one. Do not
let us exalt anyone or anything above
you. In Jesus' name I pray. Amen.

(Evening)
God, this has been a glorious day. A
day we have shared the good news, a
day of harvest, a day of sanctification
by your Spirit. "Now may our Savior,
Jesus Christ, and God our Parent, who
loved us and through grace gave us
eternal comfort and good hope, comfort
your hearts and strengthen them in
every good work and word." In Jesus'
name I pray. Amen.

MONDAY, NOVEMBER 12
(Read Luke 21:5–11)

(Morning)
O Great Spirit, I see the beauty you have created and feel hope.
I will not let evil frighten me; I will not be deceived,
for you are the good news. You are my Defender.

(Evening)
O Great Spirit, the sun sets, and the heavens come alive with light. All the universe
holds beauty. Thank you for the gift of life so that I may behold all these things.

Jesus, you said the time would come when the stones of our temples would be
thrown down. The signs are present today. Many of our temples are no longer
adorned with beautiful stones. They have been burned by those who hate, or
they have been neglected and abandoned. Yet hope prevails. The faith and hope
you have given us through words and signs over centuries churn within us, and
so we defy. We rebuild. I cannot think of anything more promising, more excit-
ing, than to be a Christian and to know you. Praise the Creator!

(Morning)
Creator of my life, with my mind and with my heart, I absorb the sins
of the world, the sins of the people, and give them to you.
(Prayers of Intercession)

(Evening)
Gracious and forgiving Spirit, thank you for what has been good
and for being the keeper of my fears.
(Prayers of Intercession)

"Fear defeats purpose, and so, with purpose, I strive for faith."

(Morning)
Great Spirit, please put faith in my heart
where remnants of fear may lie so that
my day will be filled with good. In the
name of the one who brings peace.
Amen.

(Evening)
For the gift of life, the gift of knowledge,
and the gift of forgiveness, thank you, O
Great Spirit. In the name of the one who
brings peace. Amen.

TUESDAY, NOVEMBER 13
(Read Luke 21:12–19)

(Morning)
Creator God, you surround me with beauty today. My soul yearns to seek it so that all may know you and your powers. I will wait for your words of wisdom.

(Evening)
Creator God, this day was all that you promised.
Not a hair on my head was harmed, and you kept all of my worries
so that I might do your work with a glad heart. Thank you.

Jesus, you said that not a hair on our heads would perish if we followed you. What a gift to have in our lives, to know that days filled with strife need not be burdensome if we truly believe that you will protect us. We know that we will hear sad news—another child killed, or someone, somewhere, put to death because of his or her religious beliefs. Sadly, this has always been so. Yet when our hearts are filled with the Holy Spirit, we continue our faith journey, and we seek justice because we have to.

(Morning)
As I begin this day with a clear mind, waiting to be filled
with your wisdom, be with me and those I love.
(Prayers of Intercession)

(Evening)
As I end this day in contentment, having done my best to seek your will,
I ask that you bring contentment to all others in my circle.
(Prayers of Intercession)

"Though people may betray people, God never betrays."

(Morning)
Creator God, as the day breaks and the sun shines warmth into my heart, help me shine warmth into my home and my community. In the name of the one who brings peace. Amen.

(Evening)
God, my loving Protector, I cannot live without you in a world full of strife and turmoil. This world needs you! In the name of the one who brings peace. Amen.

WEDNESDAY, NOVEMBER 14
(Read Isaiah 65:17–25)

(Morning)
Holy, holy, holy. All around me is holy. I am holy. Creator God, there is
no ugliness in your creation; ugliness exists only in the minds of evildoers.
Help me remember my holiness and that of those with whom I associate,
so that the New Jerusalem you have promised can begin here and now.

(Evening)
Holy, holy, holy. Great Spirit of all who are spiritual in mind and heart,
the awe of the morning scripture stayed with me all day.
Thank you for lifting me and setting my mind on all that can be made new.

Living, breathing Spirit of God, your words in Isaiah bring so much hope. A
new earth, new heavens, and a New Jerusalem. A place where there will be
long lives, pure joy, and no more tears. Though I have felt pain and sadness and
cried many tears, you have always been there for me. And because you have
been there for me, I believe in you and this promise. The longer I linger on this
message, the more excited I am to have been created just for this time.

(Morning)
Eternal and Great Spirit, lift me to sacred and holy grounds,
that I might be spiritually cleansed.
(Prayers of Intercession)

(Evening)
Eternal and Great Spirit, the magnitude of your work has been manifested with the
promise of a New Jerusalem. I pray for your continuing guidance to live out this glory.
(Prayers of Intercession)

"The serpent cannot survive on dust, so feed dust to the serpent."

(Morning)
The New Jerusalem beckons, O God.
Pave my pathway with gold today,
making my walk pure. Keep the vision
of a New Jerusalem before me, so I can
do my part. In the name of the one who
brings peace. Amen.

(Evening)
I take from this day what has been good
and leave the rest behind. Thank you,
Great Spirit, for all of my lessons today.
In the name of the one who brings peace.
Amen.

THURSDAY, NOVEMBER 15
(Read Isaiah 12)

(Morning)
Praise to you, O Great Spirit, Creator of heaven and earth. Sanctify me.
Wash me clean. I hold my arms out to you—draw me close.
Take me to a place where I can breathe in your strength and your Spirit.

(Evening)
Praise to you, O Great Spirit, Creator of heaven and earth.
If I have angered you in any way, I know that I have been forgiven already.
With joy this evening, I receive the comfort of my Savior.

Sometimes my weaknesses overcome me. They grow like my shadow in the twilight. Confusing thoughts swirl about in my mind. I get too big. No room for you, dear God. I forget to exalt you. How can I not praise you, the One who has comforted me time and again? Scriptures such as this in Isaiah remind me to remain humble and grateful. You, God, promise us a New Jerusalem. You promise salvation and provide a way for us to draw water from the wells of salvation, through your Child, Jesus Christ.

(Morning)
Creator God, how great is the One who can answer all prayers.
I pray for peace and serenity in a world of pain and turmoil.
(Prayers of Intercession)

(Evening)
A restful sleep is necessary for the peace of mind needed to do your work.
In this world there are many who do not have a place to rest.
God bless all those who are meek and without.
(Prayers of Intercession)

"God's anger is never very long, God's comfort is forever."

(Morning)
Today I will sing praises to the Most High, for glorious things have been done. Thank you, God. In the name of the one who brings peace. Amen.

(Evening)
For all that has been good today, I thank you, Great Spirit. For those who have helped me in small and big ways, I thank you. In the name of the one who brings peace. Amen.

FRIDAY, NOVEMBER 16
(Read Malachi 4:1–2)

(Morning)
Dearest Jesus, some days you walk beside me, some days you carry me,
and some days you have to drag me; but you never, never give up on me.
Just knowing you are with me today is enough.

(Evening)
Dearest Jesus, you were with me today, and I felt you. I needed you. I always
need you. Thank you for this very special day and for your special presence.

Prophets like Malachi encourage our faith. God, he reminds us of your anger,
wrath, and love. We leap from our idleness with conviction and begin the process of restoration when strong-willed purpose is thrust on us. We need your
love exposed to us time and again. Scripture reminds us, "The sun of righteousness shall rise, with healing in its wings," if we respond to the call. I want
to respond to your call. I want healing. Am I prepared? Am I helping you to
build a New Jerusalem today?

(Morning)
Holy Spirit of God, I want to respond to your call.
I want healing, and so I ask
for healing.
(Prayers of Intercession)

(Evening)
My soul rests in you after a long and busy day. I am so grateful to have you in my life.
(Prayers of Intercession)

"Despondency gets you nowhere. Respond, instead."

(Morning)
Holy and Great Spirit, I welcome this
new day. May your warm winds of
heaven blow softly on me and bring
sunrise into my heart. In the name of
the one who brings peace. Amen.

(Evening)
Great Spirit, make me always ready to
come to you with clean hands and
straight eyes so when life fades, as the
fading sunset, my spirit may come to
you without shame. In the name of the
one who brings peace. Amen.

SATURDAY, NOVEMBER 17
(Read Psalm 98)

(Morning)
Dear God, your mighty creation trembles. Mother Earth seems to be shrinking
with fear and trauma. We are cruel. We forget the sacredness of life.
Today teach me kindness and respect for all that you have made.

(Evening)
Dear God, your mighty creation trembles. We forget the sacredness of life.
Continue to teach me kindness and respect.

God, you are so good. Your Child, Jesus the Christ, is so good. Your Holy
Spirit is so good. I give praise to the triumph over evil that I have been given
through your Word. I praise you for all those blessed, tormented, committed,
and loyal people who wrote down your words. I can seek justice, peace, and
especially guidance from those age-old stories and words. Let us sing; let us
make a joyful noise; let us bless all of Mother Earth's living creations. Let us
prepare ourselves for the New Jerusalem.

(Morning)
You have done marvelous things for us. Thank you, God.
I praise you today and ask you to reveal your righteousness to the nations.
(Prayers of Intercession)

(Evening)
Holy Spirit, I end this day with hope and yet with some trepidation.
Salvation is needed for me, for us, here and now.
(Prayers of Intercession)

"If we do not sing, we miss the joy of praising God mightily."

(Morning)
God, thank you for those faithful old songs
and hymns that were inspired by
someone's love for you. I have a song in
my heart this morning that tells me to keep
"my mind stayed on Jesus." In the name of
the one who brings peace. Amen.

(Evening)
Holy and Great Spirit, as shadows
lengthen across the sky, I wait for the
stars to light up the heavens, for all these
things tell me how mighty you are. Thank
you for another blessed day. In the name
of the one who brings peace. Amen.

SUNDAY, NOVEMBER 18
(Read 2 Thessalonians 3:6–13)

(Morning)
Great Spirit and Creator of all, you rested on the seventh day. Some of us rest
every day. Remove from me the idleness and complacency that sometimes set in.
Provide me with the spiritual nourishment to do your work today.

(Evening)
Great Spirit and Creator of all, provide me with the spiritual
nourishment needed to continue your work.

God, Paul tells the church to keep away from those who are idle. He reminds us
that he and others became models for us to follow. He also reminds us that we
cannot wait for Christ's return in order to set the world right. There are things we
must do here and now! I have found that a structured and directed life is easier to
live. Most important, it keeps us from associating with people who are not as spiritually inclined as we are. Paul says to stay away from those kinds of people, to
detach from them. I must get busy and prepare for Jesus now.

(Morning)
Dear God, you have taught me so much through all of your prophets and disciples.
I ask you to help me become a model for others.
(Prayers of Intercession)

(Evening)
Great Spirit and Creator of us all, idleness and evil are everywhere. Help me
to stay on the path you have determined is mine, so I may witness for others.
(Prayers of Intercession)

"Idleness breeds anxiety and defeat. Prepare yourselves daily."

(Morning)
Great Spirit, I face all directions this
morning with hope and with the spirit
of willingness. In the name of the one
who brings peace. Amen.

(Evening)
Holy, holy, holy God, you've kept me
from evil, you've given me a glad heart
to do your work, and you've guided me.
Thank you. In the name of the one who
brings peace. Amen.

MONDAY, NOVEMBER 19
(Read Luke 1:68–79)

(Morning)
Holy God, guide my feet this day in the way of peace.

(Evening)
Holy God, today, I pray I have walked in the way of peace.

Holy God, an angel came to Zechariah claiming unbelievable news of the preacher's wife's pregnancy. Zechariah muttered doubt instead of praise, and his voice was taken from him. In silence he waited and watched as the miracle came to full term. Finally, when the prophecy was fulfilled, Zechariah's heart was opened to the messages of angels, and his throat, to a response of praise. Loving God, angels still visit us. Sometimes we don't believe our eyes or our ears, and we are left cynical and silent in their passing. Today, may I be open to your messengers and messages. And may I reply in a voice of faith.

(Morning)
Come, Holy Spirit, speak to me with the words of God's abiding presence.
I pray that you will bring comfort to those for whom I pray.
(Prayers of Intercession)

(Evening)
You have blessed me, O God of love, with strength and courage and faith.
This evening I lift into your presence these concerns.
(Prayers of Intercession)

By the tender mercy of our God, the dawn from on high will break upon us.

(Morning)	(Evening)
When you come to me this day, O God, let my heart and mind be open to the news you bring. Empower me to share this news with others. In Christ's name. Amen.	I thank you for the day, your surprises of grace, and your messages of hope. I pray that the sleep I find might grant me the peace I need. In Christ's name. Amen.

TUESDAY, NOVEMBER 20
(Read Jeremiah 23:1–6)

(Morning)
O Righteous Branch, reign as Sovereign in my life this day. Be thou my righteousness.

(Evening)
O Righteous Branch, now that day is done, let me rest
in the knowledge that the Messiah has come.

God, Jeremiah preached about the coming of a Messiah who will rule over a restored Israel in wisdom and with righteousness. It was your promise to a people suffering under rulers who destroyed and scattered the sheep. Imagery of shepherds who tenderly care for the sheep is imagery used throughout the Bible. You and Jesus as Shepherds are familiar and comforting to all your followers. Here we are reminded that you come to us in the counsel and care of shepherds who do not evoke fear or dismay. Rather, those whom you have ordained bring protection and peace. May I, as a representative of the Good Shepherd, seek to serve this day as one who brings others to the fold, one who is fruitful in the spirit, and one who multiplies the joy and peace of others.

(Morning)
Great Shepherd of all, I pray this morning for those
who are lost and afraid, and for those who need your guidance.
(Prayers of Intercession)

(Evening)
Loving and gentle Shepherd, this evening I bring these concerns to your throne of grace.
(Prayers of Intercession)

The sheep recognize the Shepherd, for they remember how love looks.

(Morning)
This morning, I honor the Shepherd. I pray, as I walk this path before me, that I will always and only look to you. In Christ's name. Amen.

(Evening)
I close my eyes to sleep, confident and assured of the Shepherd's love. May I rest in God's peace. In Christ's name. Amen.

WEDNESDAY, NOVEMBER 21
(Read Psalm 46:1–9)

(Morning)
Holy One, be my strength; be my refuge. Let me, this day, not be moved.

(Evening)
Even in the still of this night, I seek to find my strength in you.

Victorious God, this psalm is a song that celebrates your victory for Israel. It serves as a reminder of your majesty and power. It was also the inspiration for Martin Luther's famous hymn "A Mighty Fortress Is Our God." Though the earth may rattle and roll; though the sky may fall, the mountains may tremble, and the waters may widen and deepen; though all I know may be torn from me, God, you will remain my strength, my stronghold, my shelter, and my hope. Just your voice, an utterance, a whisper—all the earth is silenced. Even in the midst of chaos, I can believe that you are still God. As I begin and end my day in your presence, may I be mindful of your strong and powerful presence.

(Morning)
Mighty God, with you all things are possible.
(Prayers of Intercession)

(Evening)
All-powerful God, with you all things are possible.
(Prayers of Intercession)

Nothing to fear, nothing to threaten, tenderly I rest in the arms of God.

(Morning)	(Evening)
How mighty is your name, O God. I give you all praise and honor. For you alone are God. In Christ's name. Amen.	In all the world, there is none as powerful as you. All that I have needed this day, your hand has brought forth. In Christ's name. Amen.

THURSDAY, NOVEMBER 22
(Read Psalms 10–11)

(Morning)
God, in this busy day ahead of me, let me be still and know your goodness.

(Evening)
God, at the close of this busy day, let me be still and know your presence.

We busy our lives with activities and errands and relationships, all of which seem so important. Sometimes we are so cluttered and pulled that we soon find ourselves unable to sit still, be quiet, and listen for your word, loving God. We have become so accustomed to doing more than one thing at a time, even our prayers are meant to complete several tasks: praise, confession, and intercession. How might our lives be different if we honored the need for stillness? For silence? What might we hear that we miss in all the noise? What might we see? What might we find? What would change in our spiritual lives if our prayers became a simple sentence with spaces of silence? On this day, let me make the space and time to be still and ask for your presence to speak to me so that I might once again hear and know your voice.

(Morning)
In this moment of silence, I lift up to you, O God, those who need your presence.
(Prayers of Intercession)

(Evening)
In the stillness of this hour, I pray for those who need you.
(Prayers of Intercession)

God speaks to us in the stillness we allow.

(Morning)
I begin this day in moments of silence. I ask you to help me be still and know your presence. In Christ's name. Amen.

(Evening)
And now as I lie down to rest, I pray before I fall to sleep, I will find you in the stillness. In Christ's name. Amen.

FRIDAY, NOVEMBER 23
(Read Colossians 1:11–20)

(Morning)
Eternal God, let me be strengthened with all power as I give thanks to you this day.

(Evening)
Eternal God, let me rest in the knowledge
that I have been delivered, redeemed, and forgiven.

Paul wrote a letter to a fledgling church in Asia Minor. He had heard information about false teachers who were misleading the new Christians. Paul wrote an encouraging word from prison in order to strengthen the church and remind Christians of your supremacy and your image as seen in Jesus Christ. "May you be made strong," Paul wrote, "with all the strength that comes from God's glorious power." God, indeed it is your strength that empowers us to fight against temptation; stay grounded in the Word; and seek and find your voice in the midst of many voices. God, it is your strength, as demonstrated in the life, death, and resurrection of Jesus Christ, that is now my strength. As I go about the affairs of this day, may I find the strength and endurance I so desperately need in the living of these days.

(Morning)
Holy God, strengthen me this day so that I may serve you by serving others. I pray you will strengthen the hearts and minds and spirits of those for whom I pray.
(Prayers of Intercession)

(Evening)
God of power, I honor you and give you all praise.
On this evening, I have concerns I lift up to you.
(Prayers of Intercession)

The strength of a life lived in Christ is strength enough to endure.

(Morning)
Today is a new day, a day to celebrate God's presence in my life and in the world. May I be mindful of your love in all that I do and say. In Christ's name. Amen.

(Evening)
Thank you for the day, your love, your guidance, your presence. I have recognized your power and goodness in many ways. In Christ's name. Amen.

SATURDAY, NOVEMBER 24
(Read Luke 23:33–38)

(Morning)
Omnipotent God, empower me to forgive others as I have been forgiven.

(Evening)
Omnipotent God, as I have been granted mercy, I pray I have been able to grant mercy.

Jesus watched from the cross as people gawked and laughed and as soldiers cast lots for his clothes. Even from that place of great pain and a tortured spirit, Jesus was able to recognize the suffering and ignorance of others. Even from that place, he was able to pray for those who hurt him. Even from that place high upon a cross, facing his own death, the loss of his own hope, Jesus looked down not in judgment but in mercy. Through this day and every day, may I be mindful of the spirit of Christ, a spirit of mercy and forgiveness, a spirit of love and compassion. I pray I might be able to let go of the grudges that weigh me down. I pray I, too, might make the choice not to judge, but to forgive.

(Morning)
Today, I pray for my enemies.
(Prayers of Intercession)

(Evening)
This evening, I pray for those who need mercy.
(Prayers of Intercession)

As I have been forgiven, so shall I forgive.

(Morning)
Mercy is not an easy thing, O God. Empower me to show mercy to all this day. In Christ's name. Amen.

(Evening)
As the day closes, I pray for mercy and forgiveness, for I realize I have not always shown mercy. In Christ's name. Amen.

SUNDAY, NOVEMBER 25
(Read Luke 23:39–43)

(Morning)
Gentle, loving Christ, remember me.

(Evening)
Gentle, loving Christ, remember me.

The thief on the cross who asked to be remembered by Jesus when Jesus went to Paradise received much more than what he requested. Jesus said that not only would he be remembered but the thief would be with Jesus on that very day. The thief's request was simple and childlike; no lawyer's questioning; no theological debate; no trap or need to be right; no hidden agenda; just the prayer, "Remember me." Today, dear God, let that be my prayer. Simple, easy, and to the point. Jesus, remember me.

(Morning)
I remember others who need the love of Christ this day. I lift them up to you.
(Prayers of Intercession)

(Evening)
In the close of this day, I am mindful of those who need your healing touch.
(Prayers of Intercession)

Like the thief on the cross, I pray to be remembered.

(Morning)
A new day is set before me. I seek to serve. I seek to find you in the hearts and eyes of others. Let me remember you. In Christ's name. Amen.

(Evening)
The day closes around me. I remember the things I have done, and the things I have left undone. Forgive me, and may I rest in peace. In Christ's name. Amen.

MONDAY, NOVEMBER 26
(Read Isaiah 2:1–5)

(Morning)
Sovereign God, today is a new day. May I make the most of it.

(Evening)
Sovereign God, the day has come and gone.
Your presence has been magnified. Thank you.

Since my childhood growing up on a farm in north central Iowa, I have had an affinity for plowshares. I grew up using a two-bottom plow. This is rather small by today's standards, but at the time, it was quite typical. With a plow that size, one obviously spent a lot of time in the fields. It was the perfect place to soak in all of God's creation. The sky overhead. Fresh, clean air. Birds soaring. Small animals scurrying. And the sound of the plowshare turning over the earth, furrow by furrow. The turning of that blade to me was God's gift. It meant financial security for my family. It meant food for the world. It symbolized the cycle of life. If we were plowing, the resurrection of the earth for a new season of growing could not be far behind.

(Morning)
O God, Giver of all life, be with us this day—no matter where we are
—to help us appreciate all life.
(Prayers of Intercession)

(Evening)
If I have not done a good job of honoring your creation this day,
help me to do a better job tomorrow.
(Prayers of Intercession)

God, you are the Creator of all!

(Morning)
Bless me in my waking up. In the
matchless name of Jesus. Amen.

(Evening)
Bless me in my lying down. In the
matchless name of Jesus. Amen.

TUESDAY, NOVEMBER 27
(Read Psalm 122)

(Morning)
Dear God, thank you for the peace and security
only your presence and power can give and sustain.

(Evening)
Dear God, thank you for the peace and security you have maintained this day.

Everything is always changing. I hear this comment made again and again in the rural area in which I live. Most of the time it is a comment made with lament. Seldom is it said with great joy. Too often we believe security and peace come from what is known; therefore, the unknown, the changes, are often unwelcome. I wonder whether this would be so if we truly learned the lesson that you, loving God, and only you, are our peace and security.

(Morning)
O God, all Sovereign, help us to truly understand where all things come from.

(Evening)
O God, all Sovereign, thank you for having watched over me this day.
(Prayers of Intercession)

To stand firm with God is to understand where our strength emanates from, where it is nurtured, and where peace lives eternally!
(Pray the Prayer of Our Savior.)

(Morning)
God, please bless my going out. In the matchless name of Jesus. Amen.

(Evening)
God, please bless my coming in. In the matchless name of Jesus. Amen.

WEDNESDAY, NOVEMBER 28
(Read Romans 13:11–14)

(Morning)
Sovereign Jesus, the days go too quickly. Help me to savor each and every moment.

(Evening)
Sovereign Jesus, help me put this day to rest. I am weary. Tomorrow is fast upon
me. Thank you for this respite.

When my oldest child graduated from high school, I was caught off guard. It
came too fast. I wanted back, at least momentarily, that little boy I helped
raise. But time never retreats. And better things are always in store. Help me,
God, to be ever mindful of a future that is brighter than the past if for no other
reason than you are in it.

(Morning)
We may not know the hour, O God, but you do.
In your sovereign wisdom help us to prepare.
(Prayers of Intercession)

(Evening)
The day is gone; the night is at hand. Jesus, help us to seek you again tomorrow.

If you do nothing else but put on Jesus Christ, you have done more than enough.
(Pray the Prayer of Our Savior.)

(Morning)
As I stand before you, the sun also
rises. May I seek glory in your eyes. In
the matchless name of Jesus. Amen.

(Evening)
As I sit on my porch, the sun is now
setting. Have I done your will? In the
matchless name of Jesus. Amen.

THURSDAY, NOVEMBER 29
(Read Matthew 24:36–39)

(Morning)
God, keep me alert this day to your presence and to all those around me.

(Evening)
God, did I truly pay attention today, or did I just pursue my own desires and whims?

I hate getting caught off guard, and I'm not big on surprises. I must confess that they really, truly annoy me. Which sometimes makes life an interesting proposition because you can never live life without the occasional surprise. Yet I prefer to see things coming. What about the Flood? Do you suppose anybody noticed it was raining? Did anyone notice the dry land was disappearing? What about the ark? Wasn't that a little hard to miss? Almost all were swept away. I wonder what tide we cannot see. Where are my blind spots?

(Morning)
God, help me to see.
(Prayers of Intercession)

(Evening)
God, thank you for the sight you have given me this day.
(Prayers of Intercession)

The people perish without vision.

(Morning)	(Evening)
Dear God, I want to see; I want to know. Help me to discern your will for my life, and then may I have the wisdom to follow. In the matchless name of Jesus. Amen.	As I think back on the day, as I think back over my life, there are many things I might change, but accepting Jesus into my life has made all well. In the matchless name of Jesus. Amen.

FRIDAY, NOVEMBER 30
(Read Matthew 24:40–41)

(Morning)
Sovereign God, ready or not, here comes the day.
God, am I ready? Please, help me to be ready!

(Evening)
Sovereign God, we've made it through another day. You always do, but some days
I'm not so sure about myself and others. Thank you for watching over us all.

No one likes to be left behind. No one likes to be left out. It reminds me of my younger days when we would choose up teams to play baseball. The kid who ended up in right field always seemed so forlorn. He realized that nobody really wanted him on the team. Fortunately, God, you want us all. No one is to be left out. No single person is unwanted. What a gift. To be truly loved and wanted. Awesome is an understatement.

(Morning)
What's that, God? You want me? Here I am; send me.
(Prayers of Intercession)

(Evening)
I have been sent. I have been blessed. I have been cared for.
(Hum the tune "Jesus Loves Me" or another familiar hymn.)

God, you are with us always.

(Morning)
May I always be on watch for how I treat others and how I display your love to others this day. In the matchless name of Jesus. Amen.

(Evening)
God, this has been a truly amazing day. As I lay my head upon my pillow, help me in some small way to comprehend how much you love me. Help me to grasp that I am a child of God! I am a child of God! In the matchless name of Jesus. Amen.

SATURDAY, DECEMBER 1
(Read Matthew 24:42–44)

(Morning)
Sovereign Jesus, help me to be ready to meet the demands
of this day, whatever they may be.

(Evening)
Sovereign Jesus, I await your coming.

In our small town we seldom lock our doors—never during the day unless we are going away overnight. If we came home and found something stolen, we would be totally shocked. People drop things off and pick stuff up even when we are not there. God, I suppose that if the day ever comes when we find something stolen or abused, we will struggle to trust from then on. We hope that day never comes. We hope our home will always be treated with respect and dignity. I might also add that it is a home where Jesus is always welcome.

(Morning)
I look, I ponder, I wonder, what will this day bring?
(Prayers of Intercession)

(Evening)
The setting sun always sheds such beautiful light. The Child of God always sheds such beautiful light. The human spirit touched by God always sheds such beautiful light.
(Prayers of Intercession)

Behold the Light of the world.
*(Pray the Prayer of Our Savior, and hum the tune "This Little Light of Mine"
or another familiar hymn.)*

(Morning)
God, I come to you this day with my heart open wide. I am an empty vessel; fill me up. In the matchless name of Jesus. Amen.

(Evening)
Dear God, I shall strive to love you with all of my heart, soul, and strength. My all I give to you. In the matchless name of Jesus. Amen.

SUNDAY, DECEMBER 2
(Read Psalm 122)

(Morning)
Holy God, we worship you now and forever more.

(Evening)
Holy God, as the sun sets upon this day of worship, may we your people be reminded
that every day bears your mark and that every day we should give you praise!

I have always liked to go to worship. There has never been a time in my life
when I did not go to church. It has been my strength in times of trouble. It has
been my joy in times of celebration. It is at worship with the community of
believers where I experience my greatest moments of hope. God is here! Christ
is here! The Holy Spirit is here! Advent is here! Let the good times roll!

(Morning)
In your presence, most Holy One, I receive the power to go on, no matter what!
(Prayers of Intercession)

(Evening)
Give all the world the rest we need this night. Give us peace.
Give us hope as only you can do.
(Prayers of Intercession)

O God, through you, all things are possible.
(Pray the Prayer of Our Savior.)

(Morning)	(Evening)
Holy Spirit, may your presence blow across our lives this day, that we might be a clear light for the world to unmistakably see. In the matchless name of Jesus. Amen.	As I go to a night of well-earned rest, may I arise refreshed and ready to take on a brand-new day, always knowing it is a gift from you. In the matchless name of Jesus. Amen.

MONDAY, DECEMBER 3
(Read Isaiah 11:1–10)

(Morning)
Beloved God, you are a righteous Judge and Lover of peace.
How will my works seem to you today?

(Evening)
Beloved God, have my actions expressed your love, peace, and knowledge of you?

God, you have made me such that my soul seeks peace. Through the contradictions of my daily living, the storms of discontent, and the seeming abyss of despair, I seek peace. As I anticipate the coming of your everlasting peace, let me live, work, and love with a knowledge of your wisdom and power. Give me understanding. You came to bring peace, and I anticipate your return and the lasting peace you promised.

(Morning)
O precious Fruit of David, I pray for your peace as
I call upon your name and pray for those who share my life.
(Prayers of Intercession)

(Evening)
Sweet Fruit, thank you for the peace I have known today.
(Prayers of Intercession)

"Hear, O heavens, and listen, O earth; for God has spoken."

(Morning)
This day is gloriously filled with the promise of peace. Fill me, God, with your peace that I may sow seeds of peace as I live this day. In your name. Amen.

(Evening)
I have seen evidence of you today, God. I have seen your peace, wisdom, and justice, and I give thanks. In your name. Amen.

TUESDAY, DECEMBER 4
(Read Psalm 72:1–7)

(Morning)
God, do I love you enough to be merciful and fair today? Help me see injustice and have the courage to speak against it.

(Evening)
God, have my actions this day served as a reflection of your love for justice and mercy?

There are many all around me who need to know you, God. Their yearnings, moanings, and groanings reach your ear. Your Holy Spirit urges me to be my neighbors' keeper and to minister by your power, yet I hesitate. Your people need justice, mercy, peace, and understanding. Help me to be your willing instrument. Help me to be more like you.

(Morning)
Sovereign God, Judge of all creation, I seek justice and peace
for those for whom I pray today.
(Prayers of Intercession)

(Evening)
Someone received justice and was delivered today, O God. For that I am thankful.
(Prayers of Intercession)

May we judge your people with righteousness, and your poor with justice.

(Morning)
This day I have a renewed sense of righteousness, and I go forth knowing your righteousness will prevail. In your name. Amen.

(Evening)
I rest this evening in the knowledge that your righteous guidance is everlasting. In your name. Amen.

WEDNESDAY, DECEMBER 5
(Read Psalm 72:18–19)

(Morning)
Glorious God! Glorious God! Let me praise you and reflect your glory today!

(Evening)
Glorious God! Glorious God! Have I praised you with my life today?
Did someone see your glory in me?

It's always a good time to praise you, God! In all things I ought to give you glory. I ought to bless your name with every fiber of my being. You alone are worthy of the highest praise. Help me to see your glory in all I experience. I love you, God!

(Morning)
God of glory, in your glory, move miraculously in the lives of those for whom I pray.
(Prayers of Intercession)

(Evening)
God of glory, your miracles were manifest today, and I thank you!
(Prayers of Intercession)

Blessed be God's name forever.

(Morning)
Beloved God, the sun rose this morning and displayed your glory. The wind caressed my face, and I felt your glory. May your glory dwell in me even more this day so I may reflect you to all those I meet. In your name. Amen.

(Evening)
Beloved God, the sun has set today and shown your glory. The wind grows crisp and quiet. I still feel your glory. Let me rest, as all nature does, in your peace. In your name. Amen.

THURSDAY, DECEMBER 6
(Read Romans 15:4–8)

(Morning)
God, let me be a hopeful, patient, cheerful learner this day.
Let me understand and do your will.

(Evening)
God, I have gained a better understanding of your peace and precious promises today.

I seek today to know you and your ways, O God. Too often I find myself on my own path and wonder why I feel alone. You are a God who keeps promises, a God who has left us Holy Spirit–inspired words to guide us, and the Holy Spirit to bring us truth. I want to live with all my sisters and brothers in peace so we may all enjoy the fulfillment of your promises.

(Morning)
As I pray today for those whom I lift up before you, God,
let me join them in praising you and thanking you for renewed hope.
(Prayers of Intercession)

(Evening)
I thank you, God, for allowing me another day to honor you, learn of you, and love you.
(Prayers of Intercession)

**"May the God of steadfastness and encouragement grant you
to live in harmony with one another."**

(Morning)
Today is another opportunity to learn, love, and live your Word. In so doing, my hope can be refreshed. In your name. Amen.

(Evening)
I am a hope-filled child of God as I begin this evening's rest. Praise to you, my Savior! In your name. Amen.

FRIDAY, DECEMBER 7
(Read Romans 15:9–13)

(Morning)
Honored God, I am reading your Word and remembering your instructions:
to praise your name throughout the world.

(Evening)
Honored God, have I remembered to praise you and share your gospel today?

God, I often forget to praise you. In my daily list of things I want, and the pursuit of the desires of my heart, your praise gets lost or diminished. I should remember to praise you at all times. I will bring to mind that you dwell in the midst of my praise, and you will restore my hope.

(Morning)
Most honored God, today as I pray for those in my life,
I will pray that your praises will continually be in their mouths.
(Prayers of Intercession)

(Evening)
Honored God, from divine lineage, you came for me to place your faith and hope.
I thank you for restoring my hope today.
(Prayers of Intercession)

"May the God of hope fill you with all joy and peace in believing."

(Morning)	(Evening)
I begin the day with bright hope made new by Jesus Christ. In your name. Amen.	This ending day has placed more hope in my heart and mind. In your name. Amen.

SATURDAY, DECEMBER 8
(Read Matthew 3:1–6)

(Morning)
Mighty God, the One who knows my heart,
have I made a straight path in my life so you may come in?

(Evening)
Mighty God, each day, you give me another chance to turn unto you.

Loving Jesus, I recall those who have witnessed to me throughout my life. Those who told me of your coming. Those who cried out as I wandered in self-imposed wilderness. You are still there, O Rose of Sharon, in the midst of all my blindness and numbness. You send witnesses to proclaim you, and shepherds to lead me—if I simply look up. In this season, I celebrate your Light coming into the world, the Word becoming flesh. I repent and make way for you, Jesus, in all of my life.

(Morning)
Divine Shepherd, I pray you would lead the lives of those for whom I pray today.
(Prayers of Intercession)

(Evening)
Divine Shepherd, yet another day, you have continued to lead those
for whom I pray. I thank you.
(Prayers of Intercession)

"Prepare the way of Jesus, make his paths straight."

(Morning)
God, today I will make my life a straighter way for you to come in. Praise your name! In your name. Amen.

(Evening)
God, I saw you more clearly today as I let you lead the way. Praise your holy name! In your name. Amen.

SUNDAY, DECEMBER 9
(Read Matthew 3:7–12)

(Morning)
Divine Reaper, am I wheat or a husk? Do I bear fruit
that bears witness to your presence in my life?

(Evening)
Divine Reaper, today I had a chance to bear good fruit.
Did I take that chance? What kind of fruit did I produce?

God, I have received a water baptism like those who came to John. I want to call myself your disciple. I have given up my sins, yet am I reluctant to receive a daily baptism of your Holy Spirit and your holy fire? Help me to remember that the Holy Spirit and the holy fire are the means by which I work as your disciple. They are the means by which I bear good fruit. They transform me into a living sacrifice. A living fire that is strengthened, encouraged, and renewed!

(Morning)
God, this day, let your Holy Spirit rule and abide in the lives
of those for whom I pray. Let them bear good fruit.
(Prayers of Intercession)

(Evening)
God, your Spirit and fire have sustained me and those for whom I pray yet another day.
(Prayers of Intercession)

**"Every tree therefore that does not bear good fruit
is cut down and thrown into the fire."**

(Morning)	(Evening)
God, as I begin this day, let the sun remind me of your holy fire and the wind your Holy Spirit. In your name. Amen.	God, keep my soul as I sleep assured of your promises and your everlasting presence. In your name. Amen.

MONDAY, DECEMBER 10
(Read Isaiah 35:1–7)

(Morning)
Loving and healing God, strength for my fearful heart,
I open the door of my attention to you this day.

(Evening)
Loving and healing God, at the close of this day I look to you. Thank you for being
present with loving attention to me and to this world, even when we are unaware.

God, in this season of Advent waiting, I lose sight of you. I look at all that
needs to be done, and I feel anxious. I look at what others are doing in preparation for the season, and I feel driven. The holy way of your coming loses its
fragrance, and my heart becomes a dry wilderness when propelled to rush. But
you come to where I am in my fatigue and fear, and invite me to look to you.
When I gaze at you, my eyes are opened; I see my anxious ways for what they
are; and you pour springs of water on the parched ground of my being.

(Morning)
Healing God, you who come to save, open my eyes to see you
in this day, in this season of Advent waiting.
(Prayers of Intercession)

(Evening)
Dear God, as I reflect on the day, help me to see where crocuses
have blossomed, to notice the springs of water you are giving.
I rest beside the pool of your presence this night.
(Prayers of Intercession)

In the presence of your love I pray.
(Pray the Prayer of Our Savior.)

(Morning)
As I move into this day, God, you are
here. Shape the desires of my heart and
the work of my hands, so that I co-labor
with you in the wilderness of this world.
In Jesus' name. Amen.

(Evening)
I rest in you this night, O God, Giver of
streams in the desert and joy on the
way. In Jesus' name. Amen.

TUESDAY, DECEMBER 11
(Read Psalm 146:5–10)

(Morning)
Loving God of Jacob, you made heaven and earth,
the sea and all that is. I look to you for help.

(Evening)
Loving God, I come to you, thanking you for watching
over all of creation today and for caring for this tired world.

God, Jacob ran from home in fear. When we lose trust and run, you run with us. You wait to meet us when we pause for weariness and sleep. As I open my heart to receive your help, I discover you are faithful. You help me see your creating and sustaining presence beneath and around heaven and earth, and your faithful love beneath and around those who are fearful, lost, oppressed, lonely, and abandoned. You meet us and lift us up like a tender parent holding a lost and lonely child.

(Morning)
Loving and gracious God, help me to notice your goodness in this day, and help me to see others—the lost, the unwanted, and the overlooked—as you see them.
(Prayers of Intercession)

(Evening)
God of all Jacobs, as I reflect on this day, help me to see the people
I encountered as you see them. For Jesus' sake.
(Prayers of Intercession)

Humbly I pray.
(Pray the Prayer of Our Savior.)

(Morning)
Jesus, I thank you that as I once again wait in the Advent of your coming, your Holy Spirit meets me and lifts me and opens my eyes to see your presence and care. In Jesus' name. Amen.

(Evening)
Dear God, you watch over all this night with loving, tender care. Thank you. In Jesus' name. Amen.

WEDNESDAY, DECEMBER 12
(Read Luke 1:47–55)

(Morning)
God, my Savior, I praise you this day. In you I find the source of all my joy.

(Evening)
God, my Savior, help me to notice where you have been the source of my joy this day.

God of might and mercy, I listen to Mary's song today. As she sings, her song opens a door and allows me to see her heart—the inner continent where we both hide from you and long for your presence. Now you are present in her body, for she carries Jesus. Mary sings, even while she is at risk: Joseph is fearful of this scandal; Herod is violent in his opposition. Embracing the Christ child means being embraced by you. You give joy, for you, God, are ever present.

(Morning)
Mighty One, you come to us in the womb of our lives in Jesus.
Grow within me. Scatter the proud thoughts that are against you,
and bring down the powers that wage war against you within me.
(Prayers of Intercession)

(Evening)
Savior God, you are at work even as I sleep this night.
Help me to lean into your ways, your coming;
to embrace the Christ child within me; and to risk the security of your embrace.
(Prayers of Intercession)

In thanksgiving I pray.
(Pray the Prayer of Our Savior.)

(Morning)
Just as Mary sang in the house of Elizabeth, help me to discover those who acknowledge your presence and work within me and this world. In Jesus' name. Amen.

(Evening)
With Mary, I sing to you, Mighty One, in thankfulness for your help and goodness this day. In Jesus' name. Amen.

THURSDAY, DECEMBER 13
(Read Isaiah 35:3–6; Matthew 11:2–11)

(Morning)
Loving and healing God, I look for you this day. I wait for your coming.

(Evening)
Loving and healing God, as I look back over this day, help me
to see you in new ways with the loving eyes of Jesus.

Saving God, you don't come the way I sometimes wish you would. You don't come with vengeance, stomping on abusers and war makers, thieves and murderers, throwing out selfish rulers, and putting yourself in charge of governments. Maybe that is why John wavered and wondered, "Jesus, are you really the One to come?" Today the world barely notices you. But you still come to us one by one, healing, giving, restoring life, and speaking good news to us who are poor. Help me to see you today as you are.

(Morning)
Loving God, help me to notice you this Advent. And help me to keep you
at the center. May others notice your kindness, and believe.
(Prayers of Intercession)

(Evening)
Saving and healing One, be with your servants this night who are tired
and fearful, who sometimes doubt your presence and care.
(Prayers of Intercession)

In confidence I pray.
(Pray the Prayer of Our Savior.)

(Morning)	(Evening)
This day, loving Jesus, open my eyes and my ears to see and to hear your presence. In Jesus' name. Amen.	As I rest this night, I thank you that you come to be with us in gentle, healing ways. In Jesus' name. Amen.

FRIDAY, DECEMBER 14
(Read Matthew 11:2–11; James 5:7–10)

(Morning)
Present and coming God, as I awake this day, I look to you and for your coming.

(Evening)
Present and coming God, forgive me for forgetting you
and complaining against others. I thank you for not forgetting me.

Holy One, help me to live in the expectancy of your coming again. My heart grows impatient, turns to other things, forgets the age in which I live: the Advent of your coming. Gentle me into the fruitful rhythm of seedtime and harvest, for you are the Owner of the field of this world. Like seed, your loving realm is planted—oft-hidden, sometimes seen.

(Morning)
Coming God, I am not patient in suffering. Help me sit
with John the Baptist today and contemplate the signs of your coming.
(Prayers of Intercession)

(Evening)
This night, strengthen and encourage those who speak
in your name and suffer for your sake.
(Prayers of Intercession)

Patiently I pray.
(Pray the Prayer of Our Savior.)

(Morning)
As I move into this day, dear God, help me to look for seedlings that are sprouting, signs of your presence. In Jesus' name. Amen.

(Evening)
Your coming is near, Mighty One. Your presence brings healing, gentle Jesus. Gentle us into trusting sleep, renewing rest this night, for our sake and in your great love. In Jesus' name. Amen.

SATURDAY, DECEMBER 15
(Read Psalm 146:5–10; Matthew 11:2–11)

(Morning)
God, I look to you this day. I am your servant. You are my help and my hope.

(Evening)
God, as this day comes to a close, I open my heart to you.

Merciful and holy God, I ask your help as I look back over this week to see as you see. For what am I grateful? In what ways have I noticed your presence? Where have I doubted your presence? Run from your love? Where have I responded in trusting faith to your presence? How have I shown your love to others, especially those who are alone, in need, fearful?

(Morning)
Freeing God, forgive me for times when I have forgotten you, for times when I have avoided loving others as you love them and me. Healing God, open my eyes and ears to see and hear you.
(Prayers of Intercession)

(Evening)
Gentle us now into your healing presence. Bring healing and hope to all who are prisoners of impaired sight, those who are bowed down, alienated, orphaned, and alone.
(Prayers of Intercession)

In gladness I pray.
(Pray the Prayer of Our Savior.)

(Morning)
We cannot love you without your help, see you without your giving us sight, or hear you without your giving us ears to hear with the heart. Be our Healer and Help this day. In Jesus' name. Amen.

(Evening)
Gentle me now into your healing presence, O God, who upholds the orphan and the widow. Hold all that is orphaned and alone within me in your love this night. In Jesus' name. Amen.

SUNDAY, DECEMBER 16
(Read Isaiah 35:1–10; Luke 1:47–55)

(Morning)
O mighty God, my soul magnifies you, and my spirit rejoices in you.
For you have done great things, and holy is your name.

(Evening)
O mighty God, your mercy comes like streams in the desert;
your favor creates pools in the burning sand. I rest with joy,
and my heart is glad as I look to you at the end of this day.

God of goodness, Giver of joy, I thank you for making a holy way for us to walk. Thank you for your mercy for all that is lowly; you do not let us go astray. Thank you for your protection from what is wild and destructive. Thank you for lifting sorrow and sighing from our hearts and minds. And thank you for your gift of song and everlasting joy as we walk with you.

(Morning)
My soul sings, and my spirit rejoices. Help me to hear the song you give
within my heart, and to walk in joy and gladness this day.
(Prayers of Intercession)

(Evening)
As this day comes to a close, I thank you for your great strength on behalf
of all in need this day. How kind you are! I rejoice in your care.
(Prayers of Intercession)

In your mercy I pray.
(Pray the Prayer of Our Savior.)

(Morning)
Great God, joy that lasts for all time comes only from you. I rejoice with gladness and singing this day. In Jesus' name. Amen.

(Evening)
This day, Mighty One, you have lifted those who are low, filled those who are hungry, and helped those who serve you. Thank you for remembering. I praise you for your faithful, loving care. In Jesus' name. Amen.

MONDAY, DECEMBER 17
(Read Isaiah 7:1–2)

(Morning)
Sweet God of eternal life, am I prepared today to stand on your Word despite the odds? Do I have the courage today to lean on you for my needs, sweet Jesus?

(Evening)
Sweet God of eternal life, thank you for allowing me to lean on you today. Guide me safely through this night. Let me continue to lean on you.

Everything around me reminds me of the tinsel Christmas. The Christmas trees, the decorations, the imitation Santas, and the brightly colored wrapped gifts neatly tied and tucked under the twinkling, singing green pine. In all of these distractions, help me to have courage to stand in your name in the face of adversity. Let me find comfort in your presence and see your face in your people. Blessed sweet Jesus, let me stand without fear on the promises of your coming!

(Morning)
Spirit of the living God, breathe courage in my life today. Give courage to . . .
(Prayers of Intercession)

(Evening)
O God of grace, I thank you for this day. Like the house of David, have I leaned on you today for courage? Bless the courage of . . .
(Prayers of Intercession)

Leaning on God's courage, I can stand with Christ in any season!
(Sing "What a Fellowship" or another familiar hymn.)

(Morning)
As I begin this day with new courage, O God, give me courage to celebrate the coming of Jesus Christ. Allow me the privilege to encourage others to seek you in the power of the Holy Spirit. In the precious name of the Christ. Amen.

(Evening)
Thank you, God, for the small measures of success today. Let these lessons remind me of your presence. Bless me with a restful night, and rock me in your arms of courage to enter a new day of peace. In the precious name of the Christ. Amen.

TUESDAY, DECEMBER 18
(Read Isaiah 7:5–9)

(Morning)
Holy Spirit and ever-living Creator, in the rush of this season have I accepted
God's promise? Can my heart be rekindled to trust God's promise?

(Evening)
Holy Spirit and ever-living Creator, what promise did I fulfill this day in faith?
Have I accepted the rewards of your promises through faith?

In the busyness of the season, it is easy for me to forget that I am a faithful
person. There seems to be more month left than money, and there's never enough
time to do anything. This is an impossible time of year. But I must remember
to stand on my faith and remember that this holy season is also a season of gift
giving. God, thank you for the gift of Jesus Christ, our Savior. In Christ I have
hope, and in hope I live in faith. In faith I expect the miracle of your blessings!

(Morning)
Holy God, let me operate with a spirit of anticipation of a great miracle
and exercise my faith. May you give new faith to . . .
(Prayers of Intercession)

(Evening)
Gracious God of day and night, thank you for increasing my faith
and celebrating your presence today. Bless the faith of . . .
(Prayers of Intercession)

"If you do not stand firm on your faith you shall not stand at all!"
(Sing "The Solid Rock" or another familiar hymn.)

(Morning)
Sweet Creator, as I meet the permeating
light of this new day, increase my faith
in you. Let the works of my labor
illustrate your love and forgiveness.
Like the waters of the stream, let my
words increase the pool of faithful
others I greet this day, I pray. In the
precious name of the Christ. Amen.

(Evening)
Whispering Holy Spirit, as I lie down to
rest this night, remind me if I was
faithful in some way. Did I allow my lips
to speak healing words of kindness?
Release me from the thought of failure,
and bless me with a peaceful rest. In the
precious name of the Christ. Amen.

WEDNESDAY, DECEMBER 19
(Read Psalm 80:1–3)

(Morning)
Creator God of the quiet morning, touch my heart to see your help.
Can I see your mighty hand assisting me in my daily work?

(Evening)
Creator God of the quiet evening, thank you for restoring me to you this day.
Have I seen your hand at work in my life? Or was I too busy with my own life?

God of joy and peace, when I begin the day, I feel close to you. Yet in the midst of controversy, you seem silent. Am I impatient and angry today and so fail to see your work on my behalf? How often do I operate in fear, hatred, or intolerance? Intervene, sweet God, on my behalf. God, open my eyes to see you in the middle the day, healing my brokenness.

(Morning)
O blessed God whose light illuminates all things and makes them known, help me to see your mighty acts in my life. Illuminate your healing power in . . .
(Prayers of Intercession)

(Evening)
God of the vespers light, have I seen your hand at work today? At this moment as the sun disappears into the shadows, I know you have restored me. Thank you for being with . . .
(Prayers of Intercession)

"Restore us, O God. Let your face shine!"
(After sixty seconds, repeat.)

(Morning)
Today, I claim the restoration of my relationship with God. Can God's Spirit illuminate through me to restore others as I am restored? Allow me to give glory to your name this day. In the precious name of the Christ. Amen.

(Evening)
As the evening shadows greet the fading lights, I accept God's love and forgiveness. Can these gifts of restoration begin a new journey of peace and love of others in my life? In Christ I claim this peace and love this night. In the precious name of the Christ. Amen.

THURSDAY, DECEMBER 20
(Read Psalm 80:4–7)

(Morning)
Holy Spirit, Source of all goodness, let me begin this day with a spirit of peace.
Is the battle I fight within myself? Can I draw near to you and be at rest?

(Evening)
Holy Spirit, as the battle ends today, thank you for hearing my prayers. Shall I find
inner peace from my turmoil knowing you are now listening to my prayers?

God, often the confusion in life is a direct result of my inability to hear and
seek you. However, I know the very moment you turn away from me because
I actively seek your attention. Can I empty my bed of tears in your pool of
mercy and accept grace? Can I empty my life and turn it to Christ for guidance,
doing your will?

(Morning)
Searching to drink from your spiritual cup of new life, sweet Savior,
let me share in your blessing with . . .
(Prayers of Intercession)

(Evening)
As the Creator of all life, God, you have spared my life for another day.
Give me, a weary warrior of my inner battle,
rest and peace this night. Let your grace fall upon us, especially . . .
(Prayers of Intercession)

God hears my prayers and answers them!
(Sing "Have Thine Own Way, Lord" or another familiar hymn.)

(Morning)
O God, I begin this day in your care.
Can I choose not to battle with you and
accept your will? Can you help me to
accept your will and show me how? In
the precious name of the Christ. Amen.

(Evening)
Soul of Christ, I come to you for rest.
Hold me in the palm of your hand, and
renew my strength for another day.
Thank you, God, for ending my battle
and allowing me to do your will. In the
precious name of the Christ. Amen.

FRIDAY, DECEMBER 21
(Read Psalm 80:17–19)

(Morning)
Thank you, God, for this day. On this day, how can I forget who I am
and whose I am? Can I praise you today and know your presence?

(Evening)
Thank you, God, for this night. How blessed I have been today as your hand
led my life. Have I praised and thanked you for your blessings?

As I do last-minute shopping, I often forget the lives of people living in war-
torn countries; hungry children; and homeless families. O God, have I forgotten your strength and how you give us life? In this holy season of gift giving,
can I praise you for allowing us to live and have our being? Awaken my soul
today to praise you, O God, regardless of the events of this day.

(Morning)
Dearest Jesus, you lived and died for us to call on your name in love.
Let me celebrate your gift of life with . . .
(Prayers of Intercession)

(Evening)
Holy giving Spirit of God, Spirit of life, thank you for loving me
and holding me in your hand. Your signs are clear. Bless . . .
(Prayers of Intercession)

Praise God! God has given us life!
(Sing "Great Is Your Faithfulness" or another familiar hymn.)

(Morning)
Holy God of the morning dew, lift me up
to grow in life to praise you for your
grace and love. May I always draw near
to you with praise and love. In the
precious name of the Christ. Amen.

(Evening)
God of sunsets and life, be in my heart
and on my lips this night. Let me praise
you in my waking and sleeping
moments. And allow me to rest in your
peace and grace, so I may be refreshed.
In the precious name of the Christ.
Amen.

SATURDAY, DECEMBER 22
(Read Matthew 1:1–17)

(Morning)
Dear God of my ancestors, God of my enslaved brothers and sisters, let me meet the morning knowing who I am and whose I am this day. Will I see the grace of your love?

(Evening)
Dear God of my ancestors, as the day ends, thank you for the privilege
of knowing who I am. In you, have I seen the love of my brothers and sisters?
Or have I seen the rush for temporal satisfaction in toys?

In my veins runs the blood of kings and queens, thieves and robbers, and the faithful and unfaithful. The ancestral ties, retold through Scripture, remind me of who I am and whose I am. God, as your child, co-heir with Christ, can I accept your forgiveness and forgive myself for my sins? Can I claim my ancestral ties and celebrate your gift of new life?

(Morning)
Holy ageless Spirit, you move through time
and are known to my ancestors; be known to me and heal . . .
(Prayers of Intercession)

(Evening)
Holy God of grace and glory, thank you for the privilege
of working out my self-forgiveness. Forgive and heal . . .
(Prayers of Intercession)

The God of our ancestors forgives and allows me to forgive myself.
(Sing "Blessed Assurance" or another familiar hymn.)

(Morning)
Let this day be a new beginning, a new life, in Christ, seeking to forgive myself and accept the blessings of God in love. In the precious name of the Christ. Amen.

(Evening)
As the evening draws near, I thank God for forgiveness and ancestors. Let me always rest in the cradle of your love, assured of my history of forgiveness. O God, renew my love in you as I rock in your tender care. In the precious name of the Christ. Amen.

SUNDAY, DECEMBER 23
(Read Romans 1:1–7)

(Morning)
God, in the break of this day, have I seen the young woman
with child seeking a place to rest?
Will I be obedient to your call to offer love and receive discipleship and grace?

(Evening)
God, the good news of Christ is not easy. Distractions from prayer and obedience
are ramped up in the Christmas season. Have I stayed focused on my discipleship?
Did I rest in your grace in peace?

What am I willing to do today to be obedient to your Word and yield to the work of the Holy Spirit? The season of giving is clouded with mixed messages of spending money to show love. Yet didn't you illustrate supreme love through the birth of an infant, born to an unwed teenage mother? How much more can I do to illustrate discipleship today?

(Morning)
God of grace, remove the anxiety from my life.
Let me rest in you and be obedient. Remember . . .
(Prayers of Intercession)

(Evening)
Merciful God, you have blessed my life as a disciple. Let me continue
to live with Christ as my focus leading my faith. Remember . . .
(Prayers of Intercession)

Obedience of faith illustrates Jesus Christ in love!
(Sing "Give Me a Clean Heart" or another familiar hymn.)

(Morning)
In the newness of life I begin a day of
obedience to God's love with the faith of
a mustard seed. Let this faith increase,
my words encourage, my hand build up
the love of Christ. In the precious name
of the Christ. Amen.

(Evening)
As I lay my head upon the pillow of
faith and rest myself upon the bed of
grace, I thank God for guiding me. In
obedience to your love, blessed Christ,
I submit this day to your care. In the
precious name of the Christ. Amen.

MONDAY, DECEMBER 24
(Read Hebrews 2:10–13)

(Morning)
Loving God, help me this day to prepare myself
to accept your most gracious gift. Jesus enters our lives.

(Evening)
Loving God, on this holy night, we look to the manger where Mary gave birth
to our Savior. May we ponder anew the wonder of this gift and sing our hallelujahs.

We thank you, God, that you make yourself incarnate through Jesus the Christ,
the pioneer of our faith. You share in the suffering of all your children. Help us
to be renewed during this holy season as we receive Jesus.

(Morning)
God, our Parent, forgive us our failure to know and accept the fact
that we are your children and that Jesus, your perfect Child, is our brother.
Let us live this day in trust close to you.
(Prayers of Intercession)

(Evening)
On this Christmas Eve, may we be filled with your glory
as the gift of Jesus comes into our world.
(Prayers of Intercession)

**The one whose name is Emmanuel, God-with-us,
is born this night. Thanks be to God.**

(Morning)
May the glad tidings that are about to
break forth fill us with peace and joy
this day. Make us heralds of the good
news. Thanks be to Christ. Amen.

(Evening)
O holy night, *buena noche*, may all the
nations hear in their own tongues that
your love, God, fills the whole earth
with peace and joy. Thanks be to Christ.
Amen.

TUESDAY, DECEMBER 25
(Read Hebrews 2:14–18)

(Morning)
Emmanuel, God-with-us, at the beginning of this Christmas Day, before the bustle and the distractions begin, center my prayers in gratitude for your birth in Jesus.

(Evening)
Emmanuel, God-with-us, now and forever we thank you for family and friends gathered, for the loving care and preparation that made this a joyous day, and above all, for your presence among us.

"Because he himself was tested by what he suffered, he is able to help those who are being tested." We are ever grateful to you, God, that because you came into our lives in mortal flesh through Jesus the Christ, we have been given a Mediator and a faithful High Priest.

(Morning)
Give me a warm and open heart this day, O God, that I may truly celebrate the heights and depths of your unfathomable love in the gift of Jesus, your Child.
(Prayers of Intercession)

(Evening)
I rejoice that I have been part of this wondrous day.
Help me to be worthy of your blessings.
(Prayers of Intercession)

**Gracious God, grant that we may learn to live
in your holy presence and carry out your will.**

(Morning)
Use me, God, in your service, and give me a voice to sing songs of praise on this Christmas Day. Thanks be to Christ. Amen.

(Evening)
Now the day is over. May we never be weary of praising you and singing, "Glory to God in the highest," for the gift of Jesus given to us this day and forevermore. Thanks be to Christ. Amen.

WEDNESDAY, DECEMBER 26
(Read Matthew 2:13–18)

(Morning)
God, as I awaken, I remember the joy and exultation of yesterday
and give thanks that so precious a gift has been given.

(Evening)
God, protect your people from the evil caused by jealousy and rage.
Console those who suffer loss. To those like Rachel, weeping for her children,
who find no consolation, give of your peace and love.

Help us to deal with the wicked, knowing that you, O God, will ultimately be victorious. In suffering, give us sure knowledge of your presence and abiding love. Help us not to lose courage and stamina to fight against the Herods of this world.

(Morning)
Loving God, sustain me this day in the light brought forth by the birth of Jesus.
(Prayers of Intercession)

(Evening)
Protect me this night from the evil so rampant in our world. Give me rest to
strengthen my resolve to combat those who oppose your will.
(Prayers of Intercession)

**Almighty God, the world is new with the coming
of Jesus and the Holy Spirit.**

(Morning)
Save me from temptations this day. Let me not waste your marvelous gifts, given that we might live this life abundantly. Thanks be to Christ. Amen.

(Evening)
Through these long nights, may I be mindful of all the Rachels who are weeping. Help me to be some small instrument in saving your suffering children. Thanks be to Christ. Amen.

THURSDAY, DECEMBER 27
(Read Psalm 148:1–6)

(Morning)
God, now Christmas week begins. Let me not be so caught up in the trivialities
of holiday preparation that I fail to hear the music of the spheres.
All creation is singing praises to you.

(Evening)
God, as I close my eyes, fill me with thanksgiving that I have been included
in your creation to love, protect, and enjoy it forever. Help me, God,
to be worthy of this gift of life by acting as your steward on this earth.

Creator God, help me to fathom the wonders of your work. All nature celebrates. Even the trees clap their hands. Let us make this week a time of praise and thanksgiving for your whole creation and especially for the gift of Jesus, Emmanuel, God-with-us.

(Morning)
Loving God, sustain within me the understanding that I am vitally connected to all
your creation. Help me to live all my life with that awareness within me.
(Prayers of Intercession)

(Evening)
Be with me, Gracious One. Fill me with your presence this night
and throughout my days.
(Prayers of Intercession)

Praise our God from the highest heavens and even to our inmost being.

(Morning)
God, I praise the new day and give
thanks for all the opportunities ahead to
serve and honor you. Thanks be to
Christ. Amen.

(Evening)
As I close my eyes, may I know even in
my dreams the majesty of the wonders
wrought by you, the God of us all.
Thanks be to Christ. Amen.

FRIDAY, DECEMBER 28
(Read Psalm 148:7–14)

(Morning)
Creator God, in wonder we perceive the changing seasons.
Make us aware of those who depend on your sun's rays for warmth and light.

(Evening)
Creator God, give us peace and rest this night.
Restore our energies to do your will when the new day arrives.

Young men and women, children, and old ones praise you, everlasting God. Help us to fathom our part in the vast, unending nature of your creation. As Christmas nears, we sing of these wonders. We rejoice that in the midst of our longest night, Jesus, the true Light, was born for us all.

(Morning)
Emmanuel, surely this day you are with me.
Help me to strive to be your true disciple, for you showed me the way.
(Prayers of Intercession)

(Evening)
On this longest night, fill us with your Holy Spirit, giving us new hope
amidst the sorrows and injustices of our world.
Ease the pain of all who suffer, and let them feel your presence.
(Prayers of Intercession)

Sing praises to our God through all our days.

(Morning)
Let not this day be wasted; it is precious in your sight. Let me live it doing your will. Thanks be to Christ. Amen.

(Evening)
Carry me into a peaceful sleep, knowing that when I awake, I shall be renewed to journey ahead in God's way. Thanks be to Christ. Amen.

SATURDAY, DECEMBER 29
(Read Isaiah 63:7–9)

(Morning)
O God, as I start this day, clear my mind. Help me grasp the meaning of your presence with us. May I know the strength of your redeeming love.

(Evening)
O God, I was carried this day in the knowledge of your goodness. Now, as I close my eyes, I pray that all people may know your love and mercy.

Our world awaits your coming through Jesus Christ, our Savior. Give to your people thankful hearts, that we may be carried by a steadfast faith and lifted to do your will. May these not be idle words but convictions that direct our lives.

(Morning)
Merciful God who knows the suffering of your children,
be with us this day as we seek to be your instruments in healing.
(Prayers of Intercession)

(Evening)
Through all our days and nights, be with us. Break into our lives. Help us in our striving to be the people you sought to create in your own image.
(Prayers of Intercession)

**"In all their distress God was distressed;
the angel of God's presence saved them."**

(Morning)
Jesus Christ, who brings light into our world, help us to show forth the love and compassion manifest in your life. Thanks be to Christ. Amen.

(Evening)
O God, Giver of all good gifts, we thank you this night for the abundance you have showered upon us. We ask for renewed strength to use these gifts in your service. Thanks be to Christ. Amen.

SUNDAY, DECEMBER 30
(Read Matthew 2:19–23)

(Morning)
O God, as I awaken from the dreams of night, allow me to be aware of the angels who would warn me of wrong directions. May I live this day attuned to your words.

(Evening)
O God, guide me with your wisdom as I review this past year. I give thanks for all the blessings and ask forgiveness for the ways I have failed to follow your path.

Let us remember Mary and Joseph, who by heeding the warnings of danger protected the precious Child by carrying him to Nazareth. There he grew to be the pioneer of our faith. May we also heed the signs of evildoing around us. Help us to be among the protectors of your children throughout the world.

(Morning)
Help us to act this day against evil. Protect us from the dangers
inherent in the principalities and powers of our world.
(Prayers of Intercession)

(Evening)
As we close each day, may we read the Bible and grow from the study of its wisdom.
(Prayers of Intercession)

**The leader and provider of our faith, Jesus Christ,
be our guide throughout our days.**

(Morning)
In the morning light, we raise our voices with hymns of praise for the living presence of your Child, Jesus Christ, in our lives. Thanks be to Christ. Amen.

(Evening)
This day comes to a close as we seek the rest that will give us strength to be disciples tomorrow and throughout the new year ahead. Thanks be to Christ. Amen.

MONDAY, DECEMBER 31
(Read Isaiah 63:7–9)

(Morning)
Savior, thank you for your kindness toward me.
As I look toward a new year, you are worthy to be praised.

(Evening)
Savior, thank you for your compassion toward me. You alone deserve all honor.

Dear Redeemer, there are not enough words in my limited vocabulary to tell of your goodness and faithfulness toward those who worship you in spirit and in truth. If I had ten thousand tongues, I could not praise you enough for your loving-kindness throughout this past year. In my distress, you are there to comfort me; in my rejoicing, you are there smiling at me, not because I deserve it, but because you are Love. Help me to continually seek your face, your path, and your way—every day.

(Morning)
Use every experience I face today to bring me closer to you.
(Prayers of Intercession)

(Evening)
Thank you for ordering my steps, my home, my career, my life.
(Prayers of Intercession)

"I will recount the gracious deeds of God."

(Morning)
Savior, I wake with my heart and mind steadfast upon you. You are worthy to be praised for all you have done for me. Thanks be to Christ. Amen.

(Evening)
I rest in your loving arms, knowing that your angels are encompassed all around me in the dawn of another year. Thank you for your love. Thanks be to Christ. Amen.

Contributors

Roberta R. Arrowsmith, D.Min., Th.M., is associate pastor of Newtown Presbyterian Church in Newtown, Pennsylvania, and a certified educator with the Presbyterian Church (USA).

Joan Brown Campbell is the former general secretary of the National Council of the Churches of Christ in the United States of America.

Beth P. Clark, D.Min., has been an interim minister specialist for thirty years. She is a member of the United Church of Christ.

Linda Cloutier-Namdar is certified as an accredited church educator in the United Church of Christ. She serves as the director of children's and youth ministries at the First Congregational Church, United Church of Christ, in Burlington, Vermont.

Lynn A. Collins, M.Div., is the national officer for Black Episcopal Ministries at the Episcopal Church Center. She is an Episcopal priest and a candidate for the doctor of ministry degree. Mother Collins has led workshops on spirituality, leadership, and church growth.

Davida Foy Crabtree, D.Min., is conference minister for the Connecticut Conference of the United Church of Christ.

Bill Dalke is conference minister, Rocky Mountain Conference, United Church of Christ. Prior to his current position, he served twenty years as a pastor in Maine.

Nehemiah Davis pastored churches in Robstown, Corpus Christi, and Cuero, Texas, before becoming pastor of Mount Pisgah Baptist Church in Forth Worth, where he has served for more than thirty years. He also writes for the National Baptist Publishing Board.

Lillian Valentin de Rico is an ordained United Church of Christ minister and pastor of Faith Community United Church of Christ, Oakland, California.

Curtiss Paul DeYoung is president of the Twin Cities Urban Reconciliation Network in Minneapolis–St. Paul and author of *Coming Together and Reconciliation*.

Sandra K. Edwards is director of the African American Ministries Program at McCormick Theological Seminary.

Lynne Simcox Fitch is a graduate of Grinnell College and Pacific School of Religion. She has served as a campus minister and conference minister for the United Church of Christ since her ordination in 1972.

Paul E. Forrey is pastor of Sunset Congregational Church in Miami, Florida.

Steven P. Gordon is senior minister of the Newtown Congregational Church in Newton, Connecticut.

Priscilla Anderson Gray is the associate minister at Wheeler Avenue Baptist Church in Houston, Texas, and coordinator of its Evangelism Team.

Stephen C. Gray has served churches in Alabama and Nashville, Tennessee. He is currently conference minister of the Indiana-Kentucky Conference, United Church of Christ.

Jeffrey Hammonds is the pastor of Hebron United Church of Christ in Winston-Salem, North Carolina.

Mary Ruth Harris is an ordained minister in the United Church of Christ.

Helen M. Hayes is a member of Euclid Avenue Congregational Church in Cleveland, Ohio.

Juanita J. Helphrey is minister for racial justice programs, United Church Board for Homeland Ministries, United Church of Christ.

J. Lynne Hinton is pastor of First Congregational United Church of Christ in Asheboro, North Carolina. She is author of *Meditations for Walking* and *Friendship Cake*.

Randy Hyvonen is one of two conference ministers for the Washington-North Idaho Conference, United Church of Christ.

Susan J. Ingham is the conference minister for the Iowa Conference, United Church of Christ.

Nicole P. Johnson is a writer, teacher, and sign-language interpreter who is currently pursuing a doctorate in education.

Steven D. Johnson, Ph.D., is the minister for United Church of Christ Related Colleges, Academies, and Theological Seminarians, United Church Board for Homeland Ministries, United Church of Christ.

Leontine Turpeau Current Kelly is a retired bishop in the United Methodist Church. She was the first African American woman elected as bishop of this denomination.

Carmen N. Lanning, Ph.D., is a professional writer with more than thirty years of teaching experience, mostly on the college level.

Madeline McClenney-Sadler is an ordained minister in the Baptist Church. She is a doctoral student at Duke University.

Gene E. Miller is conference minister of the South Dakota Conference of the United Church of Christ.

Mark Henry Miller, D.Min., is conference minister of the South Central Conference of the United Church of Christ.

Wendy J. Miller is a campus pastor and faculty member of the Eastern Mennonite Seminary.

Donald W. Morgan is program associate with the United Church of Christ, Back Bay Mission, in Biloxi, Mississippi.

Donald E. Overlock is now enjoying retirement on Cape Cod after twenty-two years in the parish and eighteen years with the Massachusetts and Penn Northeast Conference of the United Church of Christ.

Marilyn Pagán is an ordained United Church of Christ minister serving in Chicago, Illinois. She and her two daughters, Jet'aime and Tatiana, use *The Book of Daily Prayer* as a part of their nighttime devotions. Her daughters helped her with her contribution to this edition.

Linda M. Peavy is associate publisher and director of marketing of Judson Press in Valley Forge, Pennsylvania. She holds an M.B.A. in management.

Ralph C. Quellhorst, D.Min., serves as conference minister of the Ohio Conference and the Indiana-Kentucky Conference of the United Church of Christ.

Tyrone Reinhardt is an ordained United Church of Christ minister living in Hawaii.

Cally Rogers-Witte is the conference minister of the Southwest Conference of the United Church of Christ.

Sarah Daniels Roncolato is an ordained minister in the United Methodist Church.

Paul Hobson Sadler Sr. is the minister of evangelism for African American and Native American Indian Church Development, United Church Board for Homeland Ministries, United Church of Christ.

Lucy B. Samara is director of Outreach Ministries at First Congregational Church of Burlington, Vermont. She also serves on the Vermont Conference/United Church of Christ's Department of Mission.

Jack Seville, D.D., is the conference minister of the Northern Plains Conference of the United Church of Christ.

Sameerah L. Shareef is associate pastor at St. Stephen's Community Church, United Church of Christ, in Lansing, Michigan. She is also a certified nurse-midwife.

V. Erika Smith is a doctoral student at Case Western Reserve University in Cleveland, Ohio. She attends Parkside Church in Chagrin Falls, Ohio.

Gail Stringer is pursuing a master's degree in early childhood education at Cleveland State University in Cleveland, Ohio.

Kent J. Ulery is the conference minister of the Michigan Conference of the United Church of Christ. He is a member of the Haslett Community United Church of Christ.

Pete Velander is president and publisher of Logos Productions, Inc., an independent, ecumenical publishing house.

Gretchen Wagner is pastor of First United Church of Christ in Austinburg, Ohio, and serves as a spiritual director in the Ohio Conference of the United Church of Christ.

Helen B. Webber is retired. She is a member of the United Church of Christ.

Paul L. Westcoat Jr. is conference minister of the Penn West Conference, United Church of Christ.

George S. Worcester is the conference minister of the Nebraska Conference, United Church of Christ.

Flora Slosson Wuellner is an ordained United Church of Christ minister, an author, and a retreat leader.